BATTLE READY FOR THE 21ST CENTURY

BATTLE READY FOR THE 21ST CENTURY

Edited by

Lieutenant General AK Singh

&

Brigadier Narender Kumar

Centre for Land Warfare Studies

PENTAGON PRESS LLP

The Centre for Land Warfare Studies (CLAWS), New Delhi, is an independent Think Tank dealing with contemporary issues of national security and conceptual aspects of land warfare, including conventional and sub-conventional conflicts and terrorism. CLAWS conducts research that is futuristic in outlook and policy-oriented in approach.

CLAWS Vision: To establish CLAWS as a leading Think Tank in policy formulation on Land Warfare, National Security and Strategic Issues.

Centre for Land Warfare Studies
RPSO Complex, Parade Road, Delhi Cantt, New Delhi-110010
Phone: 011-25691308 • CLAWS ARMY NO : 33098 • Fax: 011-25692347
email: landwarfare@gmail.com • website: www.claws.in

First Published in 2021

ISBN 978-93-90095-26-1

Published by
PENTAGON PRESS LLP
206, Peacock Lane, Shahpur Jat,
New Delhi-110049
Phones: 011-64706243, 26491568
Telefax: 011-26490600
email: rajan@pentagonpress.in
website: www.pentagon-press.com

Printed at Aegean Offset Printers, Greater Noida, U.P.

Dedicated to

The Officers of the Indian Armed Forces

Contents

Foreword

The three grave crises that overtook India in 2020 – a pandemic, an economic downturn and a military confrontation – are going to have far-reaching and deleterious consequences, not just for the country's long-term socio-economic development and overall growth, but even more so, for its security. While a contracting economy will aggravate many existing or latent socio-economic problems, shrinking defence-budgets may be inadequate to sustain even current force-levels; leave alone, modernising or re-equipping our military.

Given this appalling prospect, it will take 'out of the box' thinking and extraordinary measures to set the country back on the path of a slow and painful recovery. During this interregnum, it will be the military's task to uphold the nation's sovereignty and territorial integrity. The current predicaments, thus, provide an opportunity for military thinkers to seek responses, to numerous security challenges – current and foreseeable - that loom before the nation. The compendium of essays, that you hold in your hands, is a manifestation of this worthy endeavour.

Resort to application of force, or waging of war, has been, and must remain, a measure of last resort, because even the victor pays a heavy price, in the ultimate reckoning. Therefore, the decision to go to war should come, only after statesmen and diplomats have tried their best, and exhausted all other avenues of dispute-resolution. However, the blunt view that the outbreak of hostilities signals a failure of statesmanship and diplomacy, has to be moderated in the light of Prussian military strategist, Clausewitz's description of war as, *"...nothing but continuation of policy with other means."*

If war is, indeed, a politico-military enterprise, it must be waged with the aim of achieving a more stable and enduring peace than that which existed before the conflict. This places two onerous responsibilities on the shoulders of the political leadership: firstly, to lay down, for the military, clear aims for which war is being waged, and secondly, to specify the desired 'end-state' to be achieved, before war-termination. Unfortunately, in India, these stipulations have been honoured more in the breach than in observance. By this omission, the politician seems to have absolved himself of the responsibility of addressing the military's 'ends-ways-means' conundrum. The reason is not far to seek.

India's post-independence political establishment, of all hues, has shown remarkable indifference, towards vital issues of national security; invariably according precedence to pursuit of electoral politics. Consequently, India alone, among major powers, has suffered from the lack of an institutional process which generates defence reviews, policy white papers and national security strategies. This serious void has inhibited our capacity to predict threats and evolve appropriate responses, engendering an 'ostrich syndrome,' that has prevented the funding and creation of requisite military capability. Lacking strategic assessments, of adversary intentions as well as of our own capabilities, it is not surprising that the decisions of India's civilian leadership have often been flawed.

To this lacuna have been added the shortcomings of our Ministry of Defence (MoD), which has been singularly unhelpful in resolving the 'ends-ways-means' dilemma of the Indian military. For 70 years, the management of national security, by the MoD, has been undertaken by a civilian bureaucracy, lacking adequate comprehension, of matters related to national security as well as military technology. Consequently, issues such as strategic-planning, organisational reform, defence production, technology upgradation, and even the basic provisioning for war has seen gross neglect. Lethargic MoD processes have also slowed capital acquisitions and completely stalled India's military modernisation for decades.

Against the backdrop of these significant handicaps, India's handling of national security challenges has left much to be desired. Starting with the 1999 hijacking of Indian Airlines flight IC-814 to Kandahar, the early years of this century, saw successive security crises, catching India by surprise; unprepared and invariably in the reactive mode. While India's display of forbearance, in the face of repeated provocations, may have garnered international applause, it was frustrating and demoralizing for the Indian citizen as well as the military.

All this changed on 29th September 2018, when the NDA government deployed Special Forces to deliver a punitive strike on terrorist camps located inside Pakistan; thereby breaching the self-imposed taboo that had paralysed previous regimes. The February 2019 air-strike, on a terrorist facility in Khyber Pukhtunkhwa, re-affirmed this government's resolve that cross-border terrorism by Pakistan would not go unpunished.

While these resolute actions have earned well-deserved public approval, September 2018 was a 'missed opportunity' for promulgating a national security doctrine. Such a document could have provided clear guidelines for own security planners and forces, and drawn 'red-lines' for adversaries; by sending a clear message that border transgressions – whether by military forces or by state-sponsored terrorists - would invite retribution. In my opinion, it is the absence of such a 'declaration of intent,' that has been seen as a lack of resolve by our adversaries and has encouraged adventurism, both by Pakistan and by China.

Coming to the current Sino-Indian military confrontation, China having weathered the COVIDS-19 pandemic with relatively little economic impact, has reaffirmed its revanchist agenda and expansionist intent, by actions in the Himalayas. It is, now, clear that in spite of the military asymmetry between China and India, and the active China-Pakistan nexus, Indian forces are well-placed to counter any localized offensive by one or both. However, there is also the stark reality, that if general hostilities break out, the best that India can hope to achieve, is a military stalemate on its northern and western borders. Under these circumstances, as India prepares for the long-haul, it must bring to bear, all elements of its comprehensive national power against adversaries. That is the reason why attention has been focused on the maritime domain, where it is believed that India has some options, other than 'boots on the ground,' which could reinforce India's bargaining position.

India's strategic elite must prepare to face the growing complexity acquired by warfare due to disruptive technologies and innovative strategies. Conventional distinctions between the 'weak' and the 'strong,' now, no longer hold good; as demonstrated by the 'weaponisation' of commercial airliners in 9/11 and the attacks on Saudi Arabian assets by Houthi rebels. India's civilian and military leadership must, also, note that the changing character of warfare is creating more options for pursuing strategic goals just below the threshold of traditional armed conflict – what has come to be known as 'grey-zone' tactics or 'hybrid warfare.'

Having fought five 'conventional' wars, since 1947, and having engaged, nonstop, in low intensity conflict, much of it sponsored by neighbours, India's armed forces have imbibed a sense of territoriality. It is against this backdrop, and the ongoing Himalayan confrontation with China, that we need to introspect about our capacity – material as well as intellectual - to meet future challenges in the 21st century battle-space. The recent creation of a Department of Military Affairs as well as the post of a Chief of Defence Staff, should lend a new dimension to such reflection.

By compiling and editing this valuable collection of essays, titled, *'Battle Ready for the 21st Century'* ,' Lt Gen AK Singh (Retd) and Brig Narender Kumar (Retd), both distinguished soldiers and military intellectuals, have rendered yeoman service to the cause of India's national security. Beginning with a philosophic discourse on the 'notion of victory,' this eclectic anthology spans a wide spectrum of topics, ranging from maritime and aerospace power to the impact of technology and intelligence on operations and wide-ranging commentaries on warfare in varied domains and terrains.

This book provides rich food for thought, as much for the lay reader, as for policy advisers, security professionals and academic researchers. It is my sincere hope that it will find readership and appreciation, not just amongst the military community but also in the civilian strategic and academic fraternity.

Arun Prakash
Admiral
Former Chief of the Naval Staff

1

Introduction

The Idea

The Idea of this book germinated as a follow-up to the first one edited for the Centre for Land Warfare Studies (CLAWS): *"Military Strategy for India in the 21st Century"*. The book was well received, filling a vacuum that existed on the various nuances of military strategy. The idea of the present book is to take the reader to the operational level of war and conflict in the sub-continental setting with a futuristic focus of 10-15 years.

War and Conflict have been and will always remain intrinsic to the human DNA; however, the form and instruments will continue to change, with an ever-increasing rapidity. Post the Cold War, there has been a paradigm shift in the very character of conflict. Modern-day conflicts are not merely confined to States, but have expanded to include sub-nationalities, non-state actors, terrorists, religious fanatics and ethnic interests. The battle space would encompass non-kinetic confrontations, non-contact warfare and traditional armed conflict in its hybrid manifestations. Technology is influencing the multi-domain battle space like never before. What is less certain and not easy to predict, is how technology will develop further; however, it would be safe to say that the future is unlikely to be a linear extension of present trends.

With such a complex amalgam of factors influencing war and conflict in the 21st century, it was not easy to shortlist the issues which would define this offering. A sub-continental flavour also narrowed the choices. This collection of 15 essays covers salient aspects at the operational level, combining emerging technologies affecting foreseeable ground realities, contributed by authors who have a clear understanding of their subjects and, in most cases, have been practitioners at this level of warfare and conflict. The authors have been afforded full freedom of articulation with editorial involvement only to keep it within the confines of the overall aim.

The Essence of the Armed Forces

In the 21st century, the Indian Armed Forces face a very challenging environment, which is likely to get even more complex in the next 10-15 years. Added to this are the challenges faced by human resources, linked to the dynamics of society and the soldier's interplay with it. We therefore thought it prudent to start by reaffirming the **Essence of the Indian Armed Forces,** which provides the foundation on which the Armed Forces function. This is necessary not only for the benefit of the uninitiated, but also for the uniformed fraternity, where this essence may be under stretch. The salient aspects are covered below.

Role of the Armed Forces–Remaining Relevant

Primary Role: Preserve national interests and safeguard sovereignty, territorial integrity and unity of India against any external threats by deterrence or by waging war.

Secondary Role: Assist government agencies to cope with 'proxy war' and other internal threats and provide aid to civil authority when requisitioned for the purpose.

But the Armed Forces also have a **derived role,** in which they assist in nation-building, through their contribution in various fields:

- Nation-building by providing security, and when required, essential services in remote areas.
- Employment generation.
- Enhancing India's image through their conduct and professionalism. A good example is various defence cooperation activities with many countries, as also participation in United Nations Peace-Keeping operations.
- Pool of disciplined and skilled manpower (approximately 60,000) who retire every year, enriching society. It is a different matter that we are still not able to optimise this asset because of fixated mind sets.
- Contribution to sports, environment, etc.

In recent times, the secondary role has assumed prominence even as the challenges of the primary role have grown significantly. Moreover, the Armed Forces are being dragged in as 'First Responders' for a variety of tasks which clearly lie in the civil domain, because of the non-performance of the other instruments of the state. The answers to this dilemma are not easy and each case has to be dealt on merit, while ensuring that the task does not impinge on the core values and dignity of the organisation. The bottom line is that the Armed Forces need to remain relevant whenever the nation calls, and therefore, the senior military leadership needs a good politico-military understanding and rapport in difficult situations.

Core Values

• **Apolitical:** The Armed Forces, as an institution, do not have any political preference, but serve the government of the day and the Constitution of the country. This is a key core value and needs to be preserved in the face of any inducement or short-term consideration.

• **Secular:** The Armed Forces live together and fight together, without any fear or favour or any consideration of religion, region, caste or creed. In fact, they stand as a beacon of harmony, earning the trust of all citizens.

• **Very professional,** with high levels of personal and professional integrity. (A true reflection of the spirit of the Constitution of India).

Tenets of Indian Military Philosophy

- India has multi-front and multi-sector/terrain obligations in a very challenging environment and with two inimical neighbours on either flank.
- India is not part of any military alliance or grouping and therefore needs an independent deterrent and versatile operational capability across the spectrum of conflict. While this may hold true today, temporary groupings with a military flavour with like-minded countries, at least on specific issues, could become the norm in the future.

Leadership

The Indian Armed Forces are the ultimate guarantors of our nation's security and well being. How this instrument of last resort performs will be determined by the leadership that steers the organisation in peace and leads it in war. While leadership is present in all walks of life, what makes it so special and different in the Armed Forces are three aspects:

- Unlimited liability covenant (unwritten) between the organisation and the individual, where you give yourself up to the Armed Forces and carry out assigned duties without any ifs and buts. In return, the organisation and the nation commit to look after you (and yours) in life, injury or death.
- Leadership in the Armed Forces is not about profit/loss, but about life and death issues. Therefore, the motivation has to be on a higher level and leaders have to lead through personal example/influence, both direct and indirect, to make their command achieve the seemingly impossible.
- Being the last resort of the nation, the Armed Forces have to win every time, time and again—there being no runners-up in war.

Military leadership is not about event management or entrepreneurship. It is about life and death; about standing up and being counted; taking charge when the chips are down and placing yourself in the face of danger before ordering your subordinates to do so. It is about trust, loyalty, integrity and esprit de corps. And finally, it is about that unique bonding and motivating factor—Regiment Spirit.

In the 21st century, we need military leaders who are steadfast and visionary, who measure up to the highest standards of military skills that modern warfare demands, who possess the strength of character and mental resilience to carry the burdens that modern warfare conditions impose. My recipe for such a military leader is: **"Humility in his persona and Arrogance in his uniform"**, based on his integrity, competence and commitment.

Responsibility—Authority—Accountability

This is one of the most important ethos on which the Armed Forces function. While this should be the basis of all government functioning, it is not so in India, where accountability is rarely owned/established. However, whatever the state in the civil segment of society is, in the Armed Forces it can be no other way. The Indian soldier trusts the hierarchy implicitly and will risk his life willingly based on this trust. The officers of the Indian Armed Forces have always led from the front and walked the talk. There are aberrations, but these are few and far between for such a large organisation. The result is that the Armed Forces have always responded and performed, earning the respect and confidence of the citizens across the board. The ethos of 'Responsibility—Authority—Accountability' is central to the optimum performance of the Armed Forces and they should never be shy of enforcing both personal and professional accountability, even if it remains alien to the rest. The Chetwode motto so aptly guides the leadership. Its essence is:

- The Country first, always and every time.
- The Men you command come next.
- Your own ease, comfort and safety, comes last, always and every time.

And may I conclude by saying—it can be no other way.

The Editors take this opportunity to thank Director CLAWS, the authors, the publisher and their teams who provided the encouragement and support to conceptualise and see this project through. And finally, this book is a tribute to the Indian Army, to whom we all owe so much.

Lieutenant General AK Singh

2

The Notion of Victory in 21st Century Warfare

Lieutenant General AB Shivane

ABSTRACT

The character of war over the decades has changed with evolving actors, approaches, technological progression and ideologies, often contesting the authority of the state, driven by identity politics. The question of identifying victor and vanquished in these contemporary wars is complex and ambiguous. Military success or failure in future conflict is thus replacing the notion of victory or defeat with scales of success varying from "victory, win, not lose, stalemate or status quo, not win, lose to defeat".

The present-day expeditionary forces supposedly waging, "Jus ad Bellum" intervention wars, presents another perspective that looks beyond war, to examine whether outcomes in these events are consistent with victory. The truth is that exiting and ending those wars has proven far more elusive and the consequences more disastrous, than initiating them and the battlefield mission itself. In the Indian subcontinent, India's prospective geopolitical options and threat environment were profoundly altered by the partition of India giving birth to a belligerent fundamentalist Pakistan and the uncertainties of the rise of hegemonic China. Each war post-independence, had a separate casus belli, a different course of action and a different outcome in shades of victory or defeat. These wars theoretically should have resulted in enduring peace, but this has not happened.

In the Indian context of a future conflict with Pakistan, the politico-military objectives will have to be carefully calibrated, and the notion of military victory will be a combination of degradation of combat potential, selective value spatial gains and a decisive psychological edge. A status quo would be a notion of victory for Pakistan and defeat for India. The notion of victory against proxy war will be defined by a strategy of military compellence, through punitive strikes with escalatory dynamics inbuilt, along with politico-diplomatic dissuasion and economic coercion, to keep Pak's proxy war cauldron subdued, and ensuring positive control within the Valley. On the other front, managing the rise of China and deterring its multi-domain aggressive dominance, remains a strategic and primary challenge for India. The notion of a military victory against China, should it escalate into conflict, would thus rest on ensuring the status quo by denying China its military and political objectives. While the strategy must aim at a credible deterrence, the acme of skill would lie in winning without fighting.

The challenge thus arising is to rethink the notion of victory in 21st Century warfare. Historian Christopher Hill once wrote, "The ever-changing character of war demands that every generation must also rethink its understanding of military victory."

EVOLVING NOTION OF VICTORY

Fight for the sake of duty, treating alike happiness and distress, loss and gain, victory and defeat. Fulfilling your responsibility in this way, you will never incur sin.

—Bhagavad Gita, Quote 2.38

General

The mystic flavour of a decisive victory in battle is a historic relic of the era of the epics, the *Mahabharata* and the *Ramayana*. It continued to gain some currency and acceptability until the cold war era and thereafter developed a different flavour, with greater pragmatism along with the passage of time. The rapid transformation in society, culture and globalisation brought with it changes in geopolitical and geo-economic dimensions, which have affected warfare and the notion of victory. While the traditional linkages between war, victory and politics remain, the mechanisms, politics and end states driving them have transformed and evolved with changing times. Carl von Clausewitz, on contemporary wars, had noted that every age has its particular kind of war and associated victory with "its own limiting conditions and its own peculiar preconceptions." Ironically, many have misinterpreted the nature and character of war, based on Clausewitz's contemporary thinking. The nature of war is the unchanging essence of its moral and physical characteristics. However, its character has changed with evolving actors, approaches, technological progression and ideologies often contesting the authority of the state, driven by identity politics. Post the cold war, major changes in the goals of war, the rules of war, the players and the target of war, have reshaped character of contemporary conflicts and the notion of victory. Traditional state-centric wars have been blended by the emergence of non-state actors and proxies, with a wide variety of interests and their perceptions of reality, combined with a greater focus on changing cultures and ideologies. The outcome of these modern conflicts is no more conducive to erstwhile clear-cut endings, thereby demanding that the notion of victory or defeat be formulated and achieved in a more nuanced way in these changing contexts. Whilst the character of war and the notion of victory has undergone a profound change, it has not provided the luxury of a corresponding reduction in maintaining capabilities the spectrum of conflict in the 21st century demands the maintenance and commitment of greater and smarter resources. What constitutes victory or the converse defeat in these contemporary wars and future conflicts is increasingly complex, subjective and often open-ended. Thus, victory may be seeking a shade where it is perceived as avoiding defeat, strategic messaging, retaining positive control or even status quo or simply a better peace than what existed. However, while decisive victories and end states may well be a historic relic, they remain necessary postulates towards which militaries focus their effort, resources and actions. Thus, while the flavour and ingredients of victory have changed with revolution and generation of warfare, its foundational construct remains essential for strategic guidance.

War, Politics and Victory

Victory as it applies to nations, states, military campaigns and more importantly, the course of politics, takes the relevance of a term describing a condition, which is part of a larger process. It is drawn through the dynamics of time, space, force, information and cultural change. The question of identifying victor and vanquished no more finds entirely straightforward answers. Contemporary definitions of victory tend to relate to a comparative or competitive successful outcome rather than victorious battles. The eventual victory will have to be sought through diplomacy and bargain, reinforced by the quality of leverage, the position of strength provided by a military advantage. The quality of end states achieved versus those preconceived would rest on the strategic notion of such bargaining power to make the adversary conform to one's will. Ironically, in reality, it often fails to impede the opposition's will and ability to resist or resume hostilities. The complexities surrounding contemporary war, diplomacy and strategy thus necessitate redefining the notion of victory and defeat in varying shades. Victory and defeat, although opposites are not binary. The lexicon of decisive victory is as ambiguous as the perplexity of decisive defeat. Victory consists not solely of overcoming the enemy forces; it must include the attainment of the political objective for which the war was waged. Defeating an opponent militarily is not identical to achieving the object of war, the reason for which the war was fought. Thus, success or failure in war is replacing victory or defeat with scales of success varying from *"victory, win, not lose, stalemate or status quo, not win, lose to defeat"*. These scales are closely related yet independent variables that can be used in analysing and understanding conflict. Simply stated, the outcome could be better, status quo or worse, which could change with the passage of time and perceptions of adversaries.

Taxonomy of Victory

Victory can be classified in multiple ways though all not so enduring. It usually is employed with tactical, operational, strategic, or political connotations. At the tactical level, it essentially pertains to battles/strikes, at the operational level victory it refers to a victory that decides the outcome to a campaign, though not necessarily to the war as a whole. A victory in one theatre might be offset by a defeat in another. In contrast, a strategic victory should be one that decides who wins the war militarily. Such a strategic military victory or defeat while certainly providing the political arm with the necessary leverage, may or may not always achieve the desired political end state for a nation's victory. It may not always be necessary to "render the enemy militarily powerless," in order "to impose one's will on the enemy". After all, the war was initiated towards the achievement of the nation's political aim. Military strategic success or strategic advantage, that may fall notably short of the decisive military defeat of the enemy, may well suffice to achieve the political objective, along with others tools of victory, namely, diplomatic, economic, social, informational and political. The idea of erstwhile decisive military victory, therefore, should not be equated necessarily with the annihilation of the enemy. The focus will be more on the achievement of political objectives, rather than destruction of the enemy's combat potential. Thus, "destruction/annihilation", may be replaced by a more plausible term "degradation". The key issue is that the continuing power of physical and psychological resistance of the enemy lies below the winnability scale.

Thus, strategic success or strategic advantage assumes a more plausible term in contemporary conflicts requiring a "Complementary and Comprehensive Approach".

End State and Victory

The next compelling issue is the relationship between the end state defining victory/defeat. In contemporary wars, end states are visualised as strategic guidance in terms of war objectives in time, space and force, with well-defined centre(s) of gravity. In reality, the "end state" of conflicts has often evolved and changed in ways that none of the participants ever anticipated at the commencement of the war. Even in circumstances where the victor has successfully destroyed the opposing military, bringing the conflict to a successful end is more often than not a fallacy. War ends in victory when the vanquished accepts the outcome and transforms their belligerence towards the victor. Further, as contemporary conflicts have become a contest of narratives, as much as a violent struggle, perceptions of war will shape the perceived victory. Perceptions of the actors in and out of conflict will vary with time and according to their beliefs and manipulation. Around–the- clock media coverage, transparency and social media plausibly affect perceptions. Victory in contemporary conflict is thus inherently ambiguous, subjective and transitory. The formulation of victory in the 21st century thus requires more long-term, abstract, and complex and less tangible and immediate terms perspectives. A victory in the true sense implies that the state of peace and tranquillity of one's people, is better after the war, than before. In particular, the US-led wars in Iraq (1991, 2003-2011) and Afghanistan (since 2001) have led to interpretations that look beyond war to examine whether outcomes in these events are consistent with victory and the desired end state.

Global Contemporary Conflicts and the Notion of Victory

The present day-expeditionary forces waging supposedly, *"Jus ad Bellum"* intervention wars, present another perspective that looks beyond war, to examine whether outcomes in these events are consistent with victory. The wars in Iraq and Afghanistan began as regime-change operations and then transformed into more open-ended phases with US-led coalition forces stalemated, at best. The truth is exiting and ending those wars has proven far more elusive and consequences more disastrous, than initiating them and the battles fought itself. Clausewitz asserted that 'the defeated state often considers the outcome merely as a transitory evil, for which a remedy may still be found in political conditions at some later date'. Apparently defeated adversaries and populations may not accept their 'defeat' and the peace on the victor's terms; thus, perceived victory may not end violence but can mark a transition to a long-drawn insurgency. This is the case with Iraq and Afghanistan where the answer remains elusive to the question "How the Good War went Bad?". The continuums of these apparently endless wars make one ponder whether the notion of "victory" has any meaning in respect of contemporary warfare or is it nothing more than an enduringly dangerous myth. Welcome to an era where wars never end.

Operation Desert Storm or Gulf War 1 (1991), was not the strategic masterpiece that many at that time heralded. The outcome of the war illustrated the gap that separates battlefield success from victory. The US-led coalition forces were successful at forcing Iraq out of Kuwait but the end of the war saw Saddam still alive, in power, and unremorseful. Saddam Hussein actually viewed the Gulf War as a victory for Iraq, because US forces had stopped short of entering Iraq and threatening his regime. In ending the war unilaterally before Saddam had been chastened, the Bush Administration condemned the USA to a long-term presence in the Gulf in an effort to contain Iraq. The great losers of the Gulf War were the people of the region, who suffered the consequence of a victory that was incomplete and indecisive. Subsequently, the coalition presence and the sanctions imposed on Iraq due to Saddam's defiance, in the end, served as a rallying cry for jihadists such as Osama bin Laden against the USA and others. The 9/11 catastrophe financed by the al Qaeda terrorist organisation of Saudi fugitive Osama bin Laden was possibly a retaliation for America's involvement in the Persian Gulf War and its continued military presence in the Middle East. Victory in any shade remained elusive in this war.

The Iraq War Operation Iraqi Freedom (2003), was waged by the USA and several coalition allies, to rid Iraq of its weapons of mass destruction, as well as to topple Saddam Hussein's regime and replace it with a democracy. The coalition achieved a decisive victory against Iraqi military forces, which led to the collapse of Saddam's regime, but it struggled subsequently to secure the peace. The power vacuum following Saddam's demise and the mismanagement of the Coalition Provisional Authority led to widespread civil war between Shias and Sunnis, as well as a lengthy insurgency against coalition forces. Many of the violent insurgent groups were supported by al-Qaeda. Ironically, the invasion was far less perilous and costly to US forces than the subsequent occupation. Moreover, the majority of the Iraqi public by then had come to view the US military forces as foreign occupiers rather than liberators. A comprehensive study, commissioned by former Army Chief of Staff Gen. Ray Odierno in 2013, spans the strategic consequences of this invasion through the US withdrawal, the rise of the ISIS, and the influence of Syria and Iran. The key issue of defining victory as in Gulf War-1 remained—"Tactical Victory, Operational Success but Strategic Failure."

Operation Enduring Freedom (Afghanistan), remains the United States' longest war. The American-led international effort to oust the Taliban regime in Afghanistan and destroy Osama bin Laden's terrorist network based there began on October 2001. Over the past 19 years, More than 2,300 US military personnel have lost their lives there; over 58,000 Afghan soldiers and police have been killed in the conflict, along with 38,000 civilians and an estimated 42,000 anti-government insurgents. Washington has spent close to $1 trillion on the war. Although the al-Qaeda leader Osama bin Laden is dead and no major attack on the US homeland has been carried out by a terrorist group based in Afghanistan since 9/11, the USA has been unable to end the violence or hand over the war to the Afghan authorities with assured peace. At the end of 2019, *The Washington Post* published a series titled "The Afghanistan Papers," a collection of US government documents that included notes of interviews conducted by the special inspector general for Afghanistan reconstruction. It reveals that senior US officials failed to tell the truth about the war in Afghanistan throughout the 18-year campaign, making rosy pronouncements they knew to be false and hiding unmistakable evidence that the war had become unwinnable. The war seems an unresolved dilemma with elusive victory once again for the US Forces with no military solution in sight and the Taliban viewing it as a victory through the lens of status quo. The greatest fear that remains to the Afghan people and the world at large is that a frustrated exit might be worse than the status quo. Pretending that the Taliban can be defeated and that a constitutionally bounded, democratic, and competent Kabul-based government can be left in its place is unrealistic both in time and in space. The US notion of victory thus remains questionable in Afghanistan. Osama bin Laden being killed in Abbottabad right inside Pakistan under their nose was certainly a strategic messaging of intent and capability, but the larger issue of al-Qaeda and the ISIS remained. Wars end when one side is destroyed, or when one or both give up what they were fighting to achieve. The history of military conflict in Afghanistan has been one of initial success, followed by long years of floundering and the ultimate failure or status quo at best. Is this the notion of victory by expeditionary forces and unilateral intervention operations?

Syrian Conflict declared by the United Nations as the "worst humanitarian disaster since the Cold War," is another example, which has defied the notion of victory. The revolution which snowballed around issues of social inequality and repression ended up in a zero-sum game. The Syrian civil war was never just about Syria with its complexities of players and proxies and an open-ended turbulent future. Tragically, despite all the bloodshed and destruction and the exit of the USA, the conflict is no closer to a resolution today than it was when the revolution began in the spring of 2011. No single warring party or proxies have the military strength to declare military victory. With no clear military victory in sight, a political compromised solution is still the best bet to see comparative peace and stability. Victories have also been proclaimed in the recent wars in Iraq, Afghanistan, and Libya, only for violence to continue unabated. Syria's devastating civil war is no exception to this illusive notion of victory. If there is a perceived gainer, if not victor, it is Russia, which has regained a pivotal position not only in Syria but in the whole of the Middle East.

Israel's "Mowing The Lawn" Strategic Doctrine is a unique notion of victory and has many lessons for nations, including India. Whereas Israeli strategists traditionally focused on procuring decisive battlefield victories against adversaries, recent experiences in Gaza have led them to adopt a different approach. Instead of supposing that the Israeli Defence Force (IDF) should aim to vanquish its enemies once and for all in direct combat, it advocates that the IDF must treat the threat from Israel's enemies in the same way that a gardener approaches the mowing of a lawn: that is, as a recurrent task that can never be fully completed but must instead be returned to at regular intervals. As such, it reflects an acceptance of the fact that Israel will not achieve a decisive victory over its foes any time soon. In its place, it proposes that the best Israel can hope for is provisional gains; namely, the degradation and short-term containment of its enemies that require constant and recurrent punishment. Israel is thus acting in accordance with a "mowing the grass" strategy. The use of force is not intended to attain impossible political goals, but rather is a long-term strategy of attrition designed primarily to debilitate the enemy's capabilities and retain positive control. However, critics of this strategy have cautioned that the periods of *interbellum* calm has been used consistently to regroup and enhance capabilities by Hamas. Thus, while war is fought in spurts of strikes, the larger issue of making the adversary change its belligerence remains unresolved. This is another view of the notion of victory by not "cutting the head" of the adversary, but keeping the "head down".

INDIAN EXPERIENCE AND THE NOTION OF VICTORY

India's national security canvas, if not irretrievably perilous, is stressed and susceptible to conflict with its neighbouring rivals. Post-independence, India has fought five conventional wars. Four of these wars were against Pakistan in 1947-48, 1965, 1971 and 1999 (limited) while it fought one against China in 1962. Of course, there was Sri Lanka, Maldives and many other stand-offs, skirmishes, and surgical strikes too. The sub-conventional threat confronting the Indian state essentially stems from Pakistan-sponsored proxy war, although insurgencies in northeast India and naxalism also impose a security burden. These conflicts are a rich repository of the changing notion of victory over the years in the Indian context too. Each war had a separate *casus belli*, a different course of action and a different outcome in shades of victory or defeat. These wars theoretically should have resulted in enduring peace, but this has not happened in the Indian context. The confrontation between India and Pakistan continues unabated as also the disconcerting calm with periodic sparks with China. Ironically nuclearisation of all three antagonists has also greatly impacted the connotation of the desired end states and the notion of victory.

Operations in Jammu and Kashmir 1947-48. The first war between India and Pakistan was fought over the possession of Jammu and Kashmir. The war was a limited affair—limited in its goals, in a limited theatre, with limited means and thus battles were essentially tactical in nature. Pakistan relied on a self-created and nurtured insurgency in J&K to realise its political goals. This had only limited success, but its results encouraged

Pakistan to rely on militancy as a means for its revisionist culture. While there were many resounding victories like at Zojila and Badgam for India, yet India was defending and driving back Pakistan aggression with success in partial spatial terms. Ironically, it led to the birth of POK and a turbulent LC. From Pakistan's perspective, it achieved its intended end state to a certain extent. Pakistan secured one-third of the strategic area of J&K which also provided it with the strategic depth against India and, more importantly, the base for the insurgency. This metamorphosed into a proxy war in the late Eighties sowing the seeds of a prolonged no-war-no-peace situation. The liberation of Jammu and Kashmir from the tribal raiders supported by the Pakistan Army was a remarkable feat achieved by the Indian Army under extremely difficult circumstances. Most neutral assessments agree that India emerged victorious from the war, as it successfully defended most of the contested territory, including the Kashmir Valley, Jammu, and Ladakh. The notion of victory at the strategic level was however adverse to India with the partition of J&K and the emergence of a perpetual hot border. Indian losses in the war totalled 1,104 killed and 3,154 wounded; Pakistani, about 6,000 killed and 14,000 wounded. India gained control of about two-thirds of Kashmir; Pakistan, the remaining one-third. The notion of strategic victory remained ambiguous and the belligerence of the adversaries continued unabated.

Sino-Indian Conflict 1962. The Sino-Indian conflict of 1962 is a scar in Indian military history. It is remembered for India's decisive defeat and the betrayal of Hindi-Chini-Bhai-Bhai. The invasion inflicted immense psychological political shock on India. The shock value of China's blitzkrieg, physically and psychologically, dented the response by the poorly equipped and ill-prepared Indian Army forcing it to retreat. The Chinese victory resulted in control of Tibet and created the foundation for a strong relationship between Pakistan and China. The 1962 humiliation resulted in a politico-military awakening and rise on India's military capabilities and a strong relationship with the Soviet Union. Thus, the Indian military was undoubtedly better prepared during the 1965 and 1971 wars against Pakistan. In an important sense, the subsequent skirmishes and face-off at Nathula 1967, Sumdorong Chu 1987 and Doklam 2017 brought out India's resolve and capabilities to withstand any Chinese coercive actions. The 1962 war, however, did not settle the fundamental border dispute that divided India and China and thus China failed in its strategic aim of resolving the main cause. The notion of military victory was clear with India defeated and China victorious.

Indo-Pak Conflict 1965. Fifty years ago, Pakistan muddied the waters by initiating a spate of belligerent actions in the area of the Rann of Kutch that led to a war between India and Pakistan on the former's Western borders. It is said that 1965 was the first real war between the two countries that precipitated a feeling of permanent hostility. India claims it was the victor. Equally vociferous is Pakistan's claim to victory. Neutral military historians grade it as a 'stalemate'. The battles fought were essentially tactical with the operational level of war conspicuous by its absence on both sides. In the final balance, the outcome of war should be whether the political aim set was achieved. Pakistan started the war with the explicit aim to wrest J&K from India by force. In that, it failed miserably. Minor tactical gains and territorial gains are not sufficient to claim victory. Since India was in a reactive mode in a war that was thrust upon it, denying the belligerent achieving any of his stated objectives was, therefore, a victory by all accounts. In the aftermath of the war, the situation was back to square one with both sides incurring huge losses in lives and material. There were gains and losses of territory. However, in mere figures, both casualties and territorial losses were in India's favour. The notion of victory at the strategic level was again ambiguous and inconclusive, though the scales rested in India's favour. Although the two countries fought to a standoff, the conflict is seen as a strategic and political failure for Pakistan, as it had neither succeeded in fomenting uprising in Kashmir nor had it been able to gain meaningful support at an international level. India won by not losing...Pakistan lost by not winning. In the end, the Tashkent Agreement restored the status quo denying India the limited advantage it had spatially gained.

Indo-Pak War 1971. 1971 was an exceptional year for India for the development and exercise of its national power dynamics. It had won a decisive military and strategic victory and a *Jus ad Bellum* war for India, which gave birth to a new nation. The military leverage not only created a new nation but had 97,000 war prisoners and over 13,000 sq. km. Pakistan territory on the western front. It is a different story of not converting this leverage for long-term strategic advantage. For the first time after the independence of India, there was complete synergy between the political executive and its military power. India made it clear that its ambitions were not territorial, nor revengeful or expansionist but that its national interest was supreme. The notion of victory was unambiguous in a full-scale war on two fronts. Even the superpowers were kept at bay and India emerged as a regional power of global standing. It was a resounding and decisive victory for India at all levels. The world including Pakistan accepted that India was both just and victorious.

Sri Lanka 1987. Op Pavan was India's Vietnam-like quagmire; an ill-advised hurried war that ended in retreat without achieving an end state. In 1990, less than three years after India sent in an Indian Peace Keeping Force (IPKF), it was pulled out, leaving India frustrated and embarrassed. The bravery and tactical engagements were indeed creditable but beyond that, there was no notion of victory. The Indians were fighting a limited war against the LTTE, while Prabhakaran was fighting a total war against them. Indians were fighting a blind conventional war while LTTE was fighting a 4GW on home ground. India lost 1,240 soldiers in 32 months; a high price without strategic victory. A year after the withdrawal, the Tigers assassinated former Indian Prime Minister Rajiv Gandhi, who had sent in the military. Ironically, the civil war, which India had hoped to end through its campaign, lasted another two decades before the Sri Lankan military crushed the Tigers. The scars from that illogical intervention continue to shape India's approach to foreign military action, including Afghanistan. The IPKF's negative experience exposed to India the limitations of using coercive military power to change the domestic affairs of its neighbours. From a military perspective also, the IPKF operation was a failure because it failed to separate the LTTE from the Sinhala forces, much less disarm them, and bringing them into the political process. The notion of victory was clear; India failed to achieve what it had set for at all levels—military, political and strategic, and ended up sacrificing the precious lives of soldiers.

Kargil 1999. Pakistan's 1999 Kargil misadventure was an emergence of limited war in the Indo-Pak context under the nuclear umbrella. India called it a victory by way of achieving the vital national interest of restoring its territorial integrity. Pakistan called it a military victory by catching the enemy napping, but political failure to capitalise initial gains and succumbing to international pressure to withdraw. India convincingly achieved its military objective of removal of intrusions and politico-diplomatic objectives of enhancing India's image as a responsible nation with restraint, willing to work for enduring global peace. This was also the first media war in the Indian context which gave rise to nationalism and euphoria. However, India missed the opportunity to exploit success by entering Pakistan territory, with exhibited restraint giving credence to nuclear deterrence. The Kargil conflict *de facto* gave an impression of the inviolability of the LC, almost akin to the International Border. However, besides the glaring intelligence failure at all levels, it had several long-term strategic consequences for India. A new deployment, a mountain division, an erstwhile reserve for conventional war, got deployed on the Kargil heights in high altitude areas around the year at a high human and economic cost. In addition, suicide and fidayeen attacks emerged in the Valley, which were absent in the pre-Kargil era. The Valley heated up for a different blend of proxy war. The notion of victory for India was achieved, but at a high cost against enemy irregulars and paramilitary force (NLI), accepting limited wars driven by nuclear holocaust and redeployment of forces to another high ground.

Era and Aura of Surgical Strikes. The transactional trajectory of Indian response strategy from Risk Aversion and Strategic Restraint of Kargil, to Risk Aligned and Symbolic Retribution post-Uri, to Risk Acceptance and Punitive Retribution post-Pulwama, has incrementally reformatted the Asian strategic security calculus and global security paradigm. Balakot marked a new normal exhibiting certainty of response even in the fog of an adversary's traditional deniability with an uncertainty of intensity and medium, as part of the strategy of punitive deterrence and assured retribution, exhibiting strategic autonomy. It demonstrated the nation's resolve, strong political will and multi-domain military capability for a comprehensive punitive response to national security threats. Ironically, it simultaneously also gave rise to the concept of hyper-nationalism and politicisation of military operations. Certainly, it achieved its aim of strategic messaging to Pakistan and the world, of the emergence of a decisive, bold India. However, the notion of victory even at a tactical level was ambiguous with Pakistan airstrikes and claims and counter-claims of achievement of tactical and operational objectives. Each side claimed it a victory of sorts with its own information warfare, but certainly, India's strategic messaging was clear and unambiguous. However, at the end of the day, the challenge of deterring Pakistan from fuelling a proxy war in Kashmir remains. India has not yet found a lasting formula of dealing with it. The surgical strikes were mooted as the solution, but they have clearly not worked in entirety, though partially and temporally it has restrained Pakistan, only to recalibrate its pitch. It also exposed chinks in the armoury of both sides and saw the emergence of a new "tit for tat "dynamics. So, the status quo continues until effective mechanisms are found to tackle the problem of Kashmir.

CALIBRATING THE FUTURE NOTION OF VICTORY IN THE INDIAN CONTEXT

India's prospective geopolitical options and threat environment were profoundly altered by the partition of India giving birth to a belligerent fundamentalist Pakistan and the uncertainties of the rise of a hegemonic China. The strategic triangle of India-Pakistan-China is symbolised by disparate ideology yet mutually influencing relationship, deeply rooted and intertwined in historical contradictions. This strategic triangle and its periphery also bear the shadow of major world powers, their interests and personal agendas. Besides, this triangle has the discredit of the largest warring militaries, disputed border acting as flashpoints, nuclear brinkmanship, a quest for competing strategic space and proxy war creating strategic fragility. This has led to mistrust, collusive interplay and a fragile oscillating balance between a revisionist Islamic republic struggling for survival, a stable democracy with the recent upsurge of ideology-driven nationalism and an expansionist fast-growing communist state challenging strategic stability. India's internal front also remains active. India's struggle with insurgencies began soon after independence, and it has had its share of successes in dealing with these movements, but challenges remain, particularly in Jammu and Kashmir, the North East and Left-Wing Extremism. India thus faces a turbulent and fragile strategic environment with multifarious threats and challenges. The notion of victory in future conflicts for India, in the foreseeable future, will thus have to be theorised in this environment with a foundational edifice of strategic autonomy.

Pakistan. All-out conventional wars are unlikely to be fought among nuclear powers, be it with Pakistan or China. India has called Pak's bluff of the nuclear bogey with responses to Kargil and Balakot; this must be retained. Pak's continued obsession with Kashmir and revisionist ideology will continue to fuel a proxy war in Kashmir with spillover possibilities to the heartland. Pakistan would, however, attempt to calibrate the proxy war under the nuclear overhang, to prevent a conventional face-off with India. Thus, surgical strikes and border exchanges will continue to be the new normal. The possibility of our punitive response escalating into an all-out war cannot, however, be ruled out. Thus, limited wars with limited objectives and restricted time duration, essentially in the LC sector or disputed boundary will gain ascendancy. Should it overflow over to the IB sector, it will require careful calibration of objectives and end states in terms of time, space and force domain. The notion of victory for a limited war and conventional response will be defined more by the desired end state of psychological gains of the capture of value territory, degradation of Pakistan combat potential and ensuring own territorial integrity. This would imply, most importantly, qualitative gains of value territory in incremental time cycles in the Pakistan Punjab Sector and POK, with well-defined periodic end state at the end of each operational cycle. This would make the cost-benefit of proxy war cost-prohibitive for Pakistan, thereby discrediting the Pakistan Army and the nation in the eyes of their own people and the world. India must accordingly adopt a strategy of "Punitive Deterrence" to exploit its conventional edge and hone its response capability by Integrated Battle Groups. The success of counteroffensive(s) and any resultant *'quid pro quo'* gains by Pakistan are likely to be claimed as a victory by Pakistan. Thus, in case of a future conflict with Pakistan, the politico-military objectives will have to be carefully calibrated, and the notion of military victory will be a combination of degradation of combat potential, selective value spatial gains and a decisive psychological edge. A status quo would be a notion of victory for Pakistan and defeat for India. Collusive support from China, more likely passive to dissuade pull out from the northern or eastern fronts, will have to be built into the war dynamics.

The notion of victory against a proxy war will be defined by assured retribution through punitive strikes and aggressive domination to keep Pak's proxy war cauldron subdued, and ensuring positive control within the Valley. Obsession with Kashmir and revisionism is an essential DNA of Pakistan's culture and ideology as a nation. Thus, rather than change what is unchangeable, making it untenable is a better option. India's politico-military aim must be synergized to deter Pak from waging a proxy war, while simultaneously addressing the internal fault lines in Kashmir. India has to enforce "Strategic Compellence" on Pakistan to achieve her political aims and deny Pakistan her political objectives. Militarily, another surgical strike would not be enough to deter. The most important aspect to understand about deterrence is that it is not a one-way action, but rather involves a reciprocal relationship between the two players in which perception and actions are crucial operational components. Specifically, the adversary must agree to be deterred by the capability, credibility and communication of the response. A strategy of proactive punitive deterrence should be built around politico-diplomatic dissuasion, economic coercion, and military compellence based on political isolation, economic sanctions, and calibrated military actions to "Hit Hard, Hit where it hurts and Hurt where it lasts". This would involve a comprehensive and comprehensive approach of punitive military response as deterrence, complemented by diplomatic, economic and political acumen to expose Pakistan. Exposing Pakistan's nefarious designs globally and its recognition as a hotbed of breeding terrorism and must be the foundational pillar of this notion of victory. As regards the internal dynamics within the Valley, these will have to be complementarily better managed politically with effective governance and addressing the ideological divide, fault lines and mistrust with people as the Centre of Gravity, while the security forces create a facilitating environment to usher in lasting peace.

China. China presents a long-term, and multifaceted challenge to India. Relations with China while being managed from competition to cooperation, have all the potential to flare up to a future confrontation. While dealing with China has always remained one of India's biggest foreign policy challenges, today the asymmetry in economic and military capabilities between the two Asian giants is expanding rather than shrinking. The challenge is greater in the non-contact, non-kinetic, informational, digital allied domains. China's military-focused infrastructure development in Tibet, modernising of its armed forces and investment in futuristic battlefield systems has created a wide gap in combat capabilities on the Northern front. China has also developed an all-weather relationship with Pakistan, which it employs as a proxy against India. This collusive support remains a reality and challenge for any future conflict for India, be it a one- or two-front conflict. China sees India as not only a regional competitor but a major geostrategic player in the Indo-Pacific and a global anchor meant to contain its rise. This has been further aggravated by growing strategic convergence between India and the USA and formulations such as 'Quad' and Indo-Pacific, seen by China as part of a containment strategy. Active disputed borders on India's land and maritime periphery, to nuclear weapons, and incremental expansion in the Indo-Pacific exemplify China's hegemonic design. China not settling the boundary dispute holding it as a Damocles' Sword, leaves no doubt that undercurrents of conflict remain. Managing the rise of China and deterring its unilateral aggression in the region thus remains a strategic challenge for India. Thus, countering the threat from China is based more robustly on conventional deterrence with unlikely nuclear posturing. India's current strategic deterrence against China is thus based on dissuasive deterrence edging towards credible deterrence, with a build-up of adequate infrastructure and military response capability opposite it. This essentially is a defensive and limited offensive strategy based on ground holding deployments for ensuring territorial integrity, backed by the limited offensive capability for a *quid pro quo* gain in preselected areas. This strategy is not punitive but conflict prevention deterrence by developing capabilities. The strategic construct of this strategy 'to raise the cost of military intervention' is more political than military. China's periodic forays in peacetime by way of transgression will have to be denied any psychological gains with due resolute military deterrence and astute political decisiveness to preserve its core national interests. This would be an important aspect of strategic messaging. Thus, managing China both in peace and war requires collaborative military, economic, informational, diplomatic and political levers to deter its revisionist designs. While China may continue to ignite sparks, India will need to do much more in these domains to build up such levels of capacity that the military opposition withers without conflict—in the mould of Sun Tzu's classical dictum of 'winning without fighting.' The notion of a military victory against China thereby rests on ensuring the status quo by denying China its military and political objectives. This would amount to politically subduing Chinese politico-military objectives and therefore a notion of defeat for them in the eyes of their own people and more importantly the world. This is something the world would welcome and China detest.

Conclusion

Clausewitz recognised war's ability to change its appearance in more than a superficial manner. Though victory can be hideously costly in modern war, it invariably accomplishes far less than it is intended to achieve and is not an entirely vacuous concept. Victory may be seen in the context of achieving or denying an adversary politico-military objectives/end states, at least cost and minimum time and thus indicative of a better outcome than what existed before the war. Sometimes the status quo for an adversary also constitutes a victory. What is of antiquity here is not the general concept of victory itself, but the notion that victory is a product of decisive battles. Instead of yielding an absolute victory for one side and, conversely, an undeniable defeat for the other, modern armed conflicts are prone to descend into protracted, drawn-out endgames. Success is a matter of perspective which varies with the perception of the players involved and nations at large. Victory in such conflicts no longer rests on the ability to inflict massive destruction but on the ability to wrestle popular support away from one's opponents.

However, decisive victories may well be a rare beast, but they are also widely postulated as the desired end states toward which all militaries should strive. As such, it continues to guide our thinking about what war can achieve, when it should be employed, by what means it should be conducted, and how and when it should be concluded. More simply, it is the balancing of desired outcomes with allotted resources and military ingenuity. Thus, it is clear, warfare and victory/defeat, irrespective of the changing complexion, have a bonded relationship which cannot be divorced from one another. The challenge arising from this is to rethink how we define military victory in 21st century warfare. Historian Christopher Hill once wrote, "The ever-changing character of war demands that every generation must also rethink its understanding of military victory".

NOTES

1. Clan O'Driscoll, "The Myth of Victory in Modern Warfare", *Quartz*, available at https://qz.com/1758673/are-modern-wars-unwinnable/.
2. Collin Randall, "A Dynamic Theory of Battle Victory and Defeat", *Cliodynamics Journal*, available at https://escholarship.org/uc/item/5mv6v0r1.
3. Raymond G. O'Connor, "Victory in Modern War", *SAGE Journal*, available at https://journals.sagepub.com/doi/pdf/10.1177/002234336900600406.
4. Ove Pappila, "The Nature of War Today", available at https://www.kkrva.se/wp-content/uploads/Artiklar/084/kkrvaht_4_2008_5.pdf.
5. Lieutenant General A.B. Shivane, *"Operational Art: Western Front—Concepts, Means and Methodologies"*, Seminar Army War College on Operational Art.
6. Lieutenant General A.B. Shivane, "Hit Hard, Hit where it hurts, Hurt where it Lasts", available at https://nationaldefence.in/breaking-news/hit-hard-hit-where-it-hurts-hurt-where-it-lasts-need-a-paradigm-shift-in-proxy-war-response-strategy/.
7. Lieutenant General A.B. Shivane, "Hit Smartly, Hit Vulnerabilities, Hit when it is Hot", available at https://nationaldefence.in/breaking-news/hit-smartly-hit-vulnerabili

ties-hit-when-its-hot-lt-gen-a-b-shivane/.

8. Lieutenant General A.B. Shivane, "Six Strategic Messages: Post 26/02 Air Strikes", available at https://nationaldefence.in/breaking-news/six-strategic-messages-post-26-02-air-strikes/.
9. Lieutenant General A.B. Shivane, "Pulwama to Balakot: Myths, Realities and Challenges", available at http://www.spslandforces.com/story/?id=603&h=Pulwama-to-Balakot-andndash;-Myths-Realities-and-Challenges.
10. Lieutenant General A.K. Singh and Lieutenant General Raj Shukla, Chapter 3. *"Changing Nature of Conflict in the 21st Century"*, Military Strategy for India in the 21st Century, KW Publishers.
11. Colin S. Gray, *"Defining And Achieving Decisive Victory (2002)"*, Strategic Studies. Institute, available at https://archive.org/search.php?query=creator%3A%22 Strategic+ Studies+ Institute%22
12. Brigadier Mohammad Iftikhar Zaidi, *"The Conduct of War and the Notion of Victory: A Theory and Definition of Victory"*, PhD Thesis, Cranfield Defence and Security University, available at https://www.semanticscholar.org/paper/The-conduct-of-war-and-the-notion-of-victory-%3A-a-of-Zaidi/0d091e0f566f191fd816fc83ad51a21ec8e4db43).
13. Zachery Tyson Brown, " Unmasking War's Changing Character", Modern War Institute at West Point, available at https://mwi.usma.edu/unmasking-wars-changing-character/
14. Gabriella Blum, "The Fog of Victory", *European Journal of International Law*, 2013, vol. 24, no. 1, 391-421, available at https://papers.ssrn.com/sol3/papers.cfm?abstract_id=2246774).
15. H. Cordesman, *"The "End State" Fallacy: Setting the Wrong Goals for War Fighting"*, Centre for Strategic and International Studies (CSIS), available at https://medium.com/center-for-strategic-and-international-studies/the-end-state-fallacy-setting-the-wrong-goals-for-war-fighting-15214f0416f.
16. Iraq War, Afghanistan, Syria, Sino India and Indo Pak Wars, Operation Pavan, Operation Vijay, Wikipedia.
17. Afghanistan: *"What is an Acceptable End State, and How Do We Get There"*, Hearing Before The Committee On Foreign Relations, United States Senate, One Hundred Twelfth Congress, First Session, available at https://www.loc.gov/item/2011508069/
18. Carter Malkasian, "How the Good War Went Bad, America's Slow-Motion Failure in Afghanistan", *Foreign Affairs Journal*, available at https://www.foreignaffairs.com/articles/afghanistan/2020-02-10/how-good-war-went-bad.
19. "The Afghanistan Papers - At War with the Truth", *The Washington Post*, available at https://www.washingtonpost.com/graphics/2019/investigations/afghanistan-papers/afghanistan-war-confidential-documents/
20. Takenori Horimoto, "India's Wars: The Indo-Pakistani Wars and the India-China Border Conflict", available at http://www.nids.mod.go.jp/english/event/forum/pdf/2015/07.pdf).
21. Chapter 3: "Case Studies of India's Wars Fought Post-Independence", available at https://shodhganga.inflibnet.ac.in/bitstream/10603/262036/10/10_chapter3.pdf.
22. Martin Sherman, *'Mowing the Lawn' Won't Cut It: My Challenge to the Begin-Sadat Center for Strategic Studies*, available at http://www.israelnationalnews.com/Articles/Article.aspx/19394).
23. Bart Schuurman, "Clausewitz and the New War Scholars", *Parameter Journal*, available at https://www.researchgate.net/publication/267637446_Clausewitz_and_the_'New_Wars'_ Scholars

3

Dynamic Military Strategy

Lieutenant General AK Singh and Brigadier Narender Kumar

"The nation that will insist on drawing a broad line of demarcation between the fighting man and the thinking man is liable to find its fighting done by fools and its thinking done by cowards."

—**William Francis Butler**

Introduction

Clausewitz defined that military strategy is not a plan; it is a national security doctrine for the purposes of war. If analysed empirically, military strategy is a tool to channelise hard power to secure national interests. This tool becomes imperative if there is an uncertain security environment. Dynamic military strategy provides the ability to a military force to renew and alter its process of execution of war, especially when there are deep uncertainties and threats loom large. Under the prevailing security environment of the 21st century, military strategy needs to be dynamic, to be able to provide options to the leadership in an ambiguous security environment. A dynamic strategy would assist military leaders to weigh in risks that may arise due to conflict situations and empower them to execute military plans amid uncertainties. There is a necessity to understand that planning a military campaign or operation is not a strategy and these are two different processes. However, scenario planning is the fulcrum to formulate a dynamic strategy. In modern full-spectrum wars, dominant battle space awareness will no longer be just buzz words. The "Clausewitzian friction of war, articulated centuries ago and emphasizing deception, manipulation, and information operations, will not just live but thrive in the 21st century.[1] In view of the above, futuristic strategies would be aligned to ensure denial of dominance and battle space awareness to even digitised forces of the adversary. China is fast digitising its forces to integrate multi-domains to add speed, security, lethality and a disabling impact on enemy forces by simultaneously developing contact and non-contact warfare capabilities.

Thucydides said, "Peace is a temporary truce in a war that is continuously going on." India is at war since 1947 as no other nation has fought so many conventional and sub-conventional conflicts post World War–II. Incidentally, each of these wars was different from the others. India has faced conventional wars (1962, 1965 & 1971), local wars (Kargil & Sri Lanka), proxy war in Jammu & Kashmir (J&K) and sub-conventional conflicts (militancy in Punjab, insurgency in the North East and Left Wing Extremism, or LWE). The character of war is rapidly changing; the threat is from conventional and sub-conventional forces, contact and non-contact warfare, with the spectrum of conflict ranging from land, air, sea, space to cyber, information and cognitive domains. Technology has made wars ambiguous and multi-domain has made it even more lethal.

A two-front challenge in the Indian context is a reality with both the Line of Actual Control (LAC) and the Line of Control (LoC) becoming active. To deal with such an uncertain security environment, there is a need to put in place dynamic military strategies backed by robust military capabilities. The fact of the matter is that building capability is a military science and employment of that capability is an art inherent to military leadership. The analytical base line needs to be widened and this is possible when the military becomes part of policy formulation in meeting the challenges of an uncertain security environment. The big question is why is India's response to security challenges reactive or transactional and generally restricted to the tactical level? The answer lies in the fact that India has not adequately invested in the intellectual component of war fighting and contestation of ideas with potential adversaries. This void can only be filled when there is a grand strategy, national security strategy and military strategy in place to align the instruments of power for a holistic response to a full spectrum or limited threat of a hybrid nature.

Political and Diplomatic Leaders Need to Understand the Nuances of Application of Military Power

Understanding how to leverage smart power to secure vital national interests is indeed fine statecraft. Ironically, political leaders and diplomats in India have not invested adequately in understanding the nuances of employment of military power in pursuance of national interests. India laid emphasis on moral power that failed to protect India from external aggression. It is therefore imperative for our strategic leaders and diplomatic community to understand that "hard power occupies the pole position in statecraft". Political leaders and diplomacy should be aware that soft power has limitations and they can only be overcome by hard power. Things are changing, with India not hesitating to use its military power to signal its strong intent to both the adversaries, in very recent face-offs. But this needs to be persisted within an institutional framework through the articulation of NSS and a dynamic military strategy.

War is only a branch of political activity; it is in no sense autonomous.[2] 'War is not an act of 'blind passion,'[3] it is dominated by the political objectives. Thus preparation for war cannot be left to the Generals alone; political and military leaders are co-equal in the process to develop capabilities and preparation for war. The US President George Washington declared, 'If we desire to secure peace, one of the most powerful instruments of our rising prosperity, it must be known that we are at all times ready for war.'[4] Political leaders in consultation with military and diplomacy should lay down the objectives of war. How the military power is applied on the ground to achieve political objectives is the responsibility of the military leaders. It is not brute force alone that can be employed to safeguard and secure a nation, but it is how smart power is carefully nurtured and then utilised for the preservation and enhancement of the nation's long-term social, economic and political objectives. Joseph Nye, of the Centre for Strategic and International Studies (CSIS) of the USA, describes smart power as: "an approach that underscores the necessity of a strong military, but also invests heavily in alliances, partnerships, and institutions of all levels to expand influence and establish legitimacy.[5]

Leveraging military victories to achieve political objectives is a nuanced skill of statecraft. India lost an opportunity and fell short of achieving political objectives by unilaterally halting the advancing army without liberating the entire J&K in 1947-48, against the advice of the military leadership. Similarly, soldiers captured the strategic pass of Hajipir in 1965, but political leaders lost it on the negotiating table on the ill advice of the bureaucracy. Last but not the least, after having captured 93,000 prisoners of war in East Pakistan in the 1971 war, India repatriated all of them without adequate strategic returns. This happened due to a poor understanding of the application of military power and failure to leverage military victories to achieve strategic objectives. If the political and diplomatic corps is ill-educated on issues of employment of the military in war, it is likely to diminish the security interests of the country, and military victories may go in vain.

At the same time, the problem with military influence in policymaking is that military commanders often tend to see foreign affairs purely through the security lens. The military leaders too lack sufficient understanding of diplomacy as a political tool, and are thus more inclined to rely on force to conduct statecraft.[6] However, this characterisation disregards the diverse responsibilities of modern military leaders, which require a broad strategic perspective. Today's complex threat environment requires that military leaders understand the employment of diplomacy as a political tool and as part of statecraft.[7] Diplomacy will become effective and relevant only if it is backed by strong military capabilities. In fact, diplomacy and military power are two sides of same coin. Disproportionate emphasis on diplomacy or instrument of force may often lead to flawed policy outcomes and as a result, a nation may either punch below its capabilities or miscalculate the political aspirations and strategic reach. To win wars, it is important for military leaders to correct the Army's political blind spot.[8] We need to be more cognisant of how to deftly leverage force and reconfigure its use in the obtaining politico-strategic environment.

Grand Strategy and National Security Strategy is a Pre-requisite for Formulation of Military Strategy

Some time ago, grand strategy was considered a mother source for formulation of national security and military strategy. But over a period of time, grand strategy became an academic exercise that could be bypassed to formulate national security strategy. In fact, for policymakers, grand strategy defines a nation's vision of its place in the world, its international role, guides the alignment of means and ends, and serves as a polestar for discrete foreign policy decisions.[9] Liddell Hart stated that, "The crux of grand strategy lies therefore in policy, that is, in the capacity of the nation's leaders to bring together all of the elements, both military and non-military, for the preservation and enhancement of the nation's long-term (that is, in wartime and peacetime) best interests."[10] Barry Posen draws on a similar strategic tradition and offers an even more succinct definition: Grand strategy is "a state's theory about how it can best cause security for itself".[11]

Grand strategy is an overarching academic tool that broadly defines the objectives of national security strategy and military strategy. Some scholars argue that grand strategy works best on predictable terrain—in a world where policymakers enjoy a clear understanding of the distribution of power, a solid domestic consensus about national goals and identity, and stable political and national security institutions.[12] It is in an environment where power is becoming more about the ability to disrupt, block, disable, veto, and destroy than it is about the ability to construct, enable, repair, and re-build[13]. Under such circumstances grand strategy is becoming an imperative to secure national interests. In the absence of grand strategy and national security strategy, military response to a security challenge becomes more of a transactional tactical response to an emerging strategic and operational security challenge. The states are likely to confront a disorderly, cluttered, and fluid realm that is not in harmony with grand strategy's supposed virtue: a practical, durable, and consistent plan for the long term. To operate successfully in such an environment, states would have to constantly change their strategies.[14] To overcome this limitation of linear thinking, a dynamic military strategy holds immense value.

A National Security Strategy or Policy (NSS or NSP) is a key framework for a country to meet the basic needs and security concerns of citizens and to address external and internal threats to the country.[15] Lt Gen D.S. Hooda, a former Army Commander, flagged key themes that NSS must endeavour to achieve: "assuming our rightful place in global affairs", "achieving a secure neighbourhood", "peaceful resolution of internal conflicts", "protecting our people" and "strengthening our capabilities".[16] Lt Gen Phillip Campose, a former Army Vice Chief, states that "The Indian 'national security strategy', in the current context, must not only deal with threats to our strategic autonomy as well as the external military threats to the nation, it must also deal with internal threats, threats to our core values and other non-traditional threats that face the nation.[17] Our national security should not be handled in an ad-hoc manner when the threats to internal and external security are so pronounced. There is a need for enunciating a NSS considering the changing character of war, technological developments and increasing threat from hybrid and grey zone warfare. Once the grand strategy and NSS is formulated, it becomes a foundation for evolving the military strategy. Defining NSS would facilitate focussed capability building and articulation of appropriate military doctrines to meet the threats and challenges of the future. It would enable better training and preparedness so that our defence forces are able to operate and deliver optimally in the future.[18] It is evident that without defining grand strategy and NSS, India's response to threats or black swan events will remain largely ad hoc in nature.

Future Battle Space will also be contested in the Non-kinetic and Non-military Domain

Future battle space will be contested in an informationalised environment. There is a need to have a greater understanding of this aspect of war fighting to formulate a dynamic military strategy to fight wars under such ambiguous conditions. Nations like China and Pakistan may not always engage in direct military confrontation since they have developed non-contact and non-military capabilities through which they can achieve their objectives of war without employment of hard military power. Today, revisionist powers and rogue regimes are using non-military tools such as predatory economic practices, propaganda, political subversion, proxies, and the threat or use of military force to change facts on the ground[19] to create strategic instability.

The peace-war paradigm has ceased to exist between India and Pakistan and now China and India. It is now a paradigm of war and the contours of conflict are suggestive of the fact that India will always remain in competition/confrontation, and it is just the intensity and the nature of that competition that will determine the type and nature of contest (military or non-military). Most strategic analysts agree that non-contact and non-kinetic wars make good economic sense because they do not impose a high economic burden unlike conventional wars, and achieve their goals without much bloodshed. Indeed,' 'successful wars" of the future may be those that conclude without firing a shot.[20]

The most critical aspect of the contest in the information domain is employment of technology, especially big data, artificial intelligence (AI), cognitive modelling of media, data analytics, robotics, human machine teaming, net-centric connectivity and even biotechnology. The strategic and operational leaders will face a decision dilemma on what means to employ to achieve their goals and objectives. The dynamic military strategy will have to also cater for dealing with non-contact, non-military and non-kinetic warfare by developing suitable capabilities through harnessing technology. The question comes up who should be the coordinator of this warfare? The basic principle of fighting modern wars is unity of command and an integrated operational plan executed by a structured organisation to achieve simultaneity and synergised response. Ideally, such operations would require political clearance since they are executed at a strategic level; however at the military level it should be coordinated by theatre commanders when they come into existence. Till then, Headquarters Integrated Defence Staff should be coordinating these operations by designating a lead service in a particular theatre. It may be even prudent to create hybrid warfare organisations where cyber, robotics, autonomous surveillance systems, space, communication and irregular/Special Forces' actions may be coordinated.

The Need for a Dynamic Military Strategy for India

In developing and justifying capabilities to deal with unpredictable security challenges, each defence service in the Indian context is assuming its own matrix of threat without examining the analytical models involving multi-domains whereas the threat, especially from China and Pakistan, is now multi-domain and two-front. Events such as the Kargil Conflict 1999, Mumbai 26/11, Doklam and Pulwama attack and standoff with the People's Liberation Army (PLA) in Ladakh in 2020 warranted profound strategic planning for a structured response. Most of the current response options are primarily based on operational plans prepared for a theatre of war and not as part of enunciated military strategy. India's response in most cases till now appears to be reactive and not a part of predefined strategy. Such a reactive policy is suggestive of the fact that Higher Defence Organisation (HDO) does not have a National Security Strategy to appropriately align instrument of force to deal with the security challenges. Interestingly, Prime Minister Modi in his address to the Combined Commanders Conference in 2015, stated that, "In a world of rapid changes, India faces familiar threats and new ones. Our challenges cover land, sea and air at the same time. It includes the full range, from terrorism to conventional threat to a nuclear war. Our responsibilities are no longer confined to our borders and coastlines. They extend to our interests and citizens, spread across a world of widespread and unpredictable risks."[21]

Though it is a policy indication suggesting that the Indian Armed Forces should prepare military strategy for conventional and sub-conventional wars and develop expeditionary capabilities, the sanctity of such a policy directive becomes binding if it is documented in National Security Strategy or Grand Strategy. In nutshell, the Military Strategy provides an overview of our strategic challenges to give broad guidelines on how India should employ the military to keep the nation and its interests safe. The following conditions necessitate implementation of a resilient military strategy in the Indian context:

(a) Sub-conventional/asymmetric security challenge may not always require a conventional military response, because a nation cannot go to war to a black swan event. The attack of 26/11, Uri terror attack and Pulwama suicide attack are black swan events where two nuclear neighbours could have clashed in conventional/local wars. Thus, there is a need to develop strategy that guides military or non-military actions short of war to prevent and respond against such unpredictable events that have serious consequences for national security.

(b) Hybrid threats could necessitate the military stepping in even before diplomacy. The Uri terror attack and the Pulwama suicide attack did not give any time and space for diplomacy to intervene. Under such circumstances, the HDO needs to keep the military in the loop so that it is not found wanting at a critical juncture.

(c) India may not be having territorial expansionist designs, but under the current security environment, it has become imperative to protect vital national interests even beyond territorial boundaries. Thus, the development of expeditionary capabilities is essential, especially to protect the Indian Diaspora, energy security and economic interests that lie in distant geographic regions, especially the Indian Ocean Rim countries.

(d) India should not feel guilty of developing military power that ensures the security of the nation and dissuades adversaries or prevents subversion of national security. There is a need for India to emerge out of its "defensive crouch" and display no hesitation in the use of military force against strategic destabilisation by hegemonic and expansionist adversaries.

(e) There is a need to understand that the adversary will not come at you by following protocols and a graduated response, but will position military power to its advantage. A standoff between the PLA and the Indian Army is indicative of the fact that all CBMs and protocols have been thrown out of the window by China and a proxy war has indicated Pakistan is no different.

(f) A two-front war is a reality and no more a fiction. There is a separate chapter devoted to this serious challenge in this book.

(g) War under a nuclear overhang is a reality that must be acknowledged and prepared for in our military strategy, to include both defensive and offensive contingencies. Such a preparation will also provide greater credibility to India's Nuclear Doctrine, especially against Pak's threat of use of Tactical Nuclear Weapons.

(h) Trade and economic interests are not a shield against enemy aggression. It is the instrument of force that will ultimately dissuade adversaries.

(i) China is making efforts to subvert the neutrality of our neighbouring states. If China succeeds, it would exploit these nations as new corridors of peril of three warfares (3W) against India. We will have to deal with this new threat and cater for a robust strategy without allowing these nations to drift away. The strategy so designed should endeavour to neutralise the Chinese 3Ws, unrestricted and non-kinetic war against India.

Essential Components of Dynamic Military Strategy for India

There is a requirement to define a dynamic military strategy that caters for a wide spectrum of future conflicts ranging from conventional to sub-conventional conflicts and multiple battle space domains. The broad purpose of military strategy is to ensure internal security, secure land, sea, space and cyber frontiers and project power to secure vital national interests beyond the territorial boundaries of India. The military should be capable of providing a safe and secure environment so that the nation is able to pursue diplomatic, informational, and socio-economic activities that promote enduring national interests.[22] As a consequence, the tenets of military strategy ought to be different for the conventional and sub-conventional spheres of conflicts. The military strategy for "conventional conflict" ideally should be based on the tenets—"Dissuade, Deter, Deny and Defeat". Similarly, against "hybrid and sub-conventional challenges" the military strategy should be—"Disrupt, Degrade and Defeat".

Strategic deterrence and escalation management. Escalation can be defined as an increase in the intensity or scope of conflict that crosses threshold(s) considered significant by one or more of the participants.[23] Lack of capabilities could also lead to an escalation dilemma, forcing the military to either avoid proportionate response or resort to unsustainable disproportionate escalation that may entail huge military and political cost. Managing escalation will require strategies tailored to the magnitude of threat envisaged and the interests likely to be trespassed. The bottom-line is development of capabilities and use of instruments of force to deter China and Pakistan. India will have to legislate deterrence that is broader than nuclear deterrence. The instrument of force to fight "New generation warfare" (NGW) would require nuclear, conventional, irregular and non-military measures for both, peacetime and war-time scenarios. India should also start thinking of the concept of "escalate to de-escalate" conflicts when the push comes to shove.

Need to create future ready military force. In an increasingly volatile security environment, the Indian armed forces need to be prepared to conduct a broad range of contemporary operations while also continuously anticipating the requirements of future conflicts. India is in a situation where its armed forces should be prepared for war at all times, "while concurrently becoming future ready". Execution of war should be based on current challenges but planning, structural transformation and development of technology should be to fight "New Generation Wars" (NGW) so that the military is war-ready for future conflicts in an acceptable timeframe. Integration and jointness is key to create future war ready military.

Creation of capabilities for employment of non-military and non-kinetic forces in hybrid wars. General Valery Gerasimov had stated that, "The role of non-military means of achieving political and strategic goals has grown, and, in many cases, they have exceeded the power of force of weapons in their effectiveness".[24] The China-Pakistan strategic nexus would endeavour to create strategic destabilisation of India through unrestricted and asymmetric warfare. Both these nations have developed potent capabilities to employ non-military and non-kinetic forces against India. Therefore, it is high time India incorporates the use of non-military and non-kinetic forces to effectively disrupt, degrade and defeat the dark forces since the employment of conventional forces against non-kinetic and non-military forces may be an unwise strategy.

Improving operational agility. Agility has been defined as the combination of robustness, resilience, responsiveness, flexibility, innovation, and adaptation.[25] In simple words, it is the ability of a military to mobilise faster than the enemy to deny initiative. A military must be operationally agile; this can be achieved if there is suitable infrastructure and strategic mobility based on land, sea and air. Agility is not only in moving men, material and fire power to the battle field rapidly, but it also includes organisational agility, conceptual agility, physical agility and sustaining agility to maintain momentum of operations. Synergy and interoperability among various Services and domains will be the cornerstone of fighting future wars that require agile forces. Resource-informed planning cannot be overlooked and is considered an essential component of operational agility. Combat imagination and combat innovation is key to improve operational agility.

Technology a significant tool to align strategy to national security objectives. On the one hand, innovations in artificial intelligence will see a more rapid collection, analysis, and distribution of critical information down to the lowest levels to support our war fighting efforts.[26] On the other hand, quantum computing by China may threaten communication and guidance systems by encryption/decryption of electronic information. Cyber penetration will be a major threat especially in the conduct of war and employment of high technology modern war fighting support systems. Autonomous weapon systems will prove to be a game changer in future conflicts but the defensive shield against drone swarm attacks would also require high-end technological capabilities.

Maintain a secure and effective nuclear deterrence. India needs to maintain an effective nuclear deterrence especially when both our northern and western neighbours are nuclear armed. This includes Triad capabilities and robust command and control systems that can function without disruption and destruction during the adversary's first strike. Readiness profile and rapid transition of command and control from peace time to war time to oversee conventional and nuclear conflict will be the key to maintain second strike and punitive deterrence.

Development of capabilities. The ultimate yardstick of national power is the ability of a nation to deliver military capabilities at the point of decision. There are four pillars of developing military capabilities: first, leverage technology to create favourable conditions during war; second, military doctrine and concept of operations that define the broad principles of application of military power; third, modern military structures that are capable of dealing with threats across the spectrum of conflict; and fourth, military infrastructure that actually is responsible for delivery and sustaining combat power in the battle space.[27] It is not possible to match China in development of military capabilities, rupee for Yuan. We need to however, spend significantly more to at least sharpen our conventional and asymmetric capacities, as also optimise by way of defence reform and structural overhaul.[28] The other areas that require focus at this stage is to build non-contact, non-kinetic and high-end technology-military capabilities, since future wars are going to be fought in these domains.

Empowering strategic and operational military leadership. In the chaos and uncertainty of modern wars, strategic and operational military leaders must be empowered to take the initiative and take decisions without looking over their shoulders and execute operational plans boldly. The key to prepare a nation to deal with uncertain security challenges is empowering the strategic and operational military leadership so that the armed forces are able to adapt to changes in circumstances quickly enough to win future conflicts.[29] The Indian armed forces are fighting multi-front conflicts including conventional, unrestricted, hybrid and grey zone conflicts. These are wars of ideas and intellect. Thus, a military leader should always think ahead of his time and beyond the horizon. For effective implementation of dynamic military strategy, military leaders must empower themselves with prudence, intellect, and ethics. Prudence is both a moral and an intellectual virtue and a leader having both these values would not seek victory alone, but would always seek the enduring good of the nation. Aquinas says, "The direction of war requires leaders with prudence as well as fortitude."[30] In fact, NGW can be won by leaders who are creative, adaptive to technology and have developed prudence with profound professional knowledge. This is even more so for military leaders in times like these, when brinkmanship and imprudence amounting to impudence seem to be the order of the day.[31]

It is an accepted fact that the quality of leadership has always been a pivotal factor in the conduct of war, especially in respect of the Indian Armed Forces. However, over the years, two significant aberrations have crept into the focus of the military leadership in India: over-emphasis on sub-conventional warfare and a pronounced Pak focus instead of looking at the major threat from China. Thus, two major strategic shifts are warranted in our higher defence mindsets: from a Pak-centric to a China-centric orientation and from sub-conventional to conventional NGW.

The armed forces have been, are and will remain crucial to the nation's security and well-being. We therefore need leaders who are steadfast, visionary and who measure up to the highest standards of military skills, leaders who have a comprehensive understanding of the challenges of modern warfare, and who possess the endurance, strength of character and mental resilience to carry the burdens that modern warfare conditions impose.[32]

Conclusion

Hard power occupies the predominant position in statecraft. Soft power is not a replacement for hard power, but the two can synergise for optimum effect. Thus, dynamic military strategy is an important tool to apply instruments of power to secure vital national interests. For too long India has adopted a "defensive crouch" and laid emphasis mainly on "moral power" that encouraged Pakistan and China to take an aggressive stance against India. For some unknown reasons, the political leadership hesitated to even articulate or have a public debate on building conventional and nuclear capabilities to deter and dissuade adversaries. India is at a critical juncture where it is faced with a two-front challenge and threat from non-state actors. Diplomacy may be good to keep the channels of engagement open, but without the backing of hard military power, it is no more a guarantee to secure our interests, especially with inimical adversaries, China and Pakistan.

War is military operations tailored to achieve one's preferred peace. In the course of war, any limits a nation may set in pursuit of victory are actually limits on your commitment to your peace. In an ambiguous and complex security environment, military strategy lays down the course of action how a nation should respond to long and short term security challenges either by choosing to fight a full spectrum war or response short of war with a view to dissuade and deter adversaries. Therefore, military strategy in an ambiguous and uncertain security environment will dictate how much cost a nation is willing to pay to remove the "obstruction in peace" by employing hard power. Achieving political goals of war requires a whole-of-government approach that aligns and harnesses all the strengths of our nation's instruments of power. To conclude,

"Military strategy is not merely codification of military agenda but an intent and willingness of politico-military leadership to use instrument of power to secure national objectives and interests".

NOTES

1. Roman Muzalevsky, Strategic Landscape, 2050: Preparing the US Military for New Era Dynamics, Strategic Studies Institute, The United States Army War College, p. 49.
2. Jordan Lindell, Clausewitz: War, Peace and Politics, E-International Relations, November 26, 2009.
3. Ibid.
4. Think/Exist (2009), "George Washington Quotes" [Online]. http://en.thinkexist.com/quotes/George_Washington/ [Accessed October 27, 2020].
5. Yoav Tenembaum, "Diplomacy Is the Art of Enhancing Power," E-International relations, February 22, 2017.
6. Sean Illing, "Is Trump hiring too many generals?," *Vox*, July 31, 2017, https://www.vox.com/policy-and-politics/2017/7/12/15923856/donald-trump-military-civilianrule-constitution-foreign-policy; Gordon Adams, "If All You Have Is a Mattis, Everything Looks Like a Nail," *Foreign Policy*, December 2, 2016, http://foreignpolicy.com/2016/12/02/if-all-you-have-is-a-mattis-everything-looks-like-a-nail-civil-militarybalance-of-power-trump/.
7. Caroline Bechtel, Warriors, Scholars, Diplomats: The Role of Military Officers in Foreign Policymaking, Centre for Strategic & International Studies. p. 5.
8. Joseph Roger Clark, "To win wars, correct the Army's political blind spot," *Parameters* (Vol. 45, Issue 4), Winter 2015.
9. Rebecca Friedman Lissner, "What Is Grand Strategy? Sweeping a Conceptual Minefield," *Texas National Security Review*, Vol. 2, Issue No. 1, November 2018.
10. According to Earle: "Strategy is the art of controlling and utilizing the resources of a nation—or a coalition of nations—including its armed forces, to the end that its vital interests shall be effectively promoted and secured against enemies, actual, potential, or merely presumed. The highest type of strategy — sometimes called grand strategy — is that which so integrates the policies and armaments of the nation that the resort to war is either rendered unnecessary or is undertaken with the maximum chance of victory."; Edward Mead Earle, "Introduction," in Makers of Modern Strategy: Military Thought from Machiavelli to Hitler, (ed.) Edward Mead Earle, Gordon A. Craig, and Felix Gilbert (Princeton, NJ: Princeton University Press, 1944), viii. For his part, Liddell Hart offered this definition: "Grand strategy should both calculate and develop the economic resources and manpower of nations in order to sustain the fighting services. Also the moral resources — for to foster the peoples' willing spirit is often as important as to possess the more concrete forms of power.... Moreover, fighting power is but one of the instruments of grand strategy—which should take account of and apply the power of financial pressure, of diplomatic pressure, of commercial pressure, and, not least, of ethical pressure, to weaken the opponent's will...It should not only combine the various instruments, but so regulate their use as to avoid damage to the future state of peace—of its security and prosperity." See: Basil Liddell Hart, Strategy (New York: Praeger, 1967), 322.
11. Paul Kennedy, "Grand Strategy in War and Peace: Toward a Broader Definition," in

Grand Strategies in War and Peace, (ed.) Paul Kennedy (New Haven, CT: Yale University Press, 1991), 5.

12. Ibid.
13. Daniel W. Drezner et. al., "The End of Grand Strategy: America Must Think Small," *Foreign Affairs*, May/June 2020.
14. Ibid.
15. "National Security Strategies: Towards a New Generation," Accessed from https://issat.dcaf.ch/ser/Learn/SSR-in-Practice/Thematics-in-Practice/National-Security-Strategies on October 4, 2020.
16. Happymon Jacob, "A blueprint for a National Security Strategy," *The Hindu*, May 23, 2019.
17. Philip Campose, "India's National Security Strategy: Imperative of Integrating Defence Policy," *CLAWS Journal*, Winter 2016, p. 16.
18. Ibid.
19. DoD, Summary of the 2018 National Defence Strategy of the United States: Sharpening the American Military's Competitive Edge, Washington, D.C., January 2018, p. 5.
20. John D. Winkler, Timothy Marler, Marek N. Posard, Raphael S. Cohen, and Meagan L. Smith, "Reflections on the Future of Warfare and Implications for Personnel Policies of the US Department of Defence," RAND Corporation, p. 6.
21. PM Narendra Modi presides over Combined Commanders' Conference on board INS Vikramaditya, December 15, 2015.
22. The National Military Strategy of United States of America 2015, p. 5.
23. Forrest E. Morgan et.al., "Dangerous Thresholds: Managing Escalation in the 21st Century," RAND Corporation, p 8.
24. Russian Armed Forces: Military Doctrine and Strategy, Congressional Research Service, August 20, 2020.
25. D. Alberts and R. Hayes, "Power to the Edge, CCRP Press," 2003, www.dodccrp.org/publications/pdf/Alberts_Power.pdf.
26. Doug Livermore, "Military trends and predictions: 2020," *Defence IQ*, January, 18, 2019.
27. Narender Kumar, "Infrastructure Voids on India's Northern Borders: Implications for India," Scholar Warrior, Centre for Land Warfare Studies, Spring 2016, p. 36.
28. Lt Gen A.K. Singh & Lt Gen Raj Shukla, "Changing nature of conflict in the 21st Century," Ch 3 in the book – "Military Strategy for India in the 21st Century", KW Publishers, New Delhi, 2019.
29. Lt Col Greg Colton, "Winning Future Wars through Developing the Intellectual Component of Fighting Power," Mad Scientists Laboratory, July 18, 2019.
30. Reed Bonadonna, "Military Command as Moral Prudence," accessed from https://thestrategybridge.org/the-bridge/2017/9/22/military-command-as-moral-prudence, published on September 22, 2017.
31. Ibid.
32. Lt Gen A.K Singh & Lt Gen V.K Ahluwalia, Ch 17 – "Military Leadership in the 21st Century", in the book "Military Strategy for India in the 21st Century", KW Publishers, New Delhi, 2019.

4

Grey Zone Conflict: An Emerging Challenge for India

Brigadier Narender Kumar

ABSTRACT

Grey zone conflict has shifted focus from the Clausewitz theory of war to Sun Tzu's "Art of War" to subdue the enemy without fighting. The conflict in the grey zone allows an adversary to remain indiscernible. A grey zone conflict challenges moral and ethical thresholds and undermines international norms, laws of armed conflicts and ethics of war fighting. The objective of the grey zone is to keep the conflict smouldering and bleed the economy, create instability and keep the conflict below the threshold of conventional war. China and Pakistan combined have been able to create corridors of peril against India to exploit the potential of the grey zone from almost all domains including immediate neighbourhood through Bangladesh, Nepal, Myanmar and Pakistan itself. Even the littoral states of the Indian Ocean can become a potential pivot of the grey zone. Thus the priority at this stage is to deny exposed flanks and develop capabilities to fight grey zone conflict in all its forms. It is everyday war and it would require technology, skills, and even collaboration with strategic partners because there will be novel threat every day.

Introduction

The era of large-scale conventional inter-state wars is nearing an end and now there is a rise of ambiguous, protracted, and indecisive conflicts in a complex environment.[1] It will be increasingly difficult to decode who is fighting against the state and how they are fighting. Dr. Tracey German of Kings College, London, says, "The global security environment in the 21st century makes it difficult for states to plan for future wars, because of the sheer pace of development of technology and communications."[2] Fusion of disruptive technologies with disruptive ideas is emerging as powerful tools of modern wars. Transnational terrorism, hybrid war and political wars have emerged as the new methods of waging modern wars in the grey zone where victory in conflict is determined not by capture of territory but by manipulating public perception through a choreographed narrative or coercive actions. Information warfare in combination with disruptive forces has made it increasingly difficult to distinguish between friend and foe, and peace and war. Grey zone challenges are inherently elusive, paradoxical and ambiguous in nature. They feature unconventional tactics, from cyber attacks to propaganda and political warfare, to economic coercion and sabotage, to sponsorship of armed proxy fighters, to creeping military expansionism.[3] The elements of the grey zone are *special forces, paramilitary, or other state-controlled forces, proxy forces (little green men of Russia or little blue men of China), information warriors, corrupt political parties and politicians, corrupt and compromised institutions of governance, economic tools, institutions shaping societies (Chinese Study Centres, Confucius Institutes) and compromised media to peddle fake news and lies repeatedly*. Grey zone conflict is best understood as an activity that is coercive and aggressive in nature, but that is deliberately designed to remain below the threshold of conventional military conflict and open interstate war.[4] In fact, political and hybrid wars are the vanguard of grey zone conflict when staged at a strategic level.

India faces a combined threat from grey zone and transnational terrorism in view of the China–Pak strategic nexus and the encircling of India in the immediate neighbourhood. China and Pakistan would exploit corridors of peril of through Nepal, Bangladesh, Myanmar and Pakistan. Thus, it is a new front that needs careful decoding and understanding of a new dimensions of war.

Conceptual Framework of Grey Zone Conflicts

It is imperative to understand that the grey zone is a conceptual space between peace and war, occurring when actors purposefully use multiple elements of power to achieve politico-security objectives with activities that are ambiguous and exceed the threshold of ordinary competition, yet fall below the level of large-scale direct military conflict.[5] The grey zone conflict challenges moral and ethical thresholds and undermines international norms, laws of armed conflicts and ethics of war fighting.

Often, states using grey zone elements as tools for proxy and maintain deniability to avoid direct confrontation. The precision attack on Saudi oil facilities in September 2019 was near impossible to execute by the rebels without state support; however, Iran and Russia remained in denial since the frontline fighters are non-state actors who claimed the strikes. There is ambiguity in conceptually defining a grey zone. Is it a battle space where rules do not apply? If it is true, in that case, it will encourage bad behaviour on all sides and raise the risk of miscalculation and escalation.[6] Though one may argue that hybrid war is a subset of a grey zone, each state however, based on their expertise and capabilities, has been defining grey zone and hybrid war differently since its application may be completely diverse in nature. Russian grey zones overlap with hybrid war, whereas for the Chinese, unrestricted war is strategically grey zone and revisionist in application without elements of hybrid warfare. However, it may not remain the same if the conditions change in the South China Sea or any disruption is encountered along the BRI.

In a grey zone, multi-domain conflicts could range from cyber, information, psychological, proxy, transnational terrorism and various forms of violent extremism in the same battle space to achieve common or even diverse objectives. However, it may also not be correct to compress every form of societal violence or internal conflict within a state as part of grey zone conflict. At the same time, societal fracture, political dissonance, communal flashpoints, compromised institutions of governance, socio-economic stress and criminal takeover of streets create a suitable environment for grey zone conflicts to be ignited. The conflict in Syria, Iraq, Yemen and Ukraine have amply displayed that when there is ungoverned territory, state sponsored non-state actors, irregular forces and transnational terror organisations exploit such fractures to achieve geostrategic and political objectives. Though criminals and autonomous non-state actors may also operate in alliance or in conjunction with state-sponsored non-state actors or irregular proxies, the objective may not be same or always political in nature. There is a generic consensus throughout that conflicts in a grey zone are often triggered to achieve political purposes intended to influence the behaviour of a target group wider than its immediate victims.

Doctrinal Objectives of Grey Zone Conflict

During the Cold War, containment by deterrence was the dominant strategy, but after the demise of the Soviet Union, the containment and deterrence strategy gave way to military intervention for regime change. But this strategy led to bleeding and states got bogged down in multiple small wars dominated by a wide variety of violent insurgencies. The big armies had no answer to such warriors who were invisible and their organisations amorphous. It gave way to evolution of asymmetric, irregular and hybrid wars that found a foothold in grey zones that were partially ungoverned. These modern wars gave an opportunity to bring conflict-induced changes to establish regimes that were/are willing to pursue the strategic agenda of the state orchestrating the conflicts. Grey zone conflict need not always be violent but the danger is that it can lead to uncontrolled chaos and instability for a prolonged period without any decisive outcome. A primary target of the grey zone is domestic or international public opinion and elements of grey zone are employed to advance a nation's interests while still aiming to avoid retaliation, escalation, or third-party intervention.[7]

Chinese grey zone strategy is more materially threatening since it uses economy, information and political warfare for opinion shaping and revisionist purposes. Russia's virtual and ephemeral approach has complicated policy responses.[8] At one end of the spectrum, China's concept of "unrestricted warfare" closely approximates grey-zone elements to achieve strategic, revisionist thinking without hybrid warfare. Then there is Russia's involvement in the Baltics and Eastern Ukraine where we see mixed elements of grey-zone conflict and hybrid warfare or what we call "hybrid balancing".[9] The third example is Israeli application of "regional hybridism", emphasizing tactical operations. The USA and NATO employ hybrid warfare in weak and fragile states and its use of "restricted hybridism" largely absent of an offensive strategic calculus embedded in grey-zone conflict.[10]

Durable disorder is the fundamental objective of grey zone conflict. Violence is not always a pre-condition of this new war but it does not preclude the option of violence either. More often, grey zone conflicts may focus on bloodless victories, where the weapon is perception, coercion, and threat of use of violence; invariably, it may not be lethal, but it is still very effective.[11] Manipulation in election to install a favourable regime may be a better option than regime change by military intervention. At the same time actors in grey zone conflicts do not hesitate to achieve their objective by violence and instead of regulars, such operations are executed by irregulars or non-state actors to maintain deniability and keep the threshold of conflict below conventional war. The annexation of Crimea and fomenting civil conflict and separatism in eastern Ukraine are a few examples of the effective use of grey zone and hybrid war. A word of caution; it is not that a grey zone or hybrid war will cease when conventional conflict gets triggered. It will continue to cause friction especially along the interior lines of communication and in the heartland.

Grey Zone a Multi-Dimensional Conflict

Many terms have been used to describe these unconventional methods of modern conflicts including "grey zone conflict", "hybrid warfare", "nonlinear warfare", "ambiguous warfare", "indirect action", "asymmetric", and "political warfare".[12] In other words, the grey zone is an ambiguous battle space where irregulars, proxy forces, state-sponsored non-state actors, transnational terror groups, criminal syndicates and groups/individuals acting as separatists or secessionists operate independently or in alliance with other stakeholders. The spectrum of conflict chosen could be cyber, information, economic, political war, violent extremism, coercion and agitation. In fact, the relation between hybrid, grey zone and political warfare is an ill-defined notion in conflict studies. It refers to the use of unconventional methods or alternative wars as part of a multi-domain war-fighting approach. These methods aim to disrupt and disable an opponent's actions without engaging in open hostilities.[13]

Hybrid warfare can be a tactical subset of grey-zone conflict deployed under certain conditions and in varying degrees.[14] There are no defined boundaries between hybrid and grey zone conflicts; it can overlap or can be employed concurrently since some of the elements of hybrid and grey zone conflicts are common and termed as hybrid balancing. Russia's involvement in the Baltics and Eastern Ukraine is where one can see mixed elements of grey-zone conflict and hybrid warfare or "hybrid balancing".[15] Yemen, Syria and Northern Iraq are engaged in ambiguous wars that are amorphous and paradoxical in nature that has prompted renewed debate about the character of future wars and conflicts. Syria and Yemen are classic examples of regulars, irregulars, state-sponsored non-state actors and transnational terror organisations operating in the same battle space. The objective of initiation of war in Syria and Yemen was to enforce a regime change. In Syria, Islamic State, a non-state group (Transnational Terror Group) wanted to establish a pan global Muslim caliphate. Russia and

Iran want to support President Asad with diverse objectives. Russia wants to maintain control over two of the Syrian bases in the Mediterranean Sea, whereas Iran wants to consolidate Shia regimes in Syria with access to the Mediterranean Sea. On the other side, Turkey, Saudi Arabia, UAE and Qatar are supporting almost 50 rebel groups including Al Qaeda affiliate Jabhat al-Nusra to overthrow the Asad regime in Syria and establish Nizam-e-Mustafa and the Shariya in Syria. The objective of the USA is to throw out the Russians from the Mediterranean Sea and keep Iran out of Syria. The spectrum of conflict that has emerged in West Asia makes it evident that there are different stakeholders operating in the same battle space with diverse objectives. In the light of the above facts, there is a need to examine two subsets of grey zone conflicts, transnational terrorism and hybrid wars because these are applied at tactical levels and invariably operate in conjunction with each other for greater impact. The significance of political war cannot be underestimated since that is also a powerful tool to give impetus to the instability.

Hybrid War a Strategy of Chaos

Hybrid and asymmetric warfare are everyday wars that developing countries are facing in military, political and economic competitive environments. A recent RAND Corporation-funded study states that while the term 'hybrid warfare' has no consistent definition, it generally refers to "deniable and covert actions, supported by the threat or use of conventional and/or nuclear forces, to influence the domestic politics of target countries."[16] Another definition says hybrid warfare is broadly characterized by "a wide range of overt and covert military, paramilitary, and civilian measures employed in a highly integrated design".[17] It is difficult to categorise hybrid war as a military or quasi-military challenge but it has elements of military and non-military domains. In fact, hybrid warfare is not a tactical or strategic challenge; it is a political issue.[18] It threatens the political stability of the state and creates fault-lines among the institutions of governance and the people that can be exploited by adversaries. Hybrid war is a vanguard for grey zone and other asymmetric forces to sneak in. Therefore, it is not only important to defend physical frontiers but also cyber, cognitive and political frontiers that may be under threat from hybrid and grey zone conflicts. Hybrid war in the Indian context is more pertinent in the case of Jammu & Kashmir, where Pakistan has actively employed regulars, irregulars, criminals (drug traffickers), cyber and religious radicalisation making it a potent hybrid threat. While India's response is very much conventional in nature it may be inadequate to fight this nuanced emerging hybrid war by Pakistan. The challenges posed by hybrid war are technological, military and non-military. Hybrid and grey zone conflicts invariably overlap and have common elements consisting of civil-military fusion. Ideal response mechanisms should therefore be simultaneous to deal with the quasi-military threats that hybrid and grey zone conflicts pose. Since technological hybridisation is separately discussed in a separate chapter, hybrid warfare will not be covered in further details in this chapter.

Characteristic	*Grey-Zone Conflict*	*Hybrid Warfare*
Level	Tactical, operational, strategic	Tactical and operational
Use of conventional military operations	Used alongside non-conventional operations.	Used alongside non-conventional operations. Usually the dominant element.
Use of non-conventional military operations	May be used stand alone or alongside conventional operations.	Used alongside conventional operations as auxiliary tactics.
Protracted engagement	One of the dominant characteristics.	May be protracted or short.
Global and/or regional revisionist ambitions	One of the dominant characteristics.	Out of scope as the concept pertains to operational and tactical levels.
Symmetry between opponents	Used under both symmetric and asymmetric conditions.	Largely used under asymmetric conditions.

Source: David Carment, *War's Future: The Risks and Rewards of Grey-Zone Conflict and Hybrid Warfare.*

Transnational Terrorism Manipulating Disruption and Disorder

Transnational terrorism has emerged as the most potent weapon in the grey zone conflicts that drive the asymmetric wars of the 21st century. There is a generic consensus throughout that transnational terrorism implies the use of violence for political purposes and is intended to influence the behaviour of a target group wider than its immediate victims. These groups may act independently or may be controlled or supported by sovereign states in different regions. Transnational terrorism in other words is the use of premeditated violence to obtain a political or social objective through intimidation of a large population beyond immediate victims. Transnational terrorism operates simultaneously across continents threatening Westphalian states and modern democratic norms of governance. Transnational terror organizations exploit flow of people, ideology, weapons and information to further their cause. Peter Mandaville wrote that Al Qaeda was the first group to be designated as a 'fifth wave' terrorist group. He argued that their initial success was because they effectively used technology, mythology and ideology.[19] Al-Qaeda was successful in expanding its influence among the Islamic Diaspora globally because it employed ideology to win loyalty and effectively used technology to indoctrinate, recruit cadres, conduct training, plan and coordinate lethal terror strikes across the globe. Urban centres communication hubs and critical infrastructure are becoming targets of grey zone conflicts. The objective of transnational terror organisations is to establish politico-religious structures that are contrary to the Westphalian state system and would impose a new moral order that would necessarily exclude those who do not follow their religious beliefs. Most of the transnational terror organisations use criminal syndicates to finance their operations, allowing them to have greater reach, influence and power. They follow a strategy of protracted warfare and employ disruptive technologies and information space to unleash terror to motivate their supporters and sympathisers and demoralise their opponents.

Transnational terrorism exploits disruption, disorder and chaos. It erodes the authority of the state, creates displacement of population, triggers public disorder, damages trade or foreign direct investment (FDI), disrupts people-to-people contact, cross-cultural interaction, development of industries and infrastructure and disrupts the education and health sectors. The displacement of population under such circumstances is a natural fallout of prolonged conflicts. The key for survival and expansion of network of transnational terror organisations is to adapt and align with regional terror organisations to achieve their objectives, subject to regional groups accepting the ideological framework. In February 2012, Al-Shabab a Somali terror organisation "pledged obedience" to al-Qaeda.[20] Similarly, Boko Haram, a Nigerian terror group, aligned itself with the Islamic State. Jamaat-ul Mujahideen Bangladesh (JMB) is aligned with the ISIS and Ansarul Islam to Al Qaeda. However, there are now even small modules based on lone wolf or family groups that have shown allegiance to transnational terror organisations. The bombers of Sri Lanka who bombed churches on Easter were followers of Sri Lanka's Tawheed Jamaat. The objective of the ISIS is to establish a caliphate from Morocco to Manila.

Ashley Tellis writes that Lashkar-e-Taiba (LeT) is one of the most dangerous transnational terror organisations in South Asia that has a global vision and international ambitions, even if it may be currently limited by capacity or focus.[21] Ashley Tellis further writes that the LeT has a distinct ideology that underwrites a program of Islamic revanchism—and justifies collaboration with other terrorist groups. On one hand, it pursues its agenda of terrorism in India and on the other, it acts as a social welfare group in Pakistan. It maintains a benevolent face at home and that of a radical transnational terror organisation abroad. Similarly, Jaish-e-Mohammad (JeM) is another transnational terror organisation that has its ambition to initiate a Deobandi jihadist movement to achieve Ghazwa-e-Hind (consisting of parts of Pakistan, India and Bangladesh). In fact, the ideological relations between al-Qaeda and JeM are even deeper, going by the close relationship that Masood Azhar has had with al-Qaeda members like Omar Saeed Sheikh and Rashid Rauf.[22]

Bio-Warfare a Potent Tool in Grey Zone

It is immaterial whether bio-weapons are intentionally triggered or negligently escape from the laboratory; what is more significant is that it leaves hazy footprints to identify the culpability of a nation or agency. There is adequate scope for deniability, whereas the same advantage cannot be attributed to the use of nuclear or chemical weapons. The source can be traced back and states can be made accountable in nuclear and chemical weapons. The corona virus has raised a few questions that the national security apparatus must find answers to and solutions as well. The virus, even if it advertently escaped from a laboratory or was intentionally released, has proved that the strongest of the economies and the strongest of military powers can come down on its knees in a matter of few weeks. The situation as it stands today is that the global economy stands collapsed, markets closed, industries have come to a grinding halt and people have been locked inside the four walls of their houses with no definite timeline for their opening up or of nations. National reserves of liquidity are exhausted, supply chains disrupted, food stocks dwindled, millions of jobs lost and the threat of loss of lives to disease is mounting in addition to death by starvation that is lurking around. At the same time, China is using its financial muscle to acquire financially stressed assets at throwaway prices globally and arm-twisting nations in need of emergency medical equipment at exorbitant prices to fight Covid-19. Using global

Institutions of governance such as the World Health Organisation (WHO) to acquire a clean chit for the spread of Covid-19 and refusing to cooperate to investigate the circumstances how the corona virus has spread is a display of arrogance and hegemony. Interestingly, one of the spokesperson of the PRC said, the 'mike is yet not fully in our control,' meaning thereby that the PRC has yet not got hold of global institutions of governance. Therefore, this pandemic has added another dimension to the new threat in the grey zone without inviting any military response or violating any rules of armed conflict. Such a threat would require nations to relook the provisions of penalising a nation for hiding, escalating, intentionally spreading and refusing to cooperate with the global community. Similarly, such a threat in the grey zone domain cannot be fought individually by a nation; rather, it would require global efforts to fight, prevent and penalise a culpable state or institution.

Corridors of Peril of Grey Zone Conflict to India

China and Pakistan have created corridors of peril to unleash grey zone conflict against India. It can be in the form of hybrid, transnational terrorism, bio-war, political war, cyber, information and psychological warfare. Both these countries together have their foothold and footprints in India's immediate neighbourhood and even in the maritime domain. The main corridor of peril of grey zone threat and transnational terrorism is from Pakistan with Chinese support. There are other emerging corridors of peril mainly through Pak Occupied Jammu & Kashmir, Peninsula India (where Islamic radicals have established footholds), Bangladesh, which is also emerging as a jihadi hub with linkages with transnational terror organisations. Nepal is new threat that has the potential to establish possible linkages with Left Wing Extremism (LWE) through Nepalese Maoists. China has traditionally exploited ungoverned Northern territories of Myanmar to support North East insurgents and it is unlikely to abandon this corridor.

India should be most concerned about unrestricted war, 3Ws and the influence operations of China. It appears at this stage that India is perilously unprepared because Indian defence security establishments continue to view war from the perspective of Clausewitz and not through the unthinkable and unexpected war that China has already embarked and initiated against allies and inimical states. China would exploit new-found corridor of peril through Nepal that is posing a serious threat to India from grey zone elements including trans-national terror access to India through open borders, pumping of fake currency and use of Nepalese Maoists to establish links with Left Wing Extremism (LWE) to create subversion and disorder in the resource-rich heartland of India. China has become willy-nilly a party to conflict in J&K and Ladakh due to the China Pakistan Economic Corridor and China would endeavour through Pakistan to keep J&K unstable and Ladakh under threat of salami slicing. At the same time, China is also using proxies, insurgents and terror organisations in the Northeast in a controlled manner to impose restrictions on India to expand its influence to the east to ensure that India's "Act East Policy" does not fructify. One cannot overrule the fact that China intends to intensify its proxy war against India in the Northeast through separatist groups.[23] Phungting Shimrang, the former chief and senior member of the NSCN-IM, has reportedly gone to Yunan province in China with two of his trusted comrades.[24] Veteran journalist-writer Bertil Lintner had said that China's role in Northeastern India is not to create instability but "to maintain instability" because it wants to keep India out of Myanmar.[25] The Chinese model of grey zone operations is a work in progress.

Chinese Grey Zone Conflict a Real Challenge to India

China's grey zone conflict is aligned to Sun Tzu's *Art of War*, that is, winning war without fighting. The grey zone concept demolishes the monopoly of the state over war and today a stealth war can be fought by mercenaries, proxies, irregulars and even through political, economic and diplomatic domains. China has altered the maritime boundary in the South China Sea not by deploying the People's Liberation Army Navy (PLAN) but by Chinese maritime militias with civil trawlers. The capabilities of these "Little Blue Men" are least known, but what they have achieved in the South China Sea is that the US Navy has no answer to these militias. China's 3 Warfare (3W) concept is based on three mutually reinforcing strategies: first, the coordinated use of strategic psychological operations; second, overt and covert media manipulation; and third, legal warfare designed to manipulate strategies, defence policies, and perceptions of target audiences abroad.[26] "3 Warfare" is the responsibility of the PLA's General Political Department's Liaison Department (GPD/LD), which conducts diverse political, financial, military, and intelligence operations.[27] China uses influence operations, political warfare and information warfare in conjunction with the 3Ws to exploit political, cultural, and social frictions in fragile states to create instability and build a favourable perception towards China. The specific objectives of the 3Ws are psychological warfare aimed to weaken the will of the adversary to compete or fight a war (conventional or sub-conventional) against China; media warfare is to tell the world good and positive stories about China to shape the favourable opinion of the people of the target countries and finally legal warfare is to bend or rewrite the unfavourable legal provisions in institutions of global governance. Influence operations are also aimed to create a favourable pro-China atmosphere by manipulating political parties by funding, investment in key competitive industries, buying stakes in financially stressed corporate sectors and acquiring high stakes in mainstream media houses. China is dominating the grey zone with tools with Chinese characteristics. Most of these tools fit into political, cyber, information and psychological warfare and the impact is such that it does not become a cause of direct confrontation yet potent enough to cause internal smouldering of the target nation.

There is a need to understand the political psychology of the Chinese leadership why China has developed such sophisticated grey zone conflict capabilities. China's leaders believe they have a narrow window of opportunity to strengthen their rule and revise the international order in their favour.[28] This revision cannot be done by military coercion or intervention through hard power and thus the only option is development of unrestricted warfare capabilities with unique Chinese characteristics that do not appear threatening yet are lethal enough to amend the behaviour of a nation and shape pro-China sentiment by using stealth war. The exclusivity of Chinese grey zone capability is that China pursues a strategy of co-option, coercion, and concealment,[29] and over a period of time, authoritarian interventions through debt traps, consumerism and resource control may become even more pervasive. As of 2018, the risk of debt distress was growing in 23 countries with Belt and Road financing. Eight poor countries with Belt and Road financing—Pakistan, Djibouti, the Maldives, Laos, Mongolia, Montenegro, Tajikistan, and Kyrgyzstan—already have unsustainable levels of debt.[30] This is how China is creating vassal states that may find it difficult to regain financial sovereignty. China would never have gained such a control over these nations through military intervention. Though the world may know it as Chinese influence operations, 3W and political warfare, it falls in the paradigm of a very sophisticated application of grey zone elements. The ulterior motive of

China is not only to strengthen its authoritarian regime within but also extend its authoritarian control over institutions of global governance and create modern Chinese vassal states. This would make nations and institutions of global governance less sovereign.

China's compelling strategic logic for developing sophisticated grey zone capabilities is that conventional war is obsolete, nuclear weapons are unusable and the future of wars is focused for durable disorder. The objective is to keep the conflict smouldering and bleed the economy, maintain instability and keep the conflict below the threshold of conventional war. India will be eventually tested by a state-sponsored grey zone/hybrid war by China and if the military hierarchy delays building capabilities and understanding grey zone conflicts, it may have serious repercussions for national security. The Corona virus pandemic has displayed that big armies and high-technology weapon systems will not provide humans security.

The Chinese grey zone activity is aimed at two levels; first to reshape the periphery of India to eliminate India's sphere of influence through a combination of strategy of non-contact war and the 3Ws. China considers that "One Mountain Cannot Contain Two Tigers". The cornerstone of China's strategy is to isolate and eliminate any competition that may prevent it from becoming the sole regional power in Asia. Though at the global stage, China is working to create a bipolar world, in Asia it is eliminating all opposition to create a unipolar Asia. China considers India as a strategic irritant that could pose a challenge in its endeavour to be the sole power in Asia. China has willy-nilly made itself a dominant partner with Myanmar, by developing and integrating it into the Belt and Road Initiative (BRI) through the China Myanmar Economic Corridor (CMEC). Similarly, Bangladesh is integrated in BRI through the maritime silk route by developing Chittagong seaport and making Bangladesh a Chinese industrial hub centre. China has been working with Nepal on two fronts, economic and political warfare. China has now given Nepal port facilities though entailing long traverse time and is now working to connect Nepal with the Tibet Autonomous Region (TAR) by rail, road, air and fibre connectivity. Second, by developing ideological bridges with the Communist Party of Nepal. Similarly, the China Pakistan Economic Corridor (CPEC) is an indicator of developing a China-Pak strategic nexus. Sri Lanka is now under a debt trap that makes it difficult to unshackle itself from the Chinese stranglehold.

Pakistan's Fusion of Grey Zone Elements & Transnational Terrorism a Challenge for India

Closer home, Pakistan is effectively engaging through grey zone activities in Afghanistan and Jammu & Kashmir with diverse strategic and political objectives. The objective in Afghanistan is to install a regime that is pro-Pak to deny India and other inimical powers space in Afghanistan. It also gives advantage to Pakistan to increase its strategic space and greater leverage to act as a land bridge to Central Asia through Afghanistan and to keep India out of Afghanistan. Pakistan has employed both the LeT & JeM that are transnational terror organisations with political and religious ambitions. Pakistan has mastered the art of using irregulars, non-state actors and regulars in a seamless manner to create social, political, economic and internal security instability in J&K in particular and in India as a whole. Pakistan has used radicalisation and religious realignment to destroy the cultural, historical and social fabric of Kashmiris by blending it with a political and religious cause. Similarly, the objective of Pakistan is to achieve a conflict-induced change in J&K to make territorial gains without fighting a conventional war. The objective of the Sino-Pak grey zone nexus is to create an unstable political, economic and social environment along its eastern and northern periphery, so that India remains an unfavourable nation as an economic hub, politically unstable so that it is engaged internally and unable to swing either towards the US-led alliance nor able to create an anti-China front in the region. The threat of Pakistan's irregular/proxy war now is moving in a direction so that it can create anti-Hindu sentiments among the Muslims of India. Pakistan's motive may not be as much to create pro-Pak sentiment but to create an anti-India sentiment.

India's Response Options

The response options can be streamlined if the extent and scope of evolving a grey zone conflict is clearly understood. Most significant for India at this stage is to recognise how grey zone competitors operate from within or from the periphery. The challenge to India comes from China and Pakistan, but even the regional neighbours could use grey zone for creating leverages as bargain tool to extract favours. Even leveraging the space for China and Pakistan in the immediate and strategic neighbourhood of India could also fall in this category. A case in point is the increasing foothold of China in building infrastructure, opening industrial hubs, developing communication (digital and surface) and opening China study centres along the Indian borders and neighbouring countries are part of a strategy of shaping the periphery to deny access to India in those areas. Before India embarks upon building response options, work is needed to be done to develop a clear understanding of the magnitude of the threat from a grey zone conflict, potential vulnerabilities, operational frameworks and strategic approaches that could be drawn upon to more consistently and effectively counter grey zone actions.[31] The grey zone conflict by China and Pakistan is driven by their respective militaries. Even the PLA has a stake in 5G, Belt and Road Initiative and China Pakistan Economic Corridor. The cyber, information, 3W and influence operations are executed by the PLA in conjunction with other civil agencies. Similarly, the ISI and Pakistan Army drives hybrid and grey zone elements when directed against India. The question is who is responsible to develop offensive and defensive capabilities to counter grey zone/hybrid threats in India? There are gaps in accountability, responsibility and capabilities. Are the three defence agencies created by the Government adequate to deal with the elaborate and sophisticated unrestricted war of China and irregular proxy war by Pakistan? The starting point has to be to develop an understanding and thereafter-defining strategy, doctrine or basic guidelines for response options and, once that is done, defining capabilities, structures and operational methodologies. Reactive policy is absence of strategy and almost counter-productive activity to fight grey zone conflict given the uncertainty inherent in the evolution of this nuanced war.

Indigenous Model Most Suitable to Counter Grey Zone Threats. Numerous models have been adopted by various countries across the globe. China's information and three Ws are the main pillars of grey zone/unrestricted warfare controlled by the People's Liberation Army's (PLA) and the Strategic Support Force (SSF). The latter appears to be a unique organization responsible for joint missions to support all services with its space, cyber, and electronic warfare capabilities.[32] Though the Russian military structure is ambiguous and unclear about command and control of such amorphous organisations, it is under the direct control of the Russian Defence Ministry and under the political supervision of the President. Similarly, the United Kingdom is now in the process of creating a hybrid warfare division under the military for calibrated and controlled response to hybrid and grey zone threats. The unique characteristics of all such organisations is that they only proclaim these organisations to be defensive in nature. It needs to be understood that the purpose of grey zone conflict is 'durable disorder' and is often planned to be protracted and could escalate into military confrontation if not managed well or some elements cross the threshold or red line. The domains of grey zone/hybrid war can spill over to kinetic end non-kinetic, traditional and non-traditional and contact and non-contact war. This is the reason why most of the countries have placed such capabilities under military control with political supervision. Moreover, since it deals with external adversaries, it falls in the ambit of military engagement for offensive and defensive operations and yet maintain deniability. Considering the nature of the threat and the structure of India's higher direction of war, India must develop its own model of countering grey zone threats with quasi-military control with civil-military capabilities fused together.

Develop Intelligence to Embrace the Threat and Dispel the Ambiguity. The subsets of grey zone, including transnational terrorism, cyber, information, political, economic, biological warfare and proxy forces require intelligence of a different nature. Cyber may need information of data and system security codes, psychological warfare may need cultural and societal information. Political warfare may need information of vulnerable links in the institutions of governance and political establishment of the country. Transnational terror counter-strategies would need information of terror networks, ideologues, support base, terror funding, and tentative targets. Similarly, information warfare may need a psychological bent of mind of the people, sensitivities, religious leanings, culture and issues that may create a sense of victimhood. In the light of the above facts, the starting point to build response options for offensive and defensive grey zone capabilities is to develop suitable intelligence organisation, adapt technology and exploit Artificial Intelligence (AI) and skilled manpower for intelligence gathering and analysis. India has multiple intelligence agencies and yet the nation finds itself handicapped by the quality of intelligence especially while dealing with bio, nuclear and non-kinetic threats. There is no need to create a de novo Intelligence organisation since the need at this stage is to identify existing tools and expertise to harness and synergise their efforts. More important is to create a flat Intelligence structure that is able to network and pass information to analysts to sift and then disseminate to stakeholders. The biggest obstacle or inability to fight this conflict is to remain in denial of the threat and allow absolute ambiguity or confusion to prevail. Thus, the task of intelligence organisations is to confront grey zone challenges by embracing the threat and dispelling the ambiguity.

Capability Development Essential for 'Grey Deterrence'. Grey zone deterrence may hold the key to a more secure global economic and political future of a country.[33] The principles of deterrence that worked against conventional military and nuclear threats during the Cold War may not apply in the grey zone because deterrence by punishment or containment is not plausible. Therefore, in a broader sense, the 'grey zone' deterrence should also deny hostile actors an opportunity to weaponise information, data and access to Services networks. The deterrence in the grey zone should also apply both in preventing escalation of direct military conflict and assuaging an actor's desire to violate international norms of behaviour[34] and good governance. In essence, '**grey deterrence**' needs to overcome transnational terrorist organisations and insurgent calculus, while operating within the international legal framework.[35] To maintain physical deterrence in the current prevailing environment in the grey zone, some conventional military units must be both re-trained and re-organized to conduct military operations at the lower end of the conflict spectrum[36] in grey zone, hybrid and cyber warfare.

Deep Operations Capabilities. India lacks deep operation capabilities and China and Pakistan have taken advantage of this void to continuously engage India in grey zone and proxy wars. Force building is an expensive preposition especially when the nation is engaged in social and economic development. Therefore, having a separate force for each of the domains may not be an ideal solution. Ideally, cyber, Special Forces, irregulars, space and information warriors are normally employed in a synergised manner by a single command authority to fight a campaign and should not fight separate tactical battles by multiple agencies with diverse command and control organisations. In the absence of such an authority/structure, India is targeting only the arrows and not the archer. The capability to target the archer will only come if India develops deep operations capability to engage with state, society and infrastructure simultaneously. Grey zone and hybrid wars require fusion of civilian and military components under one commander and organisation for synergised application. The fragmented approach is primarily because there is no formal structure of 'merging the civilian sphere with the military.[37] Therefore, this void can be filled by creating an organisation that has the capabilities to have deep operational capabilities in civilian and military affairs simultaneously.

Need Inter-operability and Established Protocols for Plug and Play. The pre-requisite for multi-domain and cross domain operations require a structure where various components of grey zone conflicts can plug and play. But for efficient usage of capabilities to plug and play, there is a need for creation of a platform. To develop adequate operational understanding, inter-operability and establish protocols for integrated operations, these elements must train and operate together under a single command authority. The creation of a military structure to fight grey zone and hybrid wars assume greater significance especially when campaigns tend to be protracted, reflecting that states are living in an era of persistent competition, confrontation and sometimes conflict.[38] The Government of India has created the Defence Cyber Agency (DCA), the Defence Space Agency (DSA), and the Armed Forces Special Operations Division (AFSOD). The question is will the AFSOD, DSA and DCA meet the challenge of fighting lethal grey zone and other asymmetric wars with their current structure? The answer is that wars are not fought in silos; wars are fought by integrating capabilities for a holistic response under a single operational command authority. The main issue is that wars are fought and won by military ethos, discipline and hierarchical structures and not by agencies, departments or corporations. That is the reason most nations, including Russia, China, Israel, the USA and now UK and Pakistan have developed counter offensive and defensive grey zone/hybrid war capabilities under military authorities with political supervision. Ultimately. The real potential of these agencies can be optimally exploited when elements of these agencies are integrated and employed in a synergised manner. The agencies can make policies, doctrine and coordinate activities of respective constituents, but employment of holistic capabilities to fight a war requires a formal military structure. The current structures created by the Government may be a good beginning but certainly fall short to fight grey zone and asymmetric wars. The structures must be so designed so that they can plug and play during conventional or sub-conventional conflicts. Moreover, engagement of the military in the next decade appears to be more in grey zone and hybrid domains than in a conventional domain. Can the alternative wars be fought by agencies independently while all the elements of grey zone warfare are so intimately integrated at the execution level? Therefore, to begin with, a hybrid warfare division could possibly be a platform under which elements of these agencies can be employed in any future conflict. The mandate of fighting external adversaries, traditional and non-traditional, rest with the Armed Forces and it must be applied even to cyber, information and irregular warfare. The Indian military must develop this capability before it becomes too late to catch up.

Chemical, Biological Nuclear and Radiation Response Capabilities. Covid-19 has made the world sit up and take note that such a biological weapon requires capabilities and expertise to identify, contain and build an emergency response. India needs to hasten up to build a dual responsibility force that can be employed both in peace and war. The time is ripe for the creation of CBRN units along with the raising of Territorial Army medical battalions that can be deployed as an emergency response force to provide medical relief. These units should have the resources and the infrastructure to even create and run temporary hospitals and quarantine facilities. CBRN companies could be a part of regular army units but medical battalions should consist of ex-army Medical Corps personnel and also civilian health workers as doctors and paramedics. The territorial medical battalion will not only be ready for deployment during pandemics or epidemics but also during disaster relief operations.

Technology a Tool to Neutralise Grey Zone Elements. As per *Business Insider*, in 2018 India was ranked among the top 20 most dangerous countries and home to 11 recognized terrorist organizations, including al-Qaeda and ISIS offshoots.[39] Non-state actors and state proxies are using technology for virtually running their operations, radicalisation and recruitment of cadres online. Technology is being used to conceal and create false identities, terror funding, use autonomous vehicles for bombing and even use drones to attack high-value targets of economic interests. Technology today has the potential to detect and disrupt attacks by proxies and enable Intelligence and security forces to track down the network of proxies and transnational terror groups. Technology can identify the enemy within and proxies far away. Technology is also required to secure data, network systems and critical infrastructure. Cellebrite's digital forensics tools can rapidly unlock, extract, decode, and analyse digital data from multiple sources, including Cloud. Being able to analyse and sort through large volumes of data fast is critical to identify terrorists and their accomplices as well as prevent future attacks.[40] Use of facial recognition systems, digital tracking of funding, use of Artificial Intelligence to sift data and intelligence analysis has become imperative to fight grey zone battles.

Conclusion

In an era of grey zone competition, nations require more than the largest economy or strongest military.[41] National security begins at home and what nations need is robust institutions of war fighting, visionary political and military leadership and resilient protocols to enforce security of humans and institutions. There are four main principles of fighting this ambiguous and paradoxical war. First, identify competitors and their strategies. Second, respond with full range of tools within the government and beyond by synergising civil-military efforts. Third, operate with allies and adopt a whole-of-government approach to bolster deterrence. Fourth, strengthen vulnerable and weak links to build impregnable walls. Grey zone war is here to stay and the best option to fight it is to understand it and bridge the fault-lines that give impetus to this conflict to increase footprints across multiple domains.

NOTES

1. Steven Metz and Raymond A. Millen, "Future War/Future Battlespace: The Strategic Role of American Landpower," Strategic Studies Institute (Carlisle, PA: US Army War College, March 2003).
2. Tracey German, How will wars be fought in the future? Oxford University Press Blog, July 20, 2019.
3. Hal Brands, Paradoxes of the Grey Zone, Foreign Policy Research Institute, February 05, 2016.
4. Ibid.
5. Christopher Paul, the Characterization and Conditions of the Gray Zone, Report Prepared by NSI, Inc, Winter 2016, p. 2.
6. John Raine, War or peace? Understanding the grey zone, Blog on IISS, April 03, 2019.
7. Ibid.
8. Lyle J. Morris, Michael J. Mazarr, Jeffrey W. Hornung, Stephanie Pezard, Anika Binnendijk & Marta Kepe, Gaining Competitive Advantage in the Gray Zone: Response Options, RAND Corporation, 2019.
9. David Carment, War's Future: The Risks and Rewards of Grey-Zone Conflict and Hybrid Warfare, Canadian Global Affairs Institute, October 2018.
10. Ibid.
11. Megan Eckstein, Pentagon's Non-Lethal Weapons Office Pushing Gray-Zone Warfare Tools, *USNI News*, September 24, 2019.
12. Stacie L. Pettyjohn & Becca Wasser, Competing in the Grey Zone, Russian Tactics and Western Responses, RAND Corporation, 2019, p. 2.
13. Andrew Dowse, Sascha-Dominik (Dov) Bachmann, Explainer: what is 'hybrid warfare' and what is meant by the 'grey zone'? *The Conversation*, June 17, 2019.

14. Carment, N 9.
15. Ibid.
16. Håkan Gunneriusson, Russia and China's ongoing 'hybrid warfare' – When does it cross the line? *Lima Charlie News*. Accessed from https://limacharlienews.com/national-security/russia-china-hybrid-warfare/ on March 08, 2020.
17. Jean-Christophe Boucher, Hybrid Warfare and Civil-Military Relations, Canadian Global Affairs Institute, December 2017.
18. Ibid.
19. Katherine E. Brown, Transnational Terrorism, Accessed from https://www.e-ir.info/2017/01/19/transnational-terrorism/ published on January 19, 2017.
20. Who are Somalia's al-Shabab? *BBC News*, December 22, 2017.
21. Ashley Tellis, The Menace That Is Lashkar-e-Taiba, Carnegie Policy Outlook, March 2012.
22. Ayesha Siddiqa, Jaish-e-Mohammed: Under the Hood, *The Diplomat*, March 13, 2019.
23. Manoj Anand, China using Ulfa against India? *The Asian Age*, April 6, 2017.
24. Biju Kumar Deka, NSCN (IM) Leaders Camping in China? Peace Talks Aside, Outfit Seeks Help to Renew Fight, Says Sources, *News 18*, November 22, 2019.
25. 'China wants to maintain instability in North-East India', IANS, *India Today*, August 26, 2012.
26. Michael Raska, China and the 'Three Warfares, '*The Diplomat*, December 18, 2015.
27. Ibid.
28. H.R. McMaster, How China Sees the World, *The Atlantic*, May 2020.
29. Ibid.
30. Ibid.
31. John Schaus, Competing in the Gray Zone, Centre for Strategic and International Studies, October 24, 2018.
32. Kevin L. Pollpeter, Michael S. Chase & Eric Heginbotham, The Creation of the PLA Strategic Support Force and Its Implications for Chinese Military Space Operations, Accessed from https://www.rand.org/pubs/research_reports/RR2058.html on March 08,2020.
33. Jack Austin, Grey Zone Deterrence – The key to a more secure future? *UK Defence Journal*, February 217,2020.
34. Stevenson, Gray Zone Deterrence: What It Is and How (Not) to Do It, NSI, June 2017.
35. Jahara W. Matisek, Shades of Gray Deterrence: Issues of Fighting in the Gray Zone, *Journal of Strategic Study*, Volume 10, 2018, p. 21.
36. David Barno and Nora Bensahel, Fighting and Winning in the "Gray Zone", War on the Rocks, May 19, 2015.
37. Sergio Miracola, Chinese Hybrid Warfare, Institute for International Political Studies, December 21, 2018.
38. Ibid.
39. Caitlin Foster, These are the world's 20 most dangerous countries, and photos showing what life is like there, *Business Insider*, November 1, 2018.
40. Ariel Watson, The Ultimate Weapon in the Fight Against Terrorism, Digital Intelligence, https://www.cellebrite.com/en/blog/the-ultimate-weapon-in-the-fight-against-terrorism-digital-intelligence/ July 25, 2018, Accessed Jan 30,2019.
41. John Schaus, Michael Matlaga, Kathleen H. Hicks, Heather A. Conley and Jeff Rathke, What Works: Countering Gray Zone Coercion, Centre for Strategic and International Studies, July 16, 2018.

5

Technology and its Impact on Changing Character of Threats and Effect of Hybridisation

Lieutenant General Anil Chait

ABSTRACT

The evolving character of conflict that Indian Security and Law-enforcing agencies face, and will face is best characterized by convergence. This includes convergences of physical and psychological forms by kinetic and non-kinetic wielding entities that may be combatants as well as non-combatants. Nation-states will therefore be increasingly challenged by the convergence of the military force and interagency community of the adversary(s), besides non state actors, with capability emerging from a long list of choices that will be available on the menu for unleashing damage without being identified. Blurring of forms and resultant synergy from simultaneous applications through multiple modes of harm from an unknown adversary is expected to pose one of the most complex challenges for the future.

Future conflicts therefore could be expected to be multi-model or multi-variant, rather than a characterization of one form of warfare. The construct along the entire curve of relationship starting from cooperation, collaboration and competition to conflict will therefore employ traditional/non-traditional threats with regular/irregular activities (including indiscriminate violence, coercion and criminal disorder) which are unpredictable in nature and can be applied selectively, and may be simultaneously in the battle space to achieve synergistic effect in the physical and psychological dimension of the conflict.

Introduction

The present narrative of global landscape, globalization and intertwined economies has made the use of conventional force as a tool of policy less attractive. Media intrusiveness and transparency has raised the bar of international law on the use of force. Spread of democratic values and norms of international behaviour have added further limitations on security establishments and architecture. Privatization of war and emergence of non-state actors motivated by radical ideologies with access to finance and open-source technology are altering the strategic context and we are progressively witnessing diminishing of the Westphalian system.

The declining threshold of national sovereignty and shrouding of real perpetrators of instability into anonymity has been visible around the globe. While weapons of mass destruction (WMD) may have reduced, the number of interstate wars fought for national interest has increasingly been replaced by intrastate conflicts involving sub-national interests. Power transition among states and diffusion of power from states to non-state actors is occurring rapidly, with power and control often being exercised by proxies.

In such a scenario, how will technology further accentuate the fault lines? This is the line of enquiry and purpose of this chapter against the backdrop of compressed geography due to revolution in an information-driven world that has made the world inter-dependent, more than ever.

Geopolitics; Economics and Geo-Technology

Technology has always been used to produce improved tools of warfare to subjugate other nations. The history of India is replete with examples where invaders exploited superior technology, tactics, and strategy to colonize the country. Threats and challenges emanating from it has the potential to impact the Grand Vision of India, or alternately, service its need in the interconnected globalized order, which is signified by an increased area of interest, enlarged area of influence—all moving along the trajectory of cooperation, collaboration, competition and conflict.

To understand the ever-shifting nature of international relations, analysts have traditionally relied upon geopolitics and geo-economics. While these two complement each other, it is the technological innovations that have the power to tilt geo-economic advantage for larger geopolitical impact. Systemic changes in the post-Westphalian world is witness to the rise of enterprises and non-state actors controlling new technologies for creating capabilities as new Power Centres. These new power centres will leverage these capabilities for geopolitical advantages through economic gains.

Industrial Revolutions

The invention of steam power—especially its mass production through the factory system, and discoveries in metallurgy, chemistry, and physics, have made a profound impact on the society of that time. The steam locomotive marked the earliest revolution in land transportation after the invention of the wheel. It enabled railroads to move troops and supplies fifteen times faster than their marching speed, while conserving the energies of men and animals at the same time. On the other hand, beyond the railhead, soldiers still marched and animals were used to pull supply wagons.

If the First Industrial Revolution used water and steam to mechanize production, the second used electric power to create mass production. The Third has used electronics and information technology to automate production. Now a Fourth Industrial Revolution is building on the third. This is characterized more by fusion of technologies that is blurring the lines between the physical, digital, and biological spheres. Applications involving Artificial Intelligence (AI), quantum computing, machine learning, nanotechnology and genetic engineering riding on communication highways are likely to impact the State, society, and its accompanying security architecture immensely and deeply.

Rapid advances in AI which implies non-biological systems performing tasks that otherwise require human intelligence—and through it, in the working of vastly improved autonomous sub systems and systems, could possess novel war-fighting and disruptive applications involving human-machine collaboration or their combat teaming. In scale, scope, and complexity, the transformation is unlike anything that humankind has experienced earlier. Manifesting, predominantly in the civilian domain, dual-use technologies are likely to entail wider ramifications with creative and disruptive applications challenging the authority of the state due to lack of control with security establishments trying to catch up.

Overall, we do not yet know just how it will eventually unfold. But as in the past, delay in understanding the transformative effect of convergence and its disruptive underpinning, is likely to overwhelm society.

Disruptive Technologies and Disruption

The decade that is knocking on our doors is already on the verge of making science fiction manifest in our homes, society, roads, and skies as viable everyday technologies. Cars/robots that can drive themselves; Additive printing that can build our houses; Look-alike meat, that is derived from plants; Robots that can be fantastic companions; Gene editing for increasing crop yield or for fixing, genetic disorders in human beings. AI-ushered advancements can also make conventional military capabilities alone count for much less and if AI-driven machines develop their own goals and possess the capability to pursue them, then unintended catastrophic consequences can follow.

These are as much a reality as are swarms that can fly or nano-bots that can cruise through the blood stream and monitor parameters to unblock arteries in human beings. While these can be a boon to society, bio-engineered synthetically developed technologies carry with them monumental consequences of pandemics. The ability to harm increases rapidly with democratized implementation. Corona virus continues to be under discussion in this regard.

Overall, what is noticeable in the shifting of science fiction from the laboratories to becoming items of daily choice are the new non attributable tools of disruption available to invisible enemies to win without fighting which Sun Tzu rated to be, the acme of leadership thus: *"The best victory is when the opponent surrenders of its own accord before there are any actual hostilities...it is best to win without fighting."*

Data and Cyber

Data, the new language of communication, has already taken the first step in a long chain of intellectual activity. To be used for public good, distillation of data into information, information into knowledge and knowledge into wisdom is needed to serve people.

Data to be called as "new oil" also requires faster processing, to become Intelligence. When humans could not cope with the immense flow of data, they stopped becoming useful. This work progressively started to be entrusted to electronic algorithms, whose capacity far exceeded the human brain. As data and its utilization continued to surge, data processing conditions started to change too. In this race between data, its processing and basis for decision-making, premium increasingly got laid on an efficient structure. This, when not done, led to challenges to the established and prevalent order of the State.

Personal data therefore will continue to be harvested and even secure networks like WhatsApp will continue to be vulnerable as mobile applications, notwithstanding their security, continue to talk to each other. As vulnerability and threats to data due to thefts in data-driven economies increases, nationalism of data resulting in its misuse by the state, can also be expected to increase. How this will eventually be used by stakeholders will depend upon their interests and accountability since manipulation can be undertaken at genome level and the tendency to monetize data will occur within "Data Commons." The new structure around data and its encryption and processing for gainful advantage will directly be an outcome of who builds, controls, and uses that data.

It is not data alone, but the entire electromagnetic (EM) spectrum that holds the key to future threats with cyber as its part. Cyber needs to be viewed in combination with EM spectrum for surveillance, electronic warfare, and high energy beam applications. CEMA (Cyber, Electromagnetic Activities), as a combined medium, therefore assumes significance for the integrated and digitized environment.

Internet and Cyber Space

The Internet revolution was meant to connect people but as BBC reported recently in January 2020, it was shut purposely 200 times in 33 countries in 2019 alone. In view of a discredited mainstream media—both print as well as electronic—people have come to rely more on social media as the primary and prompt source of information especially during periods of crises to get more comprehensive and credible information. Cyberspace has therefore turned more crucial to our daily lives as it has become a free and lawless zone, often eroding state sovereignty.

While at the UN, countries have managed to agree on norms of responsible behaviour, cyber perhaps still constitutes the most formidable global security risk as anything, everything or a network, can become a target involving things like traffic lights, railway signalling equipment, banks, power plants, nuclear reactors, dams, airports. A cyber 9/11 on the lines of the coordinated cyber-attack of 2007 against Estonia may not be far off.

Intense debate has ranged about re-structuring of the internet, but it is much harder to change an established order. In any case, by the time decisions will be made, the Internet would have morphed many times over since governments will not be able to match the pace of the technological hare. Overwhelmed by data, they cannot even process it fast enough to generate a timely vision, which is better than what the present system can perform.

Human mindscapes residing outside most existing institutional purviews and regulatory frameworks have become the battleground of information dominated effect-based operations. Information dominance and deception for the sake of dislocation has continued to guide the strategy of disrupters. We are witnessing narratives and counter narratives supported by technological means sharply dividing public opinion based on orientation, as freedom of speech and privacy laws get pushed to suit interests and generate unrest in society. Shaping narratives, supporting protests, influencing elections, promoting jihadist ideas, enabling non state actors to achieve their aim, have the potential to disturb the social equilibrium and not the purpose for which such technologies were introduced in the first place.

In the military domain, nothing differentiates IoBT from IoT, more than the battle—the B in IoBT. In either case, a physical survival can be threatened with kinetic, directed energy and electronic attacks and against its "Things" by jamming radio frequencies, destroying fibre channels, and depriving the system of its power sources. The disrupter can also threaten the integrity and availability of information, besides acquiring friendly information by violating its confidentiality. Inimical elements will attempt to violate the integrity of information by modifying it with malware, inserting rogue content and corrupting information, for supply to information-acquiring "Things" such as sensors.

Global deployment of 5G network for a hyper-connected world

Telecom networks meant for people are now connecting machines by porting data. The future will see more connected machines than humans and that is the promise of 5G and other such next-gen mobile networks. Launching an era of large-scale Internet of Things (IOT), communications with sensors are likely to be embedded in everything. At home, appliances will communicate with the owner or with other devices, bringing it closer to being a smart home. In the outside world, high-speed 5G networks will help machines communicate with each other with zilch latency to improve communications. It will also ensure manufacturing of products additively from distant locations or controlling those that are dangerous to society remotely for destructive/criminal purposes with clinical precision and effectiveness.

How the volume of data with faster downloads of speed will be handled and how will it be utilized? With 75 billion Internet of Things (IoT) devices expected to be in place by 2025, the world is already at the cusp of experiencing a technology that will change the way we live and, not knowing how we will cope with it in the short term, will be disastrous.

The impact of such connectivity will also be linked to transparency and decision cycles between attacker and defender or between perpetuator and responder. Attacker, in such a hyper connected world because of advantages of proactivity, is likely to enjoy superiority by adapting faster than responder, because of its coping process.

Nanotechnology—Science Fiction to Reality

Atoms and molecules are controlled and assembled today to do specific tasks at the molecular level. Building systems from it will revolutionize the way we live since building such clever and invisible nano-sized machines is the lofty goal of nanotechnology. Shortly, some of the nano gear will move from labs into home appliances, cars, airplanes, food, solar panels, smart cities, our bodies and whatever else can be thought off. For applications like cars, clothes, airplanes or solar panels, materials made from carbon nanotubes (a nano-sized cylinder of carbon atoms) may be employed, making performance-enhanced products, lighter, fuel-efficient and with a longer life cycle. As they become invisible through employment of stealth technology, their impact will be massive and ubiquitous as products will become relatively invisible.

Biodegradable nano materials, which can also dissolve after the task is completed makes products made from this material even more exciting. Such products, on the other hand, with gene editing, can add to significant disruption adding to the complexity of criminality, originating from the depth of creative minds. As the product range spreads, concerns about toxicity of effects and hazards to health will need to be examined in detail.

'Quantum Computing: Solving Real Word Problems

Classical computing has been the backbone of modern society. We were correctly reminded by Stefan Filipp, quantum scientist at IBM Research, that many of the world's biggest mysteries and potentially greatest opportunities remain beyond the grasp of classical computers.

To continue with the pace of progress, augmentation of classical approach is needed with a new platform—one that follows its own set of rules. The ability to manipulate properties of Superposition and Entanglement is what makes quantum algorithms fundamentally different from classical algorithms besides the multiple values of state between 0 and 1 enabling storage of different types of information.

A quantum computer can solve complex problems that would otherwise take much more time than today's computers to solve. This not only has massive implications for decoding most secured networks but provides unique technological ascendency, including hacking, to those who possess it.

The team at Google AI—a multinational company—achieved a sort of 'quantum supremacy' by developing such a chip, a 54-qubit processor named 'Sycamore' that comprises high-fidelity quantum logic gates to perform the benchmark testing. Not just Google, but several other technology giants like Microsoft, IBM, and Intel, have already joined the race to build a scalable quantum computer. Where will machines take such non-state players, and will it not give them the advantage to influence our lives by possessing knowledge supremacy? China's phenomenal advances in quantum computing and in AI, for control of world's economy and, through it the political, centre-stage, has already resulted in the USA coming up with a military strategy of "Third Offset" Thankfully, in recognition of the Dragon threat, an outlay of 8,000 Cr INR, has also been announced in India for the national mission on Quantum Technologies and applications. The mission is expected to build solutions for quantum communications, storage, and encryption.

Intelligent Robots and Cyborg Warriors leading the Change in Battle

Today's robots are largely remote-controlled with little on board intelligence. However, the inflection point is near, where artificial intelligence and deep learning will help future robots to assess situations and make on-the-spot decisions to respond, without any human intervention. This will open new frontiers on their deployment as facial recognition algorithms proceed beyond an accuracy figure of nearly ninety-seven percent.

So far, robots designed to help soldiers on the battlefield were mostly transported in backpacks and deployed on the field when required. In future as they become more adaptable in shape and hence flexible in work, applications will multiply. Equipped with a range of dual-use systems like GPS, navigation sensors and collision detection software, these robots will be able to engage in combat, autonomously on behalf of their controllers and lead the charge in the war of the future on behalf of their owners (state/non-state/Individual). They might have tank treads to tackle difficult terrain. There might be flying robots that look more like airplanes. Some might be in the form of big trucks or bulldozers or for that matter self-driving explosive-laden boats/cars employed to coerce/threaten or terrorize society with no trail behind.

While AI robots may be free of human errors, they will continue to remain susceptible to catastrophic mistakes on their own. This is a concern, which dominates the present debate as machines could become killers based on external command or on external bidding. So, will these robots be more effective in war? Hope, we do not have to find out.

Elon Musk and Stephen Hawking have been demanding a ban on autonomous weapons. Even Google had admitted the need of regulation on the development of AI as it accepts that while technology initially may reduce the human burden, its wrongful adaptation will have a negative impact. Davos 2020 issued AI principles that prohibit its use as a weapon but did not rule out selling to the military. Can it be denied that they will not fall into wrong hands?

To that extent the idea of human-machine fusion, by creating of high-tech cyborg warriors is more likely as ethical warriors and regulatory framework might not allow other kind of development to take place with impunity. With direct neural enhancement—using chip implants or wearable devices—individual senses and muscular strength are more likely to get enhanced.

The Swarm is Coming

The USA in January 2017 claimed that 103 Predix drones, after launch, communicated with each other and went about performing a series of formation flying exercises, mimicking surveillance missions. Predix drones are not pre-programmed synchronized platforms but a collective organism sharing one distributed brain for decision making and adapting to each, like swarms. Such programs are reflective of mass or numbers of the industrial age but sharing access and flow of information of present-day age to overwhelm opponents.

The types of air defence systems and missiles that are in place are neither designed to track and cope with objects of that size nor deal with such a large number—all at the same time in one designated area.

Robots too may also be able to act in self-organizing collaborative swarms in the same way as soldiers of today act in teams. Swarms will involve systems, involving varying degrees of freedom, from being remote controlled to autonomous, and act dynamically, according to prescribed rules of operations. Units of the future could even be a mixed human-robot team operating on collaborative instead of adversarial basis. While an attacker could work to a concept, the responder will have to evolve a doctrine to optimize pay offs.

Towards an Era of Singularity

We are moving towards an era, referred to as singularity—not the cosmological event where space-time collapses to form a black hole but a tipping point for humans, when machines will become exponentially smarter than *homo sapiens*. Kurzweil feels machines will also make humans smarter on their way to singularity. In one of his lectures, he maintained that machines may not be inside our bodies but by 2030 we will be able to connect our neocortex—the part of our brain that powers sensory perception, motor commands, reasoning, thought and language, to the cloud. As and when that happens, humans will move on their way to become extinct and Singularity, where machines will out-think us, will usher in an era of abundance and ultra-smart life.

Hybridization of Threat and Effect: India and its Neighbours

South Asia has been a key epicentre of conflict and instability in the world. Being host to a mix of indigenous peoples and migrants, the sub-continent has witnessed movement of people for several centuries and many South Asian States have rarely seen true political unity due to the accompanying clash of civilizations.

Territorial disputes, religious nationalism, fundamentalism, radical extremism, ethnic tensions, and socio-economic disparities have remained prevalent. The threat of nuclear weapons falling into the hands of non-state actors and groups such as jihadis, continues to spiral instability in this conflict-ridden regions. It appears unlikely, that a genuine cooperative security framework can ever emerge from the ashes of ongoing conflicts nuanced by technological developments.

China as a rising power lying to the north of South Asia, has developed a comprehensive industrial base over the last three decades by implementing Four Modernization themes. The industrial system covers all areas and domains, from low end simple products to high end complex systems. Two Chinese tele-communication enterprises, figure amongst the world's five leading communication equipment manufacturers. China has reportedly been testing space-based quantum communications technology along with applications for electromagnetic drives. A next-generation Artificial Intelligence (AI 2.0) plan stands published which envisages the development of artificial intelligence in accordance with numeric analogy principles. It has already made rapid progress in the hypersonic glide vehicle technology.

The exponential strategy pursued by the leading hegemony of Asia, in its quest for "imposing its will" or making others do its bidding, goes beyond the exercising of military and/or economic power. In the narrative entailing profusion of conflicts defying definition of war, a mix of kinetic and non-kinetic strategy under the perspective of comprehensive national power for global reach has been chosen by the PRC. This is more appropriate to it in the context of the geo-economics of the Belt-and-Road Initiative. Consequently, future wars to be fought and won are likely to be on the fields, which lie before, and "Beyond the Battle fields" through synergistic application of resources, overt or covert, as necessitated by wars of choice. The synergy and interdependency of means and for power to exceed limits will therefore involve clandestine bypassing of frontiers to strike at critical vulnerabilities directly and in the hinterland at appropriate time. Unrestricted warfare in such a visualisation is likely to go beyond military ideology and conventional capabilities through unconventional tactics and irregular in form. Soldiers progressively could lose monopoly on war and in so doing alter the process of war itself.

PLA as an "informationalised and later as intelligent-ised force" is headed towards a new concept of integrated war fighting for the `New Period". This construct for "War Making" and Integrated Joint War fighting incorporate fused kinetic and non-kinetic tools for:

- Domination, deterring and posturing.
- Gaining of Initiative for Striking First (GISF).

- Quick battle to force a quick resolution (QBQR).
- In Depth Strike through employment of Elite Forces and Sharp Arms (EFSA).
- Achievement of political objectives and withdrawal.

The twenty years post the publication of "Unrestricted Warfare" has demonstrated the prescience of the authors in respect of new types of conflicts today. The current trajectory of technological change is making this visualization more plausible and bringing it closer to fruition. While the speculative line of enquiry on Unrestricted Warfare was conceived mainly in the context of state-based conflict between the then asymmetrical powers, the USA and China, their central thesis remains relevant across all types of wars and phases.

The Indo-Pak strategic context, on the other hand, has been mired and coloured with the use of force and clash of ideas. Analysis of the stratagem adopted by the belligerents under the nuclear backdrop suggests that the character of war has further changed on account of politico, social, cultural, and technological changes. The warfare of narratives has gained a new momentum with more and more hate campaigns being joined from outside and inside for control of minds and surgical strikes can be undertaken even under a nuclear backdrop, if the cause is "just."

Ever since Pakistani dictator General Zia ul-Haq fashioned the instrument of proxy war against India by taking a page out of covert war, the Pakistani military has been (unofficially) at war with the Indian state and has used all possible tools (drugs/counterfeit currency/subversion/hate campaigns/violence and force) to undermine the idea of India. Strangely, it is the Indian population that has been slow in realizing that Pakistan is at war and that it is being fought on Indian soil against the backdrop of religion, two-nation theory, unsettled border, and disputable sovereignty issues.

As long as Pakistan does not come to terms with the reality of India, the employment of asymmetrical tools and irregular means backed by Qur'anic motivation will continue to be her preferred strategy and regularity of this irregular war will continue to haunt India, as she gets more and more mired in pursuing religious nationalism.

India's core values, unlike many others in the region, are premised on justice, liberty and equality along, with human rights and freedom as provided in the Constitution. These form the basis of its existence as a nation. Security, mechanisms and its accompanying architecture will strive for cohesion and internal consolidation of these values against externally inspired and internally abetted contradictions.

India and its security establishment has been slow in adapting to the change while watching China's meteoric rise, altering global dynamics. It comes as no surprise that in matters of strategic affairs, the Ministry of External Affairs has only now recognized that it needs reinvention and that a new ministerial division termed NEST denoting New, Emerging and Strategic Technologies needs to be created for meeting challenges of technology. Applauding the idea, General P. C. Katoch writing for SP has rightly remarked, that such an action "can merge technology policy with foreign policy as technologies are converging to create disruption, with drastic regional and global geopolitical consequences."

Conclusion

From the above, it should emerge very clearly that it is the technology that will guide the destiny of nations in international power relations. It will not only control the levers of economic and military powers but govern the lives of people as well. Open confrontation between the nations may be a thing of the past, as emerging technologies and domains of space and cyber will possess the potential to transform the complete character of the war.

REFERENCES

1. Shashi Tharoor & Samir Saran, *The New World Disorder and the Indian Imperative*, Aleph Book Company (January 2020), ISBN-13: 978-8194233732.
2. Akash Kapur, *India Becoming: A Portrait of Life in Modern India*, Riverhead Books (March 2013), ISBN-10: 1594488193.
3. Payal Arora, *The Next Billion Users: Digital Life Beyond the West*, Harvard University Press (March 2020), ISBN-13: 978-0674241800.
4. Lt Gen PC Katoch, *Indian Military and Network-centric Warfare*, Wisdom Tree (November 2014), ISBN-10: 8183283624.
5. Yuval Noah Harari, *Homo Deus: A Brief History of Tomorrow*, Vintage (March 2017). ISBN-13: 978-1784703936.
6. Atul Jalan, *Where Will Man Take Us? The bold story of the man technology is creating*, Penguin Portfolio (April 2019), ISBN-13: 978-0143446934.

6

Cross-Domain Synergy: Way Forward to Fight Future Wars

Brigadier Arvind Thakur and Colonel (Dr.) Michael Padgett (US Army)

Wars are not fought by the armed forces alone. Nor are the constituents of the armed forces likely to fight alone in their respective single service domains. In ancient times, some of the greatest victories could be achieved employing a single service in a single domain. Alexander the Great could achieve victory using only land forces in the 4th century B.C. and Genghis Khan could capture vast swathes of central Asia and eastern Europe in the 13th century A.D. Even Lord Nelson defeated the combined fleet of the French and Spanish navies in Trafalgar during the Napoleonic Wars of the 19th century using only the battle ships of the Royal Navy. The result was the prevention of the French from ever attacking the British mainland or disrupting British naval operations. But ever since the 1900s, modern constituents of military power like the Air, Cyber, and Space have so networked battle domains that we are now living in a world where no single service force can achieve national military aims operating in only a single domain. Of particular significance has been the recognition of the immense potential of the newer forms of domains, i.e., cyber and space that has thrown up multiple challenges in its integration and synergistic employment that has led to a serious rethink of war fighting methodologies.

Military history since the last century is replete with examples of joint operational successes. No single domain battle has achieved military strategic aims even though it may have paved ways for victories many times. Though successful, Operation Allied Force, the NATO air operation in Kosovo from March to June 1999, was found wanting by a Rand study in 2002 that felt joint operations would have perhaps yielded better and quicker results. Cross-domain synergy has thus become *sine qua non* for a field force commander to achieve operational aims.

Full spectrum warfare is not a chimera and in its brutal execution could well cause military, economic and political catastrophe to a nation ill prepared and ill equipped to handle it. India's belligerent neighbourhood, often with reckless leadership, does possess modern military hardware and could unleash a multi-spectrum war comprising land, naval, air, cyber and space-based attacks. China has demonstrated its capability, to name a few, of launching ICBMs, anti-satellite weapons and cyber attacks that could make some of our systems ineffective or to malfunction at critical junctures. Pakistan, on the other hand, never tires of flexing its nuclear muscle. India too possesses military hardware to crush the enemy's designs but needs to improve its strategic doctrines and organisational structures to meet future challenges to defend itself and to take the battle across its frontiers.

Fundamentals of Domains and Cross-Domain Synergy

Domains are those areas that are exclusively controlled by a single organisational entity. In military terms, Cross-Domain would include land, sea, air, space and cyber domains. Simply speaking, Cross-Domain implies that a force should be capable of operating effectively in any domain be it land, sea, air, cyber or space, and in doing so, it would enhance the operational effectiveness of the other domain specialists. The US Department of Defence, Joint Operational Access Concept (JOAC) defines Cross-domain synergy as, 'the complementary vice (*grip*) merely additive (*additional*) employment of capabilities in different domains such that each enhances the effectiveness and compensates for the vulnerabilities of the other.'[1] The JOAC further elaborates that Cross-domain synergy creates and exploits asymmetrical advantages inherent in a joint force—air power to defeat naval assets, naval power to neutralise air defences, ground forces to neutralise land-based threats to air and naval forces, cyber operations to defeat space systems, and so on. A joint force certainly facilitates cross-domain synergy but at the same time, a single service should also have cross-domain capabilities. The latter is where the importance of cross-domain synergy is exemplified. For example, an all-Marine Air-Ground Task Force operation is not joint, yet it typically operates in three domains.[2] If the Indian Air Force's GARUD launches special operations on land, the operation is a single service operation on multiple domains. On the other hand, not all joint activities are necessarily cross-domain, as when the Air Force and Navy team up to execute air superiority missions or Army, Air Force and Naval units share ground duties related to Air Defence (AD) or Air Traffic Control (ATC).

Multi-Domain Battles

Future wars would essentially be fought in multiple domains possibly by a joint force on their own in an independent theatre. The joint force must, therefore, understand different land, sea, air, cyber and space domains and be capable of operating effectively in all when called upon to do so. The multi-domain battle concept is not just about better integration of the operations of the services; multi-domain also requires each individual service to expand its areas of responsibility (which were traditionally the sole domain of another service).[3] This is the fundamental concept of Multi-Domain Battle. The concept of Multi-Domain Battle originated after the US think tanks realised that their traditional Air Land Battle concept (which did not fully factor in the cyber and space domains) was not foolproof considering the growing strength of their potential adversaries, Russia and China. The idea was first mooted in the US Army War College, Pennsylvania, in 2015 where the then Deputy Secretary of Defence, Bob Work, charged the US Army to review the Air Land Battle concept for future wars. Mr. Work envisioned the concept's role as the means by which the US military would fight and win, after breaking into the theatre and through Anti-Access/Area Denial defences.[4] Thus, the foundation of a new concept of war fighting was laid which is still in its infancy and would need considerable scholastic vision to fructify.

The USA, Russia, Israel and China (to name a few) already have in place joint integrated structures that facilitate cross-domain synergy. The US Defence Department has 11 combatant commands, each with a geographic or functional mission that provides command and control of military forces in peace and war. The Russians restructured their higher defence organisation in 2010 and merged the six military districts into four, (Western, Southern, Central and Eastern) which also function as "Joint Strategic Commands", by giving operational control of the units of all services to the military district commander except for strategic nuclear assets. The Chief of General Staff heads the Russian Armed Forces. He is directly under the defence minister and retains operational control over the Joint Strategic Commands and the strategic nuclear forces. Earlier, the operational control of military units had typically resided with the service commander (just like it is in India today). The Israel Defence Forces' three service branches function under a unified command, headed by the Chief of the General Staff, with the rank of lieutenant-general, who is responsible to the minister of defence.

The Chinese, in 2016, announced the formation of five Theatre Commands with Western Command being of concern to us in India. The Joint Chief of Staff commands the Joint Staff Department of the Central Military Commission that is the command organ and the headquarters for the People's Liberation Army (PLA) of China. The Chinese equivalent of cross-domain synergy is, "Integrated Joint Operations" (IJO). As the communication and network integration require highly sophisticated platforms, the PLA is being supported in its efforts by the Chinese defence industry that is supplying hardware like integrated command and battlefield management systems.[5]

Pakistan, though technologically not so advanced, enjoys a clear advantage in synergistic joint operations as its army chief is extremely powerful and the de facto theatre commander. India, meanwhile, continues with its single service independence with jointness as the glue, in activities ranging from training to operations. This requires a high degree of-cross domain synergy, as the focal area to achieve politico–military aims. With these two belligerent neighbours, India has no choice but to go in for unified command structures and take measures to synergise cross-domain operations.

Future wars would be at short notice and of short duration. To fight these high intensity, swift outcome and consolidation battles, we need a force structure that cannot wait for accretions to achieve a mission. The force or theatre commander must readily have the capability to employ the combat power in the right time and at the right place. Cyber operations, Special Forces, Air Defence, operational fires, logistics et al. from all services need to act in unison across all domains without regard to its domain specialisation to achieve decisive results. If India was to embark on a military campaign across its land or sea borders today, it would be guided by the Chairman, COSC (the CDS) consensus-based decision through the IDS and on to the individual service heads to release forces for a designated operation under a nominated theatre commander. This force would then comprise independent multi-service field units, air squadrons and naval assets with a temporary command and control structure. Time may not permit adequate integration of the components of this force and the outcome of this operation may then be found wanting. Joint structures are thus necessary to be in place to achieve the cross- domain synergy that is necessary to achieve success. There are many facets and dimensions of coming to a high degree of cross-domain synergy in an operational area, but considering the *pupate* stage India is in these matters, we will consider the four fundamental elements of cross- domain synergy that are essential to be introduced in the Indian Armed Forces post-haste.

Political Direction in Higher Defence Management—the Chief of Defence Staff (CDS)

Time and again, the political leadership of late has been encouraging the Service Chiefs and senior military leadership to enhance the jointness and synergy during the Unified Commanders Conferences and elsewhere. The need, perhaps, is to enact a law or issue detailed instructions that would formalise such relationships. The USA enacted the Goldwater-Nichols Act in 1986 underlying the principles of inter-service synergy and improving the defence Budget processes. The Indian Government initiated a constructive reformation of the higher defence management by announcing the creation of a CDS for the armed forces in August 2019 and appointing one on 01 January 2020. The CDS is now the permanent Chairman of COSC and heads the Integrated Defence Staff and the newly- created DMA (Department of Military Affairs). He has the responsibility of the Territorial Army, procurements (except capital), works relating to the services and heads the existing tri-services organisations. The CDS is also Advisor to the Prime Minister in the National Nuclear Command Authority (that controls the Strategic Forces Command), is a member of the Defence Acquisition Council and Defence Planning Committee. The CDS would thus have the space to focus on strategic calculus and inter-service coordination and be able to galvanize support with other government agencies to ensure the full backing of the whole of government effort for an impending operation. The CDS would certainly relieve pressure from individual service chiefs who presently are overburdened with the responsibilities of operational and financial planning, inter-service coordination, administration, training and myriad other duties. The CDS should also be able to enhance synergistic financial planning for acquisitions and a share of the budget pie as per global and regional security considerations without being affected by the pulls and pressures of individual services. Another field where the CDS would contribute in the integration and budget process is the amalgamation of the peacetime and operational logistics that at present is looked after by each service individually for itself. It should however, be ensured that historical and traditional service institutions remain with the parent organisation and the ethos of the individual services is not disturbed.

But the most important task of the CDS that impacts on cross- domain synergy would be the process of integrating the three services into theatre commands that would enhance jointness and cut costs. The mandate still falls short of what is necessary in the long-term analysis of defence management. The services continue to retain operational control over their units and report to the minister directly, bypassing the CDS on service and operational-related matters. The CDS should be vested with operational control to achieve a higher degree of synergy in war. This essentially is the first phase in higher defence reorganisation (before the more robust Theatre Commands come up). The service chiefs must be subordinate to the CDS who would be advised by them on service matters in addition to the staff from each of the services (at the CDS or Department of Military Affairs secretariat) before issuing instructions on operational, training and Human Resource matters. Service heads should thus become force providers and the CDS, and later, the theatre commanders, should don the role of force employers. Mohan Guruswamy, Chairman, Centre for Policy Alternatives, had also recommended to the government that the CDS must have a MoS rank, the Service Chiefs should be subordinate to him and the Defence Secretary should be Secretary in the COSC under the CDS.[6] Inequality of status between the CDS and the Service Chiefs is essential to prevent arbitrational interference of the Defence Ministry bureaucrats.

Integrated Theatre Commands

The modernisation of future battlefields demands an organisational structure to be put in place to achieve a cross-domain synergy that is seamless, responsive and efficient. This synergy could be achieved in a structural edifice that works on the principle of collective leadership and coordination as is currently the case in India or in a hierarchical system where all the resources are placed under a military commander who reports directly to the highest political authority of a country as is the case in the USA, Russia, Israel and China. Needless to say, the latter system is more efficient and dynamic. It is essential to have an organisational structure that maximises the full benefit of capabilities of systems that reside in all military branches and other related civilian organisations. When considering cyber and space operations the military faces a challenge: the difficulties of working across other government agencies as well as foreign partners. It is difficult to achieve jointness, let alone synergy, in the present system in India, wherein there are 17 commands of the three services and none of these is co-located. As a prerequisite for cross-domain synergy, Integrated Theatre Commands would optimise synergy and employment of forces by a field force commander who would have at his disposal all national military assets. Integration of logistics is a natural corollary of the Integrated Theatre Commands and would lead to reduction of manpower and costs. Such an arrangement is not only effective but would prove to be economical in temporal, spatial and resource management aspects. National military assets should be made available to a theatre commander, not only for operations but for training as well as administration during peacetime. In this phase of reorganisation, the role of the CDS may then be altered from operational control to operational coordination at the strategic level.

The concept of Integrated Theatre Commands may perhaps run into rough weather internally. The Indian Army being the most dominant service, the other services may resist change for fear of being marginalised in the decision-making loop and policy formulation process. This can be overcome by a joint cadre in future and a technical veto by key appointments in the organisation. The Air Force has its own reasons to resist such a change and would prefer to continue as at present. They do feel the present system has worked well and stood the test of time; the theatres are neither vast nor out of reach of rapid relocation of air assets. And implicit in the creation of Theatre Commands is the division of woefully short air assets that would weaken India's air defence.[7] But there is a way to counter this negative. Foremost is that the Government of India needs to make up the shortfall of Air Force inventories over a period of time. Till then, some assets could be retained centrally under the Air Chief as strategic reserves, but some of these, like Attack Helicopters, some of the transport and the Ground Attack aircraft could be allocated to the theatre commands for training and integration. In any case, no theatre would be functioning in watertight compartments and regrouping of assets can be done as and when a situation demands. A host of other issues would also need collective resolution and application to achieve an acceptable level of agreement or avoid disagreements. There would of course be many differences of opinion as to how to give shape to the new structure; it would require recommendations for the number of theatre commands (the Shekatkar Committee recommended three), subsuming the existing commands of all services under these theatre commands, division of training responsibilities, a common Defence Services Act of Parliament and other similar appraisals. We need to kick-start the process and in time, many issues may be resolved.

Informationalised Warfare: Integrated Information Systems

Establishing and integrating data networks and information platforms is paramount in achieving jointness and cross-domain synergy. The Indian armed forces currently have limited capabilities of seamlessly sharing data, information or intelligence with each of its constituents, i.e., Army, Navy and Air force. In the USA, this type of framework is established within the US Department of Defence (DoD) by the Defence Information Services Agency (DISA). DISA oversees all DoD information-sharing and protection systems. Some examples of those systems are the following:

- Maritime Domain Awareness Community of Interest.
- The Joint Functional Component Command for Global Strike and Integration.
- Defence Knowledge Online (DKO).
- The Global Information Grid (GIG).

The purpose of all the above systems and programs is to exploit attributes to support information sharing, whether implemented through Attribute-Based Access Control (ABAC) or the Role-Based Access Control (RBAC) system. In its current commercial-off-the-shelf (COTS) form, RBAC is a method of restricting network access based on the roles of individual users within an enterprise. The US Army serves as an extension of the work led by the DISA. It created the Program Executive Officer for Enterprise Information Systems (PEO EIS) to oversee the programs for information systems. The programs currently part of the PEO EIS portfolio include programs for cyber security, cyber analytics and detection, and allied information technology. The US Air Force and Navy have similar acquisition structures to oversee information management and sharing programs. But all is integrated by DISA. Together, even though complex in scope and diversity, the communications system facilitates a fair degree of cross-domain synergy in the United States military. India too could do well to emulate such a system with modifications as per organisational constraints.

The Indian Army currently uses the ASCON in peacetime and AREN during operations. The Air Force uses the AFNET which is a fibre optic-based network on which the integrated air command and control system (IACCS) rides. It also provides limited lateral connectivity to the Army and the Navy. In 2016, the DCN (Defence Communication Network) was established with the aim of seamlessly integrating the three services using a common communication platform for voice and data connectivity. DCN offers high quality voice, video and data services covering 111 entities spread across the country.[8] The reach of the DCN seems limited and there exists no role or attribute-based connectivity on a wider scale. Robust encrypted data link architecture with high bandwidth for Net-centric warfare across all domains is needed to facilitate situational awareness, to build sensors to target links and have a cloud repository for users to extract sensed information from.[9] Clearly, in the times of heightened cyber warfare threats and increasing cyber capabilities of India's adversaries, it is not too early to put our heads down and expand the DCN to extend its reach within and beyond the services.

Joint Staff and Human Resource Management

The human resource system may require considerable reshuffling in the three services to make progress in jointness and cross-domain synergy. Under the current cooperative structure, the understanding of each other's capabilities and weaknesses is very limited in scope. The following merit attention:

- Joint Staff Cadre: The jointness has to go beyond the TAC (Tactical Air Centre) at Corps level or MEAF (Maritime Element of the Air Force) at the Naval Fleet and the Joint Army Air Operations Centre at Command HQ or Maritime Operations Centre at the HQ Naval Command. These are primarily lateral links to their parent organisations for coordination. Occasional attachment of officers during exercises is also not enough for enhancing joint training. We do need to create a Joint Staff structure comprising personnel from all three services to be posted not only at HQ IDS or DMA, but at each service-specific element down to the formation level. The officers and men so selected should be the best and must benefit by this tenure for their career enhancement. A tri-service study needs to establish the outline for assignments for the selected cadre in a graduated manner over a period of time.

- Joint Training Infrastructure: More joint training infrastructure and training courses would be required. Presently this joint training is restricted to a few tri-service institutions under HQ IDS like the National Defence Academy, DSSC and National Defence College, etc., where only limited personnel can benefit. There is ample room to expand this jointness in areas such as basic training, weapons training, trade training, clerical training, junior leadership courses, intelligence, ground-based AD and increased subscription of courses by senior officers of the rank of Colonel and above in all training institutions. Common training institutions would not only enhance jointness but reduce budgetary constraints as well.
- Cross Attachment and Cross Affiliations: Cross attachment with units for a period ranging from six months to a year should be considered for officers and other ranks to other service's units and formation HQ for general duties. This system has worked fairly well for Infantry and Armoured Corps officers thus far and could be tried on a pilot basis with a few units and formations before making it mandatory for all to have at least one tenure in a sister service before being considered for career enhancement. Likewise, cross affiliations of army units with naval ships and Air Force squadrons must be done to enhance understanding of each other's organisations, equipment, ethos, capabilities and limitations. Such an arrangement exists in few numbers only because of individual efforts rather than institutionalised norms.
- Management of Senior Ranks: Should the Integrated Theatre Commands come up, it needs to be ensured that the services do not lose vacancies in the higher ranks. In fact, if three theatre commands come up, it could be an addition of more vacancies by subsuming the existing commands under the theatre commander rather than relocating the existing ones. For example, the Western

Theatre could be created at Jaipur with the existing Army's Northern, Western, SW and Southern commands as well as the Air Force's Western and SW Commands and part of the Navy's fleet at Mumbai. Overall, by integrating, there would be in any case a reduction of manpower and thus a leaner force that would certainly reduce cost to the exchequer.

US Military Approach to Cross-Domain Synergy

Various examples exist from the US history of success and failures with cross-domain synergy. Aspects of Cross-Domain Synergy can be found in past victories such as Yorktown in 1781 against the British where the combined land and sea capabilities of the USA and France resulted in the surrender of Lt Gen Cornwallis, the British Commander. Thus began both the creation of the USA by the successful use of joint operations on the ground as well as French sea operations to defeat the British and end colonial rule by Britain over the USA. In the last few decades, the USA has made significant strides in improving its Cross- Domain Synergy capabilities. In 1991, during Op Desert Storm, General Norman Schwarzkopf commanded a coalition joint force of 670,000 troops from 28 countries. The volume of improved jointness is also reflected in operations within Iraq and Afghanistan.

In 2010, the Joint Publication Capstone Concept for Joint Operations V3.0 outlined the framework for joint, cross-domain strategy for the USA. In 2013, the Joint Operational Access Concept V1.0 (JOAC) emphasised the need for shifting the focus of each service from service-specific to domain-based capabilities. The JOAC did recognise that cross-domain operations may be too complex to be practical. The most recent publication within the USA on cross-domain is the Capstone Concept for Joint Operations: Joint Force 2020. The latter postulates that cross-domain should become a core operating concept in all joint operations, from combat to humanitarian to operations other than war.[10]

The USA has moved beyond simply leveraging all elements of the defence department. Operations are now a combination of various departments and agencies within the federal government. There have been combined services, special operations, CIA, and cyber assets used in current campaigns. Space operations are also integrated in many ways, not the least of which are the intelligence gained from space-based assets. Protection of the various data systems has been enabled by joint programs, such as those advocated by the DISA above and the resultant information programs by the DoD and the various services. Intelligence- sharing within the intelligence community and inclusion of the DoD has resulted in better data sharing than ever before.

Conclusion

Cross-domain should never replace the criticality of selecting the simplest, most efficient solution to any situation. If a single service can execute a plan then so be it. But across the spectrum of modern-day warfare, jointness is fundamental to achieving cross-domain synergy. The Services must discard the mother hen's protective approach of a domain and the consequent "keep off" attitude. Cross-Domain capabilities should be applied across the spectrum of military activities like sub-conventional operations, and humanitarian operations and operations other than war (OOTW). When considering cyber and space operations the military faces another challenge: the difficulties of working across other government agencies as well as foreign partners.

A top-down approach from the highest levels of the government needs to be initiated through an Act of Parliament to synergise the effort of the services. Creation of an institution like CDS was long overdue and there is a need to hasten the process for its early embedding. Measures must also be taken to establish Integrated Theatre Commands that would enhance jointness and synergy in training and operations. Cadre restructuring for joint staffs needs expansion to enable jointness down to formation and unit levels. More inter-service postings not requiring specialist knowledge should be undertaken besides expanding the joint training institutions.

Acquisition of compatible new systems, either through imports or indigenisation, is important so that cross-domain synergy is facilitated rather than hindered by incompatible weapons systems and C3I2 platforms. In the days of predominance of informationalised warfare, it is imperative that a robust communication and data connectivity structure is implemented for the entire Armed Forces. The Defence Communication Network established in 2016 needs an upgrade to achieve seamless and rapid connectivity amongst the services.

India still has some serious work to do to address jointness and enhancing cross-domain synergy. It is time to loosen our obsession with service-specific issues alone and think beyond and allow sweeping structural changes to happen to enhance jointness and cross-domain synergy.

NOTES

1. US Department of Defence, Joint Operational Access Concept (JOAC) Version 1.0. (Washington, DC: United States Department of Defence, 2012), Foreword. http://www.defense.gov/pubs/pdfs/JOAC_Jan%2012_Signed.pdf.
2. William O. Odom and Christopher D. Hayes, "Cross-Domain Synergy: Advancing Jointness," *Joint Force Quarterly* 73 (2nd Quarter, April 2014), available at https://ndupress.ndu.edu/JFQ/Joint-Force-Quarterly-73/Article/577517/cross-domain-synergy-advancing-jointness/. Accessed 20 April 2019.
3. Dr. Manabrata Guha and Prof. David J. Galbraith, "The Multi-Domain Battle Concept: A Preliminary Assessment," Centre for Joint Warfare Studies, New Delhi, 2018. https://cenjows.gov.in/pdf/The%20Multi-Domain%20Battle_03-11-18.pdf. Accessed 19 Nov 2019.
4. Kelly McCoy, "The Road to Multi-Domain Battle: An Origin Story, Modern War Institute," *West Point*, October 27, 2017. https://mwi.usma.edu/road-multi-domain-battle-origin-story/. Accessed 18 Nov 2019.
5. Tai Ming Cheun, "Forging China's Military Might: A New Framework for Assessing Innovation," *JHU Press*, 2014. https://books.google.co.in/books?id=pQjEAgAAQBAJ&dq=china%27s +cross+domain+synergy&source=gbs_navlinks. Accessed 17 January 2020.
6. Lt Gen P.C. Katoch, "Making the CDS Effective is Crucial", *The Tribune*, Chandigarh, 29 August 2019.
7. Air Marshal Ramesh Rai, "Integrated Theatre Command, Does the Concept Suit India," *South Asia Defence and Strategic Review*, New Delhi, vol. 13, issue 4, Sep-Oct 2019.
8. Press Trust of India, "India's First Integrated Defence Communication Network Launched", 30 June 2016. https://www.ndtv.com/india-news/indias-first-integrated-defence-communication-network-launched-1426516. Accessed 18 Nov 2019. Also reported widely by other media in India.
9. Air Marshal Ramesh Rai, VM, "Multi Domain Warfare in the Indian Context," *South Asia Defence and Strategic Review*, New Delhi, Vol. 13, Issue 5, Nov-Dec 2019.
10. William O. Odom and Christopher D. Hayes, ibid.

7

Crisis Management and Escalation Control

Lieutenant General AK Singh

ABSTRACT

Pakistan has been playing a very dangerous, high-stakes game with India over the last three decades. Despite Pakistan's reckless efforts, it was the maturity of the Indian response that prevented escalation beyond a point. However the terrorist attack at Pulwama crossed India's threshold resulting in the airstrikes at Balakot, with a counter-strike by Pakistan. Two nuclear armed neighbours engaging in air combat is as dangerous as it can get. With China too, despite robust mechanisms in place, the disputed border has flared up periodically both in Ladakh and in the East, with dangerous face-offs. Against a nuclear backdrop, it is imperative for the armed forces, the diplomats and the political leadership in all three countries, to come to some common understanding of escalation control and crisis management, so that we do not get into an unintended conflict. This chapter analyses two events, i.e., Kargil and Balakot, to draw valuable lessons towards crisis management and escalation control.

Introduction

Within a span of two decades (1999-2019) India and Pakistan have clashed on at least four occasions, where the stakes were very high. Starting with the Kargil conflict in 1999, the attack by Pakistan-sponsored terrorists on the Indian Parliament in December 2001, followed by Indian mobilization for Operation Parakram; the terrorist strike in Mumbai in November 2008 and the recent suicide bomber attack at Pulwama (Jammu and Kashmir) followed by the calibrated Indian response at Balakot (Pakistan), brought both nations close to high escalation, an all-out war against a nuclear backdrop. Despite Pakistan's reckless efforts, it was the maturity of the Indian response that prevented escalation. Pakistan still continues with its proxy war in Jammu and Kashmir and there is no gainsaying when India's patience will overflow.

In the case of India and China, apart from the 1962 war, there have been a number of confrontations on the disputed border, notable being the clashes at Nathula and Chola in 1967 (Sikkim) and the recent standoff at Dokala in 2017 and in Ladakh in 2020. There are mechanisms in place, yet the possibility of escalation remains, until the border issue is settled. The facts suggest most of these clashes take place because of the deliberate provocative actions of the PLA and counter actions of the Indian Army.

It is therefore imperative for the armed forces, as also the political leadership, to understand the nuances of conflict escalation and how to control it. Whilst researching on the subject, one was surprised to find a dearth of literature on the subject in India. In the subcontinental context, two works of Stephen Cohen stand out; *Nuclear Proliferation in South Asia: The Prospect of Arms Control* (1991) and *Four Crisis and a Peace Process* (2007). Even globally, the subject of escalation came to the fore only in the 1960s, at the height of the Cold War with the possibility of a nuclear conflict looming large, more due to miscalculations than by design. There have been many studies, mostly in the context of the USA-Soviet Union standoff, the most important being 'On Escalation' by Harman Kahn, a renowned political scientist and geostrategist. With the end of the Cold War, interest in studying the dynamics of escalation has waned though enough trouble spots remain. For us, in India, which has two inimical neighbours with whom there is a disputed border, this subject assumes great importance and needs greater research and study. This is an attempt to stir that interest.

Defining Escalation

Escalation, as related to conflict, is a relatively new word and was not found in the Oxford/Webster dictionary until 1961.[1] Wherever there is armed conflict and there is an increase/upsurge in the scope, intensity or spread of that conflict it can be termed escalation. The escalation could be a calculated move by one or both sides, and more often an unintended consequence or miscalculation. A Rand Corporation[2] study talks of two meanings. The first defined escalation as a type of bargaining behaviour to raise the stakes of conflict through heightened levels of violence or broadened areas of dispute, almost akin to the notion of compellence. The second concept of escalation, on the other hand, conceived it as an involuntary process where the belligerents find themselves fighting a war of ever-increasing scope or intensity.

Spectrum of Conflict

The spectrum of conflict may be defined as a range/spread of conflict from the lower end to the highest end. Whilst there is a universality to this spectrum, regional nuances may add a variety. As far as India is concerned, the spectrum of conflict may include some or most of these escalatory steps, not necessary in a sequential order:

- Standoff on the disputed borders including use of non-kinetic resources.
- Terrorist strikes aided and abetted from across the borders, including proxy war. Could include hijacking of aircraft, ship and hostage taking.
- Cross-border operations, both on land and in the air (against specific terrorist related targets).
- Large-scale air and artillery assaults on military targets.
- Limited conflict/confined to disputed areas along the line of control (LC) or line of actual control (LAC).
- An expanding all-out conflict against a nuclear backdrop.
- Nuclear threat and possibly a localized tactical nuclear strike.
- Nuclear escalation with unimaginable consequences.

The Key Players in a Conflict

Whilst there are many stakeholders and participants in a conflict, the key players would always remain the Political, Diplomatic and Military.

- The political level remains the highest level at which major decisions regarding any conflict will be taken. This would also include decisions with reference to prevention of conflict, initiation, escalation and de-escalation. Of course such decisions will also take into account the diplomatic and military advice rendered by experts, though the decision will rest with the highest political authority. During the Kargil conflict[3], whilst the armed forces wanted to cross the Line of Control (which would have inevitably lead to escalation), the political authority, in their wisdom, did not allow this, leading to some heartburn and possibly larger number of casualties.

- The diplomatic input is increasing in importance as the world is becoming more interconnected and decisions taken by a country would often have international ramifications. Conflict prevention, keeping diplomatic/back channels open, even during conflict, assisting in de-escalation are tough tasks cut out for the diplomatic community. In international relations, escalation is also sometimes used to facilitate negotiations or put pressure on one or both sides to settle a dispute without war.[4] A study of the Cuban missile crisis of 1962 should be recommended reading for all those charged with taking key decisions in a crisis. How the two superpowers almost came to the brink of a nuclear conflict, and how the political and diplomatic leadership on both sides sagaciously pulled back, is a classic case study. Harman Kahn, whilst analyzing the superpower rivalry, tensions and crisis also states that, "as always, private communication, either direct or indirect, through principals or intermediaries, or through the use of more or less deliberately arranged leaks, all play an important role".[5]
- International concerns also get heightened, where the sides involved in a crisis are nuclear powers, as in the case of India and Pakistan. Most crises between India and Pakistan have had some involvement of the USA in defusing the crisis.
- The military leadership retains a pivotal role in any crisis/conflict as also its escalation control. In a democratic setup, the military remains subordinate to the civil–political authority and draws its military strategy from the political–strategic directive. The military leadership, however, has the overall responsibility of speaking truth to the power centres on major decisions regarding war and peace, which will be largely based on this advice. Two examples come to mind. General (Late Field Marshal) Sam Manekshaw's blunt advice to the then Prime Minister Mrs. Indira Gandhi, about postponing the intended operations against East Pakistan from April-May 1971 to later in December 1971, which was accepted by the Prime Minister. The result was a spectacular victory and the birth of Bangladesh. A more recent example is the resignation of General James Mattis, US Secretary of Defence in December 2018. The trigger was President Trump's decision to withdraw all troops from Syria. "This sudden policy shift posed a direct challenge to Mattis's beliefs. He believed that a retreat from Syria would

threaten the security of American troops elsewhere in the region, and would especially threaten America's allies in the anti–ISIS coalition."[6] One of the most revered living marines, he resigned when his advice was not accepted.

Conflict Prevention

The end of the Cold War and the advent of the 21st century has seen a resurgence of conflicts across the globe, both interstate and intrastate. The emergence of non-state actors, especially in the Middle East, has intensified conflicts in the region. The conflicts have become complex and hybrid, shades of grey have crept in; threats are not easy to quantify and, sometimes, even to identify. Modern-day conflicts are not merely confined to states but have expanded to include sub nationalities, terrorists, insurgents, religious fanatics and ethnic interest.[7] The power that technology has placed in the hands of both state and non-state actors has added a very destructive dimension.

In such an emerging scenario, it is but logical that renewed focus is placed on 'conflict prevention', as also resolution of conflicts before they escalate beyond a point of no return.

Research and studies in conflict prevention are not widespread being a young discipline. The 'Department of Peace and Conflict Research at Uppsala University, Sweden, has done extensive work and offers Bachelor's, Master's and PhD programs. There are programs in Indian universities and institutes as well, but work is still at a nascent stage. As far as conflict prevention is concerned, the term suggests different things to different people[8] ranging from 'preventive diplomacy', constructive actions undertaken to avoid the likely threat or a long-term proactive action plan to create conditions for a stable and more predictable international security environment.

The Uppsala Research Paper Number 7 suggests that there are two ways to understand conflict prevention.[9] One concerns the direct preventive action to control an emerging crisis which is in a dangerous phase of military escalation, intensification or diffusion. A second concern is the structural prevention where the idea is to create such conditions that contests and disputes hardly arise, or do not threaten to escalate into militarized actions. These actions could be through bi-lateral understanding, or in some cases, through third-party interventions by another country or a world body like the United Nations. This paper will attempt to analyse such strategies/action plans, as existing in the context of Indo-Pak issues, later in the chapter.

Escalation Matrix

Escalation ladder/matrix is the way in which the severity of conflict grows step by step. There are many steps in the escalation and the crisis/conflict need not escalate gradually, but could jump many steps. Herman Kahn in his seminal work *'On Escalation'*, has broad-based his definition of escalation to include both bargaining behaviour to increase the stakes, as also an involuntary process where the intensity increases gradually.[10] Kahn's 16-step escalation ladder, starting from the crisis, to limited military confrontation, to controlled local war, to some kind of all-out war and finally the aftermath is an objective and logical description of the escalation matrix. It is often criticized as a Western view which in the cold war context reflects a one-step-at-a-time escalation, which may prove altogether wrong in many situations existing in the 21st century.

Kahn's escalation ladder is more focused on crisis continuance, but may not hold true for simmering disputes, which move up and down the escalation ladder, for example, the ongoing proxy war in Jammu and Kashmir. This logical explanation of escalation presupposes two rational adversaries but may prove inadequate with an adversary like North Korea or the Taliban. This is a good guide, but strategic and operational leaders must retain the flexibility to deal with unexpected situations imaginatively, rather than with preconceived notions.

Crisis Management and Escalation Control in the Indo-Pak Context

The chequered history of Indo-Pak relations has seen tension, conflict and war on numerous occasions. The latest round starting with Ex 'Brasstacks', was followed by the proxy war unleashed by Pakistan, which shows no signs of abating till date. Multiple crises have occurred during the last three decades, including the limited war in Kargil (1999), Operation Parakram (2001-2002), the Mumbai blast in November 2008 and recently Pulwama, followed by the Balakot strikes by India in February 2019.

For the purpose of this chapter it is intended to analyse two events, that is, Kargil and Balakot, to draw valuable lessons towards crisis management and escalation control.

KARGIL WAR

The Facts

The proxy war in Jammu and Kashmir had been initiated by Pakistan in the late 1980s. Documents and diaries captured during the Kargil war have revealed that the Pakistan military had already put into motion the battle procedure for the Kargil War (Operation Badr, the Pakistani code name for the Kargil operation), as an extension of the proxy war, before the Lahore Declaration was signed by the two Prime Ministers in February 1999.[11]

In the early months of 1999, troops of Pakistan's Northern Light Infantry (NLI) dressed as militants (Mujahidin) infiltrated through gaps in defensive deployment in the Kargil-Dras sector and occupied some of the commanding heights overlooking the Srinagar-Leh highway, the sole lifeline to Ladakh.

The Indian hierarchy, both civil and military, was totally surprised, their initial reactions ranging from bravado to disbelief. The failure of intelligence at strategic, operational and tactical levels was complete.

It was only by May 1999 that the serious nature of the intrusions was recognised and a fierce counter-action to evict the intruders was put into motion. As the initial operations failed to achieve success, enhanced contingency preparedness was ordered on the international border, though the Strike Corps were not mobilized. After 8 Mountain Division assumed operational responsibility, things began to fall in place, and slowly but surely the Indian Army began to evict the Pakistani intruders from some of the most rugged terrain in the world.

On 24-25 June 1999, General Anthony Zinni, commander-in-chief of the US Central Command, visited Islamabad on instructions from the White House. He conveyed a blunt message, "If you don't pull back, you are going to bring war and nuclear annihilation down on your country.[12]"

With that as a backdrop, let us analyse the crisis to arrive at some evident trends in behaviour pattern and crisis management of the two sides. The nuclear status of the two countries with stark differences in their nuclear doctrines adds to the complexity of such a crisis.

Differing Perceptions

The Kargil conflict related to differing perceptions of Pakistan and India.

For Pakistan, the intrusion was a mirror image of the Indian ingress in Siachen, for India it was a flagrant violation of the Shimla Agreement.[13] Pakistan's military hierarchy went seriously wrong in assessing/ forecasting the likely Indian response to this so-called nibbling actions across the Line of Control (LC). The initial local Indian response was muddled and reinforced the Pakistani perceptions. Later, the Indian side, recognizing the serious nature of the ingress, mounted coordinated attacks with overwhelming superiority to claim victory. Pakistan was either over-confident or unwilling to expand the scope and intensity of conflict, having boxed itself into a corner by claiming these were intrusions made by the Mujahidin, not the Pakistani Army.

Self-restraint to Localize the Conflict

Some Pakistanis (especially those closely associated with its planning and implementation) considered Kargil a justifiable pre-emptive defensive move.[14] Yet, when the Indian counter-attacks began to succeed, Pakistan made no move to either reinforce or expand the conflict and did not commit its air force even during the most intense phase of the battle. It could be deduced, therefore, that where the limited aims set by Pakistan were belied, there was no attempt to expand the conflict. Whether this was a part of self-restraint on Pakistan's part is open to question. India, on the other hand, made a conscious effort not to expand the conflict, even tying the military's operational options by precluding the army and air force from crossing the LC. This political direction defied military logic and entailed the acceptance of heavier casualties.[15] As per Brajesh Mishra, India's NSA, "the middle of June was the most anxious period of the war and possibly the closest we came to enlarging the conflict area", as victory in Kargil still precluded the Indian attacks and the issue of crossing the international border to expand the area of conflict was seriously considered. The US Administration reacted to this message quite seriously.[16] This important conclusion from the Kargil conflict, where restraint was met with restraint, seems to have become a defining feature of subsequent Indo-Pak crisis, whether during Operation Parakram, the surgical strikes and even the Balakot strikes, and which can be built upon to control escalation in any future crisis scenario.

Channels of Communication

Heeding one lesson of earlier conflicts, India and Pakistan did keep communications between the two leaderships open during the 1999 war, even at the height of the crisis. The Prime Ministers had also established a back channel route, involving Niaz Naik and R.K. Mishra. This channel was terminated at the end of June when its existence became public.[17] During the crisis negotiations, the American team was also scrupulous in informing both sides of their conversations with the other side.[18]

The established channels of communicating between the DGsMO were also effectively utilized to co-ordinate the Pakistani withdrawal, including a physical meeting at Attari near Amritsar.[19] The importance of keeping channels of communication open, even during the worst phase of a crisis, was clearly a defining feature of the Kargil conflict and should be built upon by both countries. There is a caveat, however. The communication channel between civilian counterparts may sometimes prove ineffective because of the power dynamics within Pakistan. The military communication channel must, therefore, also be encouraged.

Diplomacy and Pre-eminent Role of USA

The diplomatic channels remained open, if not vibrant, during the Kargil conflict, commencing with the visit of Pakistan's foreign minister, Sartaj Aziz, to India on June 12. The visit proved fruitless, mainly because Aziz received his instructions from the Army. Prime Ministers Sharif and Vajpayee also activated the hot line on at least three occasions. India also launched a very vigorous diplomatic offensive across the world, especially in Washington. Diplomatically, the international community by and large sided with India or blamed Pakistan for the crisis.[20]

Despite Indian aversion to-third party involvement in Indo-Pak issues, the Kargil conflict proved otherwise, where both countries willingly transferred the crisis management burden on them to the USA. This was a tacit acceptance that they were unprepared to manage the dangers of escalation on their own.[21] As Moeed Yusuf argues, that during the Kargil conflict, the USA's pre-eminent position and its intermediate role was reinforced by most world powers, including Russia and China. But this may not remain so in the future context, with an assertive China and Russia pursuing their own agenda in South Asia. It would, therefore, be wise for both India and Pakistan to develop a more robust bilateral mechanism for crisis management and escalation control. Crucial to this would be acceptance by the Pakistani army that it cannot continue with its high stakes, high risk policy vis a vis India, especially in Jammu and Kashmir, an improbable but not impossible proposition. India and Pakistan need to also realise that diplomatic channels are crucial, but even more so in times of crisis. Removing/nullifying this link during crisis is the worst way to manage the escalation.

The Nuclear Backdrop

Having become overt nuclear powers in 1998, both India and Pakistan chose different paths/doctrines, and consequently varying nuclear thresholds. Pakistan's strategy of "First Use" of nuclear weapons is in direct contrast to India's doctrine, which articulates a "No First" use, but commits to massive retaliation regardless of the type/quantum of weapon used.[22] It may however be noted that both countries were nascent overt nuclear powers and had not reached the sophisticated levels of established nuclear powers. The Kargil crisis did have a nuclear dimension, although its nature is contested. At the height of the crisis, Pakistan's Foreign Secretary warned that his country would not hesitate to use any weapon in its arsenal to defend its territorial integrity.[23] There are conflicting reports of how seriously was this threat taken by India including the US allusion to some Pakistani preparation towards this end. This has been denied by both Musharraf and General V.P. Malik. It is possible that the Americans used this to convey the likely dangers to the Pakistani civil hierarchy, which was clearly in the dark. In their book *"Four Crisis and a Peace Process"*, the authors state: "There remains the possibility that Pakistan was bluffing, that it had no operational nuclear capability, but moved its assets in such a way as to raise alarm."[24] If this were true, it was a very dangerous act, open to misinterpretation, as also escalation. Some very pertinent observations can be concluded from the Kargil conflict with reference to nuclear threat and deterrence:

- While nuclear deterrence made it possible for Pakistan to unleash a sub-conventional proxy war against India, the same deterrence also offers adequate space to India for a controlled conventional response.
- The backdrop of nuclear capability was a key factor in deterring the escalation of the conflict.
- As per the book *'Four Crisis and a Peace Process'*, evidence is strong that the Kargil conflict revealed the limits of nuclear deterrence to demarcate, if not deter, an India-Pakistan conflict.[25]

Balakot Air Strikes

The Facts

The dastardly car bombing of a CRPF convoy at Pulwama (Jammu and Kashmir) on 14 Feb 2019, which claimed 40 lives, caused great dismay, anguish and anger across India and many parts of the globe. The responsibility for the attack was claimed by the Pakistan-based militant group Jaish-e-Mohammed (JeM), though the suicide bomber was Adil Ahmed Dar, a local from Pulwama district, and a member of the JeM. There were over 40 funerals across India, where brave family members, overcoming their personal grief, demanded vociferously that the perpetrators and their handlers be brought to justice. For a change, the political spectrum in India showed solidarity and offered its full support to the government.

As expected, Pakistan called on India to provide evidence to support its claim that Pakistan was involved and urged the Indian authorities to share actionable intelligence. Pakistan's Prime Minister also said that Pakistan would retaliate if India takes military action against it.[26] India handed over a dossier to the acting High Commissioner of Pakistan with specific details of the JeM's complicity in the Pulwama attack. India also expressed disappointment over Pakistan's response to its dossier saying Islamabad continues to be in denial. The Indian spokesperson also said that Pakistan should take "immediate credible, irreversible and verifiable actions against terrorist and terror organisations and abide by the commitment it gave in 2004 not to allow any territory under its control to be used for terrorism against India in any manner."

In the early hours of February 26, Indian warplanes crossed the de-facto border in Jammu and Kashmir and fired guided bombs in the vicinity of the town of Khyber, Pakhtunwa province, deep inside Pakistan. Pakistan's military was the first to announce this air strike in the morning of February 26, claiming that the payload was dropped in an uninhabited wooded hilltop area near Balakot.[27] India, confirming the airstrike later the same day, characterized it to be a pre-emptive strike directed against a terrorist training camp, which caused the death of a large number of terrorists. The following day, February 27, Pakistan retaliated, causing an Indian war plane to be shot down and its pilot taken prisoner, before being returned on March 1.[28]

ANALYSIS OF THE CRISIS

Crisis Management between Pulwama and Balakot

The suicide attack at Pulwama was a deliberate attack and severe provocation by Pakistan. Although the JeM took responsibility, their connect with the deep state within Pakistan cannot be denied. Maybe the perpetrators were themselves surprised by the magnitude of the blast and lives lost. After the surgical strike in September 2016, India had made its intentions clear that there will be a cost to provocative activity against India. Maybe the deep state within Pakistan did not take the message seriously or wanted to test the Indian resolve further.

With Indian elections looming large, there was immense pressure on the government to take strong action. There was a 12-day period between the blasts and India's strike on Balakot, enough time to defuse a crisis, or at least prevent further escalation, especially when all communication channels were open. The ball was clearly in Pakistan's court; it could have moved positively to intern the JeM leadership, more so when it had openly taken responsibility for the attack. In the prevailing atmosphere, an Indian response was inevitable, but there are lessons for both countries with reference to crisis management and escalation control. Some semblance of ground rules/understanding should be arrived at, if we are to prevent recurrence or not allow the jehadis/terrorists to create such a confrontation between two nuclear-armed adversaries.

The Air Strikes at Balakot: A Controlled Escalation

India's response through an air strike at Balakot was a well thought-out, controlled action. The use of the Air Force is high on the escalatory ladder, but the way the isolated target area was chosen, though deep inside Pakistan, was to minimise chances of a direct aerial confrontation. The choice of the target was based on strategic/operational intelligence inputs.

Until Balakot, neither India nor Pakistan had gone beyond local reactions, except at Kargil, which fell in the category of a limited war. In finding greater room for non-nuclear escalation through precision air-strikes that New Delhi was careful to label as "non-military pre-emptive actions", India tried to control the narrative and behaved in a responsible manner. The puzzle is not so much why Modi chose this option, but why previous Governments did not, although such precision strikes against identified terrorist camps was an action long advocated by many of us in India.[29]

Retaliation by Pakistan Air Force (PAF)

On 27 February 2019, the PAF conducted reprisal strikes at multiple locations across the Line of Control (LoC) exactly a day after Balakot. It is possible that Pakistan assessed the IAF strikes as having crossed a spatial threshold by attacking mainland territory and saw the IAF's use of air power as a vertical escalation it could not ignore.[30] As per Pakistan, while their aircraft were able to lock on to the targets, they were ordered to drop their bombs in an open field to avoid damage, a claim contested by India, though not an improbable explanation. As Indian fighters scrambled to take on the superior PAF package of 24 aircraft, a dogfight ensued, in which one Indian MiG-21 was shot down and its pilot, Wing Commander Varthaman, who bailed out captured by the Pakistan military. Pakistan also claimed downing another IAF SU 30 MKI, a claim rejected by India. The IAF claimed strongly that a PAF F-16 had been shot down by Varthaman before he went down, but this has been denied by Pakistan. An IAF helicopter also became a casualty as part of friendly fire near Srinagar.

POINTERS AND CONCLUSIONS

Nuclear Bogey Called-Conventional Response Space reclaimed by India

Though the Kargil war was the beginning, India's bold response at Balakot has largely called out Pakistan's nuclear bogey, though it may be premature to conclude that it has been laid to rest, as Pakistan tried to engage in some sort of nuclear signalling by convening a meeting of the nuclear command authority on Feb 26, 2020. More importantly, India has shown that adequate space exists for a conventional response to Pakistan's proxy war, though the response may have to be nuanced and not just an all-out war option. What is also evident in the 21st century is that India's patience also has a threshold and henceforth Pakistan cannot remain unmindful of India's concerns. Whilst Pakistan may not change tack so easily, yet it may be difficult for Pakistan to cross India's threshold, unmindful of the likely response. It is highly likely that India will respond with military vigour to any major militant incident in the future, with options across the spectrum of conflict. The onus of further escalation will thereafter rest on Pakistan, who has to also realise that post 9/11, the international environment is no longer conducive for such provocative rogue actions.

Crisis Management and Escalation Control

The Pulwama suicide attack clearly points to the uncontrollable nature of such incidents. Pakistan has to learn the lesson that there will be great cost to any such misadventure, in whatever form. It has to stop sponsoring such incidents through its vast Jehadi/terrorist networks if it wants to avoid future crisis. The ball is clearly in Pakistan's court.

At Kargil and post-Balakot, both countries showed reasonable maturity in not escalating the crisis, but such serious flare-ups cannot always be so carefully controlled and managed. Using the Air Force is already high on the escalatory matrix; what if there had been larger loss of aircraft on either side during the crisis, a serious escalation may have resulted.

Channels of Communication

When two nuclear-capable neighbours are involved in a serious flare-up/ military crisis, channels of communication at multiple levels become critical to crisis management and escalation control. Apart from the diplomatic channel, the DGsMO have a hotline, which is often used to convey viewpoints and clarify. There also needs to be a direct channel of communication between the NSAs of the two countries to avoid a catastrophic misunderstanding. Maybe, select formation hotlines can also be considered for the future to prevent escalation/flashpoints across the line of control. Flag meeting mechanisms need to be upgraded to hotlines with each Corps HQ. It needs restating that the genesis of the problem lies in Pakistan's attempt to push in Jehadi elements across the LC and unless that changes, communication channels will lack trust and not work.

Military Dialogue

This is perhaps one of the best, as yet untried, ways forward to break the current impasse in India-Pakistan relations. The Pakistan Army controls policy and strategy concerning India, but India's political leadership is not at ease engaging with them. Greater military-to-military contacts will therefore be helpful. The USA realised this dichotomy in their dealings with Pakistan and, therefore, their dialogue with Pakistan is led by their Central Command. One reason why the Line of Actual Control with China is comparatively more peaceful is because there are regular border meetings with the PLA. Every contentious issue, however small, is immediately taken up through a meeting between the two armies. On this count it may be worthwhile for India to take the initiative. While serving as Director General Perspective Planning, in 2008-09, I had put up such a proposal to the hierarchy, but it did not find favour. Maybe its time has come.

Third Party Intervention

Despite their stated positions, both countries have turned to the USA to defuse/control a crisis, whether it be Kargil, Operation Parakram, 27/11 Mumbai terrorist strike and even the latest Pulwama–Balakot. The Americans have played this role so far, mainly to avert an escalation beyond a point, and cap this crisis below the nuclear threshold. In this they have been encouraged by the support of most key nations like the EU, Russia and China. But the future international environment is getting more competitive and complex and such unanimity may not exist. Both countries cannot bank on third-party interventions in the future, and should, therefore, develop crisis management and escalation control mechanisms between themselves, with greater despatch.

Nuclear Backdrop

CBMs in the nuclear field as also preventing any crisis/conflict from escalating to a dangerous level where threat/use of nuclear weapons may be considered, is a vast subject. In the limited space available in this chapter, one will touch upon the salient aspects only.

India's nuclear doctrine is transparent and in sync with its pursuit of Nuclear Deterrence. Pakistan, on the other hand, has an opaque doctrine, officially not declared, but hints at usage of nuclear weapons as part of its war fighting strategy. This mismatch is certainly worrisome and would be open to misinterpretations/miscalculations. This calls for greater efforts to reinforce nuclear CBMs, as also leave no doubt as to the credibility of India's stated doctrine of "Massive Retaliation". Pakistan's operationalization of its Tactical Nuclear Weapons (TNWs) capability has made the equation unstable in its understanding. As per Dr. Manpreet Sethi (Project Head, Nuclear Security, Centre for Air Power Studies New Delhi): "In the case of TNW use by Pakistan, the Indian leadership could well decide the type and extent of retaliation, but there is no doubt that it would be assured and punitive".[31] She adds that "for this message to carry weight, it is important that there is greater transparency of the military dimension of nuclear command and control, including redundancies that assure automaticity of nuclear response",[32] India has to contend with two nuclear adversaries, one the proxy of the other, with differently stated doctrines. Though India now possesses a formidable nuclear arsenal, to deny any recognition to India as a nuclear weapon state, China does not wish to engage with India to discuss CBMs. This is a dangerous proposition and has to change sooner than later. With the rise of both China and India, nuclear deterrence and stability cannot be left in its present ambiguous state. India and Pakistan have engaged earlier in talks at the Lahore summit, as also the follow-up composite dialogue, where nuclear CBMs were also discussed and agreed upon. As of date a number of CBMs are in place, i.e., advanced notification in respect of ballistic missile flight tests, unilateral moratorium on further nuclear test explosions; non-attack of nuclear facilities, pre-notification of military exercises, non-violation of airspace, exchange of list of nuclear facilities and installations, establishing a hotline, etc.

In the nuclear field there is much scope left for enhancing CBMs. Some of the issues that could be considered are:

- Greater transparency in Pakistan's Nuclear Doctrine.
- Transparency in missiles which are nuclear-tipped, especially dual use ones which are inherently destabilizing.
- Integrity of mechanisms and personnel handling nuclear weapons to prevent them falling into unauthorized hands.
- Limiting number of nuclear weapons and their delivery means, especially SRBMs.
- Greater safety and transparency in readiness status including stage-wise upgradation.
- What is needed is a dialogue mechanism specifically on nuclear CBMs. Both countries owe it to their people to reduce the risk of any nuclear accident based on misinterpretations and miscalculations.

Conclusion

There is a lack of trust between India and Pakistan, mainly due to Pakistan's duplicity. While professing to live in peace, Pakistan has been engaged in a high-risk proxy war against India. This has brought the countries to high-risk conflict situations on a number of occasions in the last few decades. Today the battle lines are more firmly drawn, with India having called Pakistan's nuclear bluff and reclaimed the space for conventional retribution.

The ball clearly lies in Pakistan's court for the next time, the situation could escalate beyond control with catastrophic outcomes. Both countries should engage in talks with greater sincerity and develop trust. For this, multiple channels including military talks/engagement should be encouraged resulting in more effective CBMs and escalation control measures. This chapter has highlighted the salient aspects; once trust is regained through sincerity, chances of conflict situations and escalation can be minimised, and when it does occur, it can be controlled and de-escalated through a mature approach.

NOTES

1. Chapter 1, Introduction, p. 3 of *'On Escalation'* by Herman Kahn.
2. Concepts and Models of Escalation, A report from the Rand Strategy Assessment Centre, May 1985, p. 4.
3. *Surprise, Strategy and Vijay—20 years of Kargil,* A publication by the Centre for Land Warfare Studies (CLAWS), 2019
4. Herman Kahn, *'On Escalation'*, p. 12.
5. Herman Kahn, *'On Escalation'*, p. 72.
6. Article by Jeffrey Goldberg in the October 2019 issue of *Atlantic.*
7. *Changing Nature of Conflict in the 21st Century;* Chapter 3; Military Strategy for India in the 21st century. KW Publishers, 2019.
8. Conflict prevention: Methodology for knowing the unknown, Uppsala Peace Research Paper no 7, Uppsala University, Sweden, 2003.
9. Ibid.
10. *Concepts and Models of Escalation* a report from the Rand Strategy Assessment Centre, May 1984, p. 4.
11. Chapter on 'The Proxy War and Lahore Declaration' from General V. P. Malik's book; *Kargil-From Surprise to Victory.*
12. Chapter 12, *Kargil-From Surprise to Victory.*
13. *Conflict Resolution and Crisis Management-Challenges in India-Pakistan Relations* by Riaz Mohammed Khan, Stimson Centre, Washington DC, 2018.
14. *Four Crises and a Peace Process,* Harper Collins, 2008, p. 125.
15. Ibid, p. 139.
16. Ibid, p. 131.
17. Ibid, p. 146.
18. Ibid, p. 147.
19. Chapter 12, *Kargil-From Surprise to Victory.*
20. *Four Crises and a Peace Process,* Harper Collins, 2008, p. 123.

21. *How the India-Pakistan Conflict Leaves Great Powers Powerless* by Moeed Yusuf, Dec 2010.
22. Takshashika: The Indian-Pakistan Conflict Escalation Framework, July 2015.
23. *Four Crises and a Peace Process*, Harper Collins, 2008, p. 139.
24. Ibid, p. 136.
25. Ibid, p. 140.
26. *BBC News*, 19 Feb 2019, India.
27. *Economic Times News* of March 28, 2019, quoting PTI.
28. Wikipedia-2019 Balakot airstrike.
29. Climbing the Escalation Ladder: India and the Balakot Crisis, Rohan Mukherjee, Oct 2, 2019.
30 Taking stock a year after Balakot, Joy Mitra in *South Asian Voices*, Mar 2020.
31 Nuclear Deterrence and India, p. 143, Ch-7 by Dr. Manpreet Sethi of the book 'The New Arthashastra', Harper Collins, 2016.
32. Ibid, p. 143

8

Re-imagining Mountain Warfare in the 21st Century

Lieutenant General (Dr.) Rakesh Sharma

O divine art of subtlety and secrecy! Through you we learn to be invisible, through you inaudible; and hence we can hold the enemy's fate in our hands.

—Sun Tzu

ABSTRACT

Re-imagination of mountain warfare is imperative for India for the mid-term, as China as an adversary is wholly across the mountainous realm and Pakistan has its internal politics and national identity hinged on the mountainous region of J&K. ***Mountain warfare in the Indian context tends to exemplify an*** *incorrect vision of a monolithic mountain range. There are most compelling dissimilarities between the disputed mountainous border Line of Control (LOC), India has with Pakistan and the Line of Actual Control (LAC) with China. While the LOC is a heavily fortified active border, the LAC has proximate Indian forces, though relatively settled. The ongoing transformation is like a sprint in technologies, evolving at an exponential velocity, that doctrinal and strategic changes are unable to keep pace with. It has been analysed that the PLA now characterises and understands modern warfare as a confrontation between opposing operational systems rather than merely opposing armies. It implies that warfare to be pursued by PLA in mountains may not be centred on annihilation of opposing forces on the battlefield. The war on the Western front towards POK or GB is another matter entirely. While relying to avoid full-fledged conventional war, Pakistan will continue to arm itself with modern warfare capability and practice deceit. The prospective wars in the Himalayas, whenever prosecuted, will be in multiple domains. These wars may, or may not, be territorially related, and may be related to geo-political rivalries. We have to create new 'sunrise' capabilities for future warfare.*

Setting the Stage

Is mountain warfare exclusive, or is it warfare against adversaries where the land border exists in mountains? Have mountains such an over-riding effect that warfare stands rigidised and frozen in time? Future warfare is transiting to follow differing contours and has changing nature and character. It may be beyond reasoned vision to predict warfare for the entire 21st century; geopolitics and geostrategy will dictate differently. Revolutions in technology keep driving strategic and tactical change. In the past, of mountain warfare, it was stated *"...yet certain regions of the world remain largely unaffected by the full reach of advances in military technology. Thin air, cold weather, and mountainous terrain combine to create a uniquely inhospitable battlefield at high altitude. The elements of military victory at high altitude have not dramatically changed. Overwhelming fire, in concert with bold manoeuvre, continues to determine victory on the high altitude battlefield. The emergence of precision warfare has yet to dominate combat in the timeless environs of the world's highest mountains."*[1] This quote was relevant at the time of the Kargil War in 1999, fought as it was on the dizzy high altitude areas with peaks above 5,000 metres. Twenty years hence, warfare has moved on, and it is imperative to contemplate on its future scale, scope and typology. Throughout history, wars generally hinged on clashes of arms. Having remained largely unchanged for millennia, the character of war has changed radically only in recent decades. By enormously increasing information flow around the world, the Internet, small satellites, drones, improved sensors, cell phone video cameras and broadband connectivity, are transforming both war and politics. These technologies allow military forces to find targets and strike them with great precision from long distances. They open the way for cyber warfare, hacking and manipulation of foreign political systems.[2]

Wars have been a historic constant; however, warfare has always remained evolutionary. Throughout history, the nature of wars has been violent, interactive, and fundamentally political. War will remain a political act that takes place in and among societies, its specific character will be shaped by politics and societies—by what Clausewitz called the "spirit of the age". Re-imagination of mountain warfare is imperative for India for the mid-term, as China is wholly across the mountainous realm and Pakistan has internal politics and national identity hinged on the mountainous region of Jammu and Kashmir (J&K) and Ladakh. Historically, mountain wars implied engagement between opposing armed forces using kinetic force, across the mountains, and winning and losing wars was largely equated to territorial gains/losses. Currently, winning wars implies the ability to wage war comprehensively in all domains and achieve the political aim. However, if political aims could be achieved without waging a traditional conventional territorial war, then fighting an attritive war in the mountains or for that matter in the plains, deserts, skies or seas, may be uncalled for. The operational focus then can also be on employing a range of non-military instruments or non-contact kinetic instruments, in ways below the threshold of large-scale conventional military operations, if these can achieve the requisite strategic gains. This newer form of warfare that defies the traditional definition of war, changes the Clausewitzian dictum that war is an extension of politics, to political warfare being war by other means.

Hence, the future of mountain warfare cannot be exclusively imagined without studying the projected realms of warfare that would simultaneously happen. This paper attempts to re-imagine the compass of mountain warfare in the Indian context, as a wholesome effort, with the distinct dissimilarities of the border lines that India shares with Pakistan and China.

MOUNTAINS OF INDIA, HISTORY OF WARS

Mountains in the Indian context tend to exemplify an incorrect vision of a monolithic mountain range. That basic thought needs to be dispelled at the outset, at it affects strategy and tactics—each of which differs dramatically from sector to sector, ridge to ridge. The Himalayas are a great mountain system that forms the barrier between the Plateau of Tibet, and the offshoot ranges that descend to the alluvial plains of India. The Himalayan Range includes the highest mountains in the world, with more than 110 peaks rising to elevations of 24,000 feet or more above sea level. The soaring height of the Himalayan mountain range has steep-sided jagged peaks, high altitude desert like in Eastern Ladakh, deep valleys and river gorges like of the River Brahmaputra and alpine glaciers as the Siachen. This topography is deeply cut by erosion. A Himalayan mountain range appears as a gigantic crescent with a continuous snow line also constituting the sources of most of the Himalayan rivers. A large part of the Himalayas on the Indian side, however, is below the snow line with offshoots of lower mountain ranges, very differing levels of precipitation and typology of forest cover. Hence, templating mountains in a generic manner, is fraught with immense pitfalls. The mountains take immense toll on people (including soldiers), physically and physiologically. Mountains also greatly extend logistical management.

The saying goes, that the **best teacher of war is war**! Over the ages the Himalayas have been witness to invasions, from Alexander the Great in 326 BC, to seven Muslim ones from Central Asia. Zorawar Singh (1786-1841), a Rajput general of the Sikh Empire, had his legacy of conquests in the Himalayan mountains that included Ladakh, Tibet and Baltistan. Post-Independence in India, the Himalayas have witnessed substantial warfare, commencing with 1948 between India and Pakistan in Jammu and Kashmir. The surreptitious invasion of the Pakistani Army couched as tribal/ irregular invasion in 1948, was pushed back substantially due to resolute offensives, and included the capture of the lofty heights of Pir Kanthi and Ledi Gali on the Pir Panjal Range. The reverses of 1962 left indelible memories but provided the all-important experience, and goaded the preparations to ensure territorial integrity. Despite the reversal in 1962, there is saga of immense valour and raw courage in the defensive battles of Rezangla and Gurung Hill in Chushul Sector. Both in the 1965 and 1971 wars, the Army had captured the towering Point 13620 astride the Shingo River in Kargil Sector. The capture of Haji Pir Pass and the massif of Bedori in 1965 exhibited planning, valour and fortitude. The Kargil War of 1999, when Pakistan had furtively occupied the heights of Drass, Kargil and Batalik above 5,000 metres, was an epitome of courage and resilience and strength of directed firepower of Herculean proportions. The dizzy heights of Siachen Glacier and the Saltoro Range, as the highest battlefield in the world, are continually witnessing a conflict scenario since 1984.

DISPARATE OPERATING ENVIRONS, CONGRUENT ADVERSARIES, DIVERGENT WAR-FIGHTING

Mountain War-fighting across the LOC: In a Time-warp?

In examining the future of mountain warfare, it is essential to study the border regions with adversaries. There are most compelling dissimilarities between the disputed mountainous borders India has with Pakistan and China. In the J&K and Ladakh Union Territory, Pakistan has administrative control of some 83,900 square km of Pakistan-Occupied Kashmir and Gilgit-Baltistan. The LOC is the line between India and Pakistan in Jammu and Kashmir and Ladakh, which does not constitute a legally recognised international boundary, but serves as the de facto border. It was originally known the Cease-fire Line, and was re-designated as the LOC following the Shimla Agreement, signed on 03 July 1972. India constructed about 550 km of a fence barrier along the 740 km-LOC. Continuation of the LOC in Ladakh is the Actual Ground Position Line (AGPL) that divides the current positions of Indian and Pakistani troops on the Saltoro Range in the Siachen Glacier region. The Indian Army holds the heights on the Saltoro. The line extends from the northernmost point of the LOC to Indira Col. The AGPL is approximately 110 kilometres long, is across the edge of the Saltoro Range, with peaks of heights in excess of 7,000 metres.

The Shimla Agreement prohibits the two sides from altering the Lines by force, the concept of 'holders-keepers' is still valid there, which Gen Bhatia explains as 'what you have, you keep; what you hold you keep and what you occupy also you keep'. Gen Hasnain calls it the 'grabbers-keepers' concept and defines it as: 'Any side grabbing a piece of ground for a tactical advantage gets to keep it unless forcibly evicted'.[3] This contention of 'holders-keepers' was however demolished in 1999, when Pakistan had furtively and cunningly 'grabbed' large tracts in the Kargil Sector, and India launched a full-fledged offensive to evict the Pakistani forces, without violating the LOC. However, the most significant issue is that the LOC is the most heavily fortified multi-tiered defensive system in the world, with forces on either side very well bunkered, and deployed eyeball-to-eyeball. The mountainous reaches of the LOC also remain hot, regularly witnessing sparring with small arms and artillery, sometimes raids on border posts and across, and offensive actions against terrorists being pushed in by Pakistan.

It is important to note that Jammu and Kashmir is an emotive issue, an identity issue for Pakistan that binds the nation, and it is the *raison d'être* for the Pakistan Army to retain its hold on the nation. *Au contraire* to China, in contemplating Pakistan's relevant approach, it can be described as *"...to reap gains, whether territorial or otherwise, that are normally associated with victory in war"*.[4] Pakistan, without crossing established red-lines and exposing itself to the penalties and risks of escalation to conventional war, will attempt to reap success by utilising proxies. Pakistan has greatly enhanced the toolkit of information warfare—from ingenuous disinformation and propaganda to taking advantage of social media for faster dissemination, from fanning radicalisation to civil unrests. It is typical of Pakistan to be vigorous and aggressive in using strategic communication, and in doing so deliberately remain well under the threshold of conventional military conflict. Suffice it to say, in the near future, with the state that Pakistan finds itself in politically and economically, it is in no position to initiate an all out conventional war with India.

Reimagining Wars across the LAC: Modern War-fighting

The LAC is the demarcation line of the effective but disputed border between India and China. The latter occupies Aksai Chin in Ladakh, which is about 36,000 square km and has claimed territories at the eastern end of the Himalayas in Arunachal Pradesh. China also has a number of other territorial claims in Ladakh and in along Uttarakhand-Tibet border. The Indian Army has largely prepared defences along the LAC; these are not physically occupied, though the Army units are located in proximity. The People's Liberation Army (PLA) does not largely have prepared defences, though there are border outposts and pucca camps in proximity and conducts large scale offensive exercises annually on the Tibetan plateau. The LAC witnesses transgressions by the PLA in the areas claimed by China, and there are occasional stand-offs. The Indian forces faced conflict scenarios against the PLA in the Nathu La-Cho La (Sikkim) skirmish in 1967[5] and Sumdorong Chu (Arunachal Pradesh) in 1987.[6] These were robustly and successfully handled by the Indian Army. The two opposing forces have well-established confidence-building measures and military exchanges along the LAC. The LAC hence is not an active border, though the underlying contestation of a disputed border exists nonetheless.

Sun Tzu had centuries ago prophesised that *'all warfare is based upon deception.'* China is the master of ambiguity. China has consistently demonstrated preference for ambiguity, risk manipulation and controlling the narrative to win without fighting.[7] Henry Kissinger had opined that, *"...whereas Western tradition preferred the decisive clash of force, emphasizing feats of heroism, the Chinese ideal stressed subtlety, indirection and patient accumulation of relative advantage"*.[8] Psychological operations that would end in intellectual confusion to the adversary are part of Chinese philosophy. Over last three decades, many a strategy of warfare has come out of China. The 'Unrestricted Warfare'[9] did not restrict itself to terrain such as mountains; rather it nullified the boundary between battlespace and non-battlespace, with non-military methods. The Chinese 'three-warfare strategy'[10] is a form of statecraft that encompasses non-kinetic means to achieve political ends. The strategy philosophises that '*...if object of war is to acquire resources, influence and territory, and to project national will...China's Three Warfares is war by other means*'.[11]

It has been analysed that the PLA now characterizes and understands modern warfare as a confrontation between opposing operational systems rather than merely opposing armies. PLA's victory in modern warfare recognizes system destruction warfare as the current method of modern war fighting.[12] It will be won by disrupting, paralysing, or destroying the operational capability of the adversary's operational systems. This will be achieved through kinetic and non-kinetic strikes against key points and nodes while simultaneously employing a more robust, capable, and adaptable operational system of its own. Systems confrontation is waged not only in the traditional physical domains of land, sea, and air, but also in outer space, nonphysical cyberspace, electromagnetic, and even psychological domains.

Recent PLA literature suggests that there are four target types that PLA planners seek when attempting to paralyze the enemy's operational system through either kinetic or non-kinetic attacks:

- First, the PLA calls for strikes that degrade or disrupt the flow of information within the adversary's operational system. To do this in mountainous areas, the PLA will attempt to paralyze information flow, by targeting key data links and vital information network sites. By carrying out strikes against data links and vital information sites, the subsystems of an operational system can be rendered "information isolated" and therefore unable to function, or operate totally independently and disjointed.
- Second, degradation or disruption of the operational system's essential factors, which include command and control (C2), reconnaissance intelligence, and firepower capabilities.
- Third, degradation or disruption of the operational architecture of the adversary's operational system. These include the physical nodes of the previously mentioned capabilities and therefore would consist of, for example, the entire C2 network, reconnaissance intelligence network, or firepower network. Striking the operational architecture is a target-heavy approach that could require numerous successfully executed precision strikes against various components arrayed around a broad battlefield.

- Finally, disruption of the time sequence and/or tempo of the enemy's operational architecture. This is to degrade and ultimately undermine the operational system's own "reconnaissance control-attack-evaluation" process. Given these instances and others, paralyze the functions of an enemy's operational system. Operational system comprises roughly five main systems: the command system, the firepower strike system, the information confrontation system, the reconnaissance intelligence system, and the support system.[13]

STRATEGISING FOR INDIA: BUILDING CAPABILITIES

Broad Parameters of Mountain Warfare

A question that begs the answer here is whether or not future wars with adversaries across the mountains can be fought with our present military strategy formulations. Robert D. Kaplan wrote of the *"flattening Himalayas"*, the *"defeat of distance"* and that *"the high wall of the Himalayas no longer separates these two great civilizations."*[14] In India, doctrinal and strategic changes are unable to keep pace, with the transformation underway in China. Conventional Indian concepts of war in mountains hence may be unsuited from the realities of multi-domain warfare of the twenty-first century, where mountains may not be sufficient material in prosecuting wars. It must hence be fathomed that current military planners and strategists face the Herculean challenge of envisioning a war or typology of a war in the Himalayas which might be around the corner or may be many, many decades away, and adversaries that could be the same or much, much different!

The futuristic form of war-fighting will be unique modern warfare, as will be the battle-space on which conflicts will be waged. It will no longer be only a contest of annihilation between opposing military forces across high altitude mountains. In fact, if war is prosecuted by the PLA as envisaged above, the measurement of victory will not be by the time-tested parameters of captured mountainous territory (even claimed), prisoners of war or decimation of force. By the sheer breadth and depth of scientific prowess, the PLA will aim at achieving success to dictate political terms, by a modern, technological war to project international repute of an emerging super power.

India has to prepare for a modern war against China. Hence, this concept of warfare could follow the following broad parameters:

- Indian nodes and systems in high attitude areas and in plains will be rendered vulnerable and even incapacitated, which will affect command and control, and cause severe infrastructural damage. This will be by an amalgam of kinetic and non-kinetic warfare, with or without contact of opposing forces.
- Such warfare would attempt to avoid the defensive strength of the Indian Army, to avoid a slogging match and face large casualties. Territorial aggression in mountains/high altitude may be additional, after significant damage has been wrought by system destruction.
- Though the PLA may attempt to soften the strong defensive lines across the LAC, in the terrain obtaining, and in the normal prevalent weather conditions, its efficacy is questionable. However, an offensive across the high mountains cannot be deemed as obviated. As the ground ingress routes are largely unpredictable due to terrain configuration the third dimension may be utilised to turn the defences. However, the altitude, the weather and the machine capability may again preclude adequacy of lift.

The wars of post-Independence India, and the continued war-like deployment along the Himalayan Massif had hardened the Indian Armed Forces to the vagaries of mountain and high altitude warfare. To that can be cumulated the incessant employment of units in mountains and higher altitudes in counter-insurgency and counter infiltration. Be it Haji Pir, Bana Top (on Northern Siachen Glacier) or Tiger Hill (Kargil) in offensive operations; Poonch (1971), Rezangla and Walong (Arunachal Pradesh) in stoic defence, Indian Army has proven it by blood and by combating terrorism.

As has been argued above, the prospective wars in the Himalayas. Whenever prosecuted, will be in multiple domains, some evident currently and many off the horizon, under development or under wraps. It is important to strategise for disaggregated or aggregated in manner that the warfare can be prosecuted. The following broad parameters of strategising for high altitude and mountainous areas are imperative:

- Being based upon contested, unsettled borders, territory will remain an important contentious issue in future wars, though the larger basis may be related to geo-political rivalries or power struggles. The likelihood of conventional force-on-force kinetic warfare will exist, and must require simultaneous planning. It may be likely that the aggressor utilises a substantially large quantum of force on the territorial frontier of the Tibetan plateau. However, the high altitude and mountainous terrain create severe restrictions on *ad lib* movement, forced to defiles or plateaus, or utilise the third dimension. Sustenance of force will depend on narrower mountainous axes, aerial drops or make-shift landing grounds. India has the experience and the prowess for defensive and offensive operations in high altitudes.

- The end state that an adversary seeks could be territory in the mountain reaches across the LAC and LOC, implying an inevitability of ground operations. With offensive operations in the Kargil War of 1999 as a general indication, the adversary has to bring to bear major force asymmetry to contemplate operations against battle-hardened and experienced Indian troops, occupying well-constructed linear defences. In the high altitude areas obtaining on the borders, terrain analysis employing geospatial information, of heights and lows, passes and valleys, rivers and water sources, presents basic visualisation of operations to support decision making. Exploitation of natural and man-made features, and its analysis and interpretation, predict the effect of the terrain on military operations. It is obvious also that for operations in mountainous regions, there are limited axes and laterals that facilitate movement. To obviate the severe terrain restrictions, adversaries may resort to use of the third dimension. Inevitably, the aggressor has to finally capture and control the dominating heights.
- The military has to prepare for a war that will be appreciably prosecuted in mountainous regions. Operational level commanders will be concerned with employing military forces in a sector of operations to obtain an advantage over the enemy and thereby attain strategic goals through the design of battle and conduct of campaigns. Gen H R McMaster had once said, *"There are two ways to fight...asymmetrically, or stupid."* In the conventional war that will be fought asymmetrically, the design would have to be tailored for the appreciated campaign, utilising the linear

defences as pivots and employing composite Task Forces (TFs) or Integrated Battle Groups (IBGs), sized and composed exclusively for each ingress avenue. The composition of the TFs will be tailored as per the threat pattern, of infantry, scouts, armour, mechanised infantry, artillery and engineers (the latter for provision/denial of mobility). These specifically composed IBGs/TFs, working in tandem, asymmetrically, would jockey in an advantageous manner, undertake a series of operations and accomplish the common objectives in the given time and space.

- Hence, India must plan to offset and defeat any force asymmetry in the adversary's favour by degradation and by an admixture of asymmetric warfare, kinetic strike and defensive layout in tiers. Asymmetric warfare contextually should encompass using linear defended lines only as trip wires, and saturate the battle space with strong deniability by focused and imaginative ruses and subterfuges. Asymmetric warfare in manifold realms would enlarge the battle space to logistical sustenance lines and the forward lines of ingress and choke points as one whole, and that will be the key to territorial warfare in high altitude and mountainous terrains. Apparently, imaginative asymmetric warfare across the battle space will deny the adversary any technological advantage across the high altitude regions, and stalemate any territorial aggression.
- As salience and preparations for modern conventional kinetic war cannot be put on the back-burner, substantive offensive capabilities, duly acclimatised, trained and kitted, must be available for achieving 'across the hump' success and consolidation. Substantial enhancement of third dimension capability will provide requisite deterrence, and reduced salience on massed combat power.
- Intelligence, Surveillance and Reconnaissance (ISR) are critical for placing the right chess pieces in place, and execute the operational plan. For example, in such an environment as available in Xinjiang and Tibet, and in correlation to the location of the combined arms formations of the PLA, it is feasible to implement an intelligence plan based upon all strategic, operational and tactical inputs. As the PLA forces are not permanently garrisoned in the Aksai Chin area, it is likely that the mechanised infantry division in Hotan and other formations in Xinjiang or Tibet would be deployed to this area. Their movement, despite air lift availability, is arduous

and time-consuming. Larger forces from Xinjiang or Tibet have to perforce traverse between 500 to 1,500 km, along National Highway G219. The 5,050-metre Tserang Daban Pass (on Kun Lun Shan) between Yarkhand/Hotan and Mazar will have to be crossed, and must be constantly kept under surveillance. Any ingress from Xinjiang has to move along G219 that traverses between the Karakorum and Kun Lun Ranges. Similar is the 5,100-metre Jieshan Daban Pass (on G219 near Rutog in Ngari Prefecture). It will be necessary to find a via-media to circumvent a battle of the turf of disparate collection and analytical agencies. The Defence Intelligence Agency (DIA) under the Chief of Defence Staff (CDS) ought to be proactive in seeking Intelligence, even if by pre-positioning liaison staff in the NTRO and R&AW, and energising the Directorate of Signals Intelligence (SI) and the Defence Image Processing and Analysis Centre (DIPAC). The imperativeness of ISR equipment for field formations, which should include a variety of Unarmed Aerial Vehicles (UAVs), requires a detailed analysis, and hastened acquisition.

- Kinetic and non-kinetic warfare may also go well beyond force-on-force engagement on the territorial sphere. It would utilise potent long range precision guided munitions, hypersonic weaponry, drone swarms, autonomous systems and stealth operational capabilities delivered by multi-modes – ground, air or projectiles. The wars may also be wholly non-kinetic in nature, in modern warfare domains of information warfare, space and cyber space and electronic spectrum that may cripple critical national and defensive infrastructure and forces. We will also require hardening our systems against premature destruction! The Indian Armed Forces need to create a robust, capable, and adaptable operational system of its own to fight a modern war. The Indian Army has to focus on acquisition of modern kinetic and non-kinetic capabilities to withstand the onslaught from across, and have offensive capabilities to *quid pro quo* and more. We have to create 'sunrise' offensive kinetic and non-kinetic capabilities across the mountains too, with the corollary that 'sunset' capabilities, like linear war-fighting on the mountains will have to be retained at least till mid-term. This modernisation will require us to embrace information-warfare technologies, recognising that it will be the application of combinations of technologies like processing power, connectivity, machine learning and artificial intelligence, automation, autonomy and quantum computing that will achieve the disruptive effect we need. We must develop a framework of strategic capabilities against non-kinetic technological threats, like weaponised information, cyber and other subversive forms of aggression—against the adversaries. We will have to accept that multi-domain campaigns will be part of future warfighting. Hence, a joint multi-domain specialisation would indicate the right preparation for future warfare.

- In the diverse nature of the Indian Armed Forces, we require composite, integrated multi-domain task forces located regionally/ sectorally under an overall Joint Multi Capability Command, that will amalgamate the sunrise technologies. Indeed sufficient redundancies exist within the armed forces to reconfigure the same, without relying on unnecessary accretions.
- Since logistics is a singularly difficult in high altitude areas, infrastructural resilience with a modern supply chain system is imperative. Again, delivery means must also entail aerial support, even by drones, to bring about flexibility.

The war on the Western front in the mountainous areas of POK or GB, is another matter entirely. A 'one size fits all' military strategy against both adversaries will not be effective. Though some technological collusion between the PLA and the Pakistan Army is feasible, the wholesome effect of what has been portrayed through Tibet previously is unlikely. And to top it, sub-conventional warfare has the permanence of threat, especially from the western adversary. Hence, an admixture of one or all—kinetic and non-kinetic—has the likelihood of manifesting itself to assure an end state that suffices for political success, and hence to be planned for:

- The Indian Armed Forces are bound by the Parliamentary Resolution that includes POK and GB as part of J&K and Ladakh Union Territories (UTs).
- While relying on avoidance of full-fledged conventional war, Pakistan will continue to arm itself with modern warfare capability, practice deceit and continue the political aim of interfering with Jammu and Kashmir (J&K).
- A traditional conventional war across the high altitude mountains is well-nigh possible. With strong conventional strength, it must

be deemed that pro-action rests with India. In prosecuting war in the mountains, and despite the given that mountains favour defence, the Erwin Rommel quote, *'I would rather be the hammer than the anvil'*, is apt.

Developing Leadership for Mountain Warfare

Leadership on the high altitudes of India is challenging in the best of times and modern wars of the 21st century, the information age, it will be vastly different from historical experiences. Leadership is inherent in a military officer's function, and at strategic and operational levels vision is a senior leader's source of effectiveness. Unlike any time in history, it is imperative that leaders must master the consequences of new technological changes, like developments in information warfare, that are as relevant in modern, mountain warfare, as they apply to leadership practices. While sophisticated standoff weapons and sensors have greatly enhanced combat efficiency, developments in information technology have enabled greater connectivity and the information sharing among widely spread force components. In both pro-active and reactive roles, information has become time sensitive and continuous and a key to success. This military response is directly proportional to the quality of military leaders our Armed Forces need to possess. The present-day military leaders need to keep pace with the technology and put their best foot forward to learn the know-how of the technology available in the Armed Forces. As combat and combatants have transformed, the dependence on network-centric warfare will soon become so complete that disruptions and events leading to denial of infostructure that the adversaries would attempt, will become jarring in exercising command and control and exhibition of leadership.

In the mountains, hence, when warfare reaches physical pro-action or defensive, technology to complement, intuitive leadership will be a major challenge facing Indian Army leaders in the 21st century. Leaders, the led, formations, units and subunits will have to be totally enmeshed in the typology of warfare planned, that the execution with or without the infostructure must be seamless. Leaders would have to ensure skilful integration of a wide range of diverse technologies likely to be encountered in the synergistic joint operations of the future, be it application of air, space and cyber systems. Despite the sprint of technology, it cannot account for many intangibles which fall under the purview of leadership such as discipline, esprit-de-corps, motivation and morale. Even with digitisation of leadership communication, leaders will have to communicate with the led in training and combat. In finality, especially in the mountains, the human emotions of pride and determination that can be built in training and combat, should instil a sense of responsibility, through delegation and faith. In future mountain warfare, effective units and formations will be those that will perform best even in the absence or out of communication with critical leaders. Leaders must 'teach' and train in peace and professionally develop subordinate leaders and sub-units/units, to undertake fully delegated operations, if need be, in the realms of modern, mountain warfare.

Conclusion

In sum, there are momentous changes afoot in the realms of warfare. The warfare of the future may well target civilian infrastructure by even non-kinetic means, with the adversary relying on plausible deniability. The nation will demand reprisals, without even clarity on the adversary having employed covert non-kinetic means. Traditional domains of force-on-force would co-exist, and yet may have reduced salience. Technology like cyberspace has expanded the domain of warfare to an arena unheard of a couple of decades or so earlier. Similar expansion of information warfare, precision weaponry and autonomous systems and many more will continue to expand to newer vistas. Indeed the northern neighbour refers to information domination, 'winning informationised local war' and application of information technology in all aspects of war and defining military doctrine in terms of technology. It is obvious that the measure of victory in future wars will be successful paralysis over destruction! In the case of the northern adversary, for political reasons, there is no aversion to undertaking 'strategic initiative', implying initiation of war.

The Indian Armed Forces are one of the most significant custodians of national security. However, in crystallising thoughts and plans on future wars, time may not be on our side and India might already be the testing ground for military technologies, without even appreciating it. The Indian Armed Forces in concert with the elements of national power need to work to eliminate strategic and operational uncertainty, and step on the pedal. If the oncoming era is of back-end warfare—combat by programming computers, launching missiles or operating drone swarms ensconced thousands of miles away, in safe environments, then so be it! Assuredly, warfare has a future, the all-important question is the typology of warfare, and what it would take to accept it as inevitable, and assiduously work to acquire the capabilities. The strategic conclusion is that technology has fundamentally transformed the character of war, and maybe its nature too, in a significant measure! Wars in the future may be without extreme violence, aggression, destruction, and mortality, and yet cause enough suffering to achieve political success.

Sir John Chipman, heading the IISS, had once famously stated that "...the world in the 20th Century lived tactically but in the 21st Century the world will have to live strategically". Obviously then, this 21st century security visualization and technological environment is leading to the challenge of devising optimal strategies, to crafting visions, to assist in translating own 'audacious dreams and ideas' into reality.

> *"Inevitably, senior leaders, even the most effective, build a picture of what they think future war will look like and then confront combat realities that differ substantially from their assumptions."*
>
> **— Williamson Murray**

NOTES

1. Marcus P Acosta, "High Altitude Warfare: The Kargil Conflict and the Future", Naval Postgraduate School, , Monterey, California, June 2003, accessed at https://calhoun.nps.edu/bitstream/handle/10945/1043/03Jun_Acosta.pdf?sequence=1&isAllowed=y
2. Douglas J. Feith & Shaul Chorev, The Evolving Nature of War, Real Clear Defense, 07 May 2020, accessed at https://www.realcleardefense.com/articles/2020/05/07/the_evolving_nature_of_war_115259.html?mc_cid=640f1f087d&mc_eid=b103e49ea4
3. Happymon Jacob, *Line on Fire, Ceasefire Violations and India-Pakistan Escalation Dynamics*, Oxford University Press, New Delhi, 2019.
4. Hal Brands, 'Paradoxes of the Grey Zone, Foreign Policy Research Institute, 05 Feb 2016, accessed at https://www.fpri.org/article/2016/02/paradoxes-grey-zone/ on 29 Dec 2019.
5. Probal Das Gupta, *Watershed 1967: India's Forgotten Victory over China*, Juggernaut Books, New Delhi, 2020.
6. Mandip Singh Lessons from Somdurong Chu Incident, IDSA New Delhi, April 26, 2013, accessed at https://idsa.in/idsacomments/CurrentChineseincursionLessonsfromSomdurongChuIncident_msingh_260413
7. Oriana Skylar Mastro and Arzan Tarapore, 'Countering Chinese Coercion the Case of Doklam', War on the Rocks, 29 Aug 2017, accessed at https://warontherocks.com/2017/08/countering-chinese-coercion-the-case-of-doklam/
8. Henry Kissinger, *On China*, Penguin Books Ltd., London, 2012, p. 47.
9. Qiao Liang and Wang Xiangsui, Unrestricted warfare, Beijing,1999, accessed at https://www.cryptome.org/ cuw.htm
10. Stephan Halper (ed), China: The Three Warfare, Washington, DC, Office of Net Assessment, Office of the Secretary of Defense, 2013.

11. Ibid.
12. Jeffrey Engstrom, System Confrontation and System Destruction Warfare, How the Chinese People's Liberation Army seeks to wage modern warfare, Rand Corporation, Santa Monica, California, USA, 2018.
13. Ibid.
14. Robert D. Kaplan, *The Revenge of Geography: What the Map Tells Us About Coming Conflicts and the Battle against Fate*, Random House, New York, 2012.

9

Urban Warfare: An Emerging Challenge

Lieutenant General (Dr.) VK Ahluwalia

"The worst policy is to attack cities. Attack cities only when there is no alternative."[1]

—**Sun Tzu, *Art of War* (500 BCE)**

"To a soldier, the capture of a built up area is the most distasteful of operational tasks, as it restricts the power of manoeuvre and entails house- to-house fighting which is not only time consuming but 'eats up troops' and, inevitably, ends up in enormous loss of life and property to the civilian population."

—**Lt General Dipender Singh**,
Indian Peacekeeping Force (IPKF) in Sri Lanka[2] (1990)

Introduction

Sun Tzu (aka *Sunzi*), the Chinese general who is remembered as the 'sage of military', and the 'teacher of military strategy', wrote the *Art of War (Sunzi bingfa)* in the 5th century BCE. A military treatise with thirteen chapters, it covers all aspects of warfare and strategy including operations in walled cities.[3] Historically (and traditionally), most militaries are organised, trained, and equipped to operate in large and open spaces that offer plenty of room for manoeuvre, with no civilians on the battlefields. While during and post-World War II, there have been many a conventional battle fought in intense urban environments (40 per cent of operations during WWII were conducted in urban areas[4]), modern times present a picture of the world racing towards hyper-urbanisation, particularly in Africa and Asia.[5] Contrary to Sun Tzu's thoughts of attack on walled cities, and the experiences of the Indian Peacekeeping Force (IPKF) in Sri Lanka, contemporary conflicts will increasingly be fought in urban terrains, by regular and irregular soldiers, extremists, as well as violent non-state actors (VNSAs). In fact, fighting in urban environments, in a highly active information age, will further toughen the challenges in the future.

In this chapter, it is proposed to broadly study the historical perspective of the military campaigns and conflicts in urban environments, both at the regional and global levels; and the expected profile of urbanisation, including migration of population from rural to urban areas. Then, it will examine the envisaged threats, challenges and opportunities of operating in an urban environment in the next two decades, as also the role of latest technology and its impact on the character of varied conflicts, with greater focus on operations in high intensity warfare, in urban terrains.

Historical Perspective

There are several examples of fighting in urban terrains in military history—as part of high intensity and low intensity operations and/or a combination of both. First, looking back at the high intensity operations, cities and urban areas—hub of communications centres from military operations' point of view—have played a prominent role in the campaigns of World War II and a significant number of wars thereafter. Since then, the world has most recently witnessed numerous intense urban battles in just two decades of the 21st century itself: Grozny; Nablus; Baghdad; Fallujah; Bint Jbeil; Nahr al-Bared; Tskhinvali; Rio de Janeiro; Gaza; Donetsk; Sadr, Aleppo; Mosul; Marawi; Yemen, etc.[6] The world has also experienced a number of conflicts with a mix of low intensity, high intensity and blend of both forms of conflicts in recent times.

Given the complex nature of urban terrains and the intensity of operations, it would be interesting to study the broad contours of a few important battles which are spread over 50-60 years. These are the Battle of Stalingrad (1942-43), the Second Battle of Fallujah (November 2004), the Battle of Aleppo in Syria (2012-16), and lessons from Israel's Wars in Gaza, which were fought in dense BUAs against widely different oppositions, varied restrictions in manoeuvre, war fighting concepts, objectives, methods, force levels, tactics and techniques.

Battle of Stalingrad. Most historians believe that the Battle of Stalingrad (1942-1943), fought between Germany and its allies and the Soviet Union for control of the city after the Germans had reached Stalingrad, was one of the most significant and decisive battles fought in a dense built-up urban terrain. The Red Army launched 'Operation Uranus' against the Germans in November 1942. It was here that the Red Army finally stopped the advance of the Germans, by cutting off their lines of communications and surrounding them at Stalingrad. It was one of the deadliest battles of World War II, as both the Red Army and the Germans suffered very heavy losses. Germany, however, could not quite recover from the defeat, and it finally resulted in their retreat. It required ferocious close combat to clear Stalingrad, street-by-street, block by block and house by house. In fact, the Battle of Stalingrad was the turning point of World War II in Europe.

Second Battle of Fallujah. The Second Battle of Fallujah, aka 'Operation Phantom Fury', and later renamed 'Al Fajr (Dawn)', was a joint American, Iraqi, and British offensive in November and December on 2004, against the Iraqi and foreign insurgents who had taken up fortified defences. In anticipation of an American assault, Abu Musab Zarqawi, leader of Al-Qaeda (AQ) in Iraq and the resistance force of eighteen groups, organised themselves to convert Fallujah into a fortress. Of 40,000 buildings of Fallujah, 2,000 were converted into a fortress with spider-holes, sandbags and breeze blocks.[7] Before the Allied troops moved into Fallujah, it was subjected to heavy artillery shelling and air attacks. They blew up holes in walls of houses to avoid concealed sniper positions and a booby-trapped door. Yet, the Americans suffered heavy casualties due to employment of vehicle-borne IEDs (VBIEDs), piling canisters of propane, and gasoline, rocket-propelled grenades (RPG), and 7 anti-tank rockets. The Americans employed Unmanned Aerial Vehicles (UAVs) and drones to map every building and street, and the forward observation officers directed fire of 155 mm howitzers, and the forward air controllers provided effective close air support with precise accuracy. The troops were involved in heavy urban combat, which resulted in huge traffic jams due to small gaps in the streets and innovative obstacles placed by the resistance force for AFVs to manoeuvre. Two important lessons in urban warfare were the significance and effectiveness of MBTs over light armoured vehicles like Humvees and Amtracks in widely-spaced urban terrain, and the usefulness of flame throwers to minimise casualties.[8]

Battle of Aleppo. The Battle of Aleppo, fought in the largest city in Syria, was one of the longest sieges in modern warfare and one of the bloodiest battles of the Syrian Civil War.[9,10] It was fought by the Free Syrian Army (FSA) and the Sunni rebel groups against the Syrian government that was supported by the Hezbollah, Shia militias, Russia, and the Kurdish-led People's Protection Units (YPG). Despite the support from Russia and Iran, it took the Syrian regime forces over four years (July 2012 to December 2016) to recapture Aleppo.[11] 'Scorched-earth tactics' and the large-scale devastation of the city led the combatants to name it the "mother of battles" or "Syria's Stalingrad."[12] Besides displacement of hundreds of thousands of people, the battle saw the use of chemical weapons by both the Syrian government forces and the rebel forces, the dropping of cluster munitions on populated areas, targeting of hospitals and schools, intense aerial bombardment, and indiscriminate shelling and use of highly inaccurate improvised artillery by rebel forces, resulting in massive casualties and collateral damage in civil areas.[13]

Five Lessons from Israel's Wars in Gaza: The Israel Defence Force's (IDF) operations in Gaza provide an excellent example of the threats and challenges that advanced militaries face when confronting a determined hybrid adversary in dense urban terrain. Gaza is one of the most densely populated areas in the world, where the Islamic militant group, Hamas, is deeply rooted within the civilian population. After a decade of operations in Gaza, the IDF has learned many lessons about urban warfare against hybrid adversaries.[14] Raphael Cohen recounts five major lessons: airpower faces serious limitations in dense urban terrain; ground operations in urban areas are never bloodless; Western militaries cannot escape warfare; the **urban fight cannot be avoided**; and the elusive lesson: turning success into lasting victory.

Destructive Face of Urban Battles. The Battle of Mosul was a blend of conventional and unconventional forms of warfare in 2016-17, and a scene of bloody battles. It resulted in enormous casualties, collateral damage and displacement of people. The capture of Aleppo (Syria) and Mosul (Iraq) was the turning point in the Syrian Civil War and the conflict in Iraq. Similarly, in 2017, a force of about 1,000 Islamic State-affiliated Abu Sayyaf militants had occupied Marawi town (Philippines), a town of 600,000 inhabitants. The government forces required five months to clear it after intense fighting in the BUA of the city. While the entire city was almost brought down to a state of rubble, practically all the Abu Sayyaf fighters were killed. (The damage to the cities of Marawi[15] and Mosul can be seen in the photographs.)

Images of the Cities of Marawi and Mosul ***(Source: Google Images)***

India's Experience in Urban Warfare

It may be in order to briefly recapitulate the Indian Army's experiences in urban terrain combat, both during high intensity and low-cum-high intensity operations: first, during the Indo-Pak War of 1971; second, the IPKF experience in Sri Lanka (1987-89).

Indo-Pak War of 1971. During the Indo-Pak War of 1971, both the armies realised the defence potential of the urban terrain, and the difficulties to capture it. Therefore, the Indian Army bypassed a few BUAs, and cut off the Pakistani forces from the rear, especially in East Pakistan, to reach Dhaka at the earliest. However, the Indian Army's 33 Corps' operations met stiff resistance in the capture of Hilli and Bogra town. The Indian forces decided to bypass Hilli and establish a block in its rear to cut off the Pakistani forces. This action forced the enemy to withdraw from Hilli to defend Bogra. Finally, the capture of Bogra was a classic battle in a BUA. On the other axis, Pakistani 14 Division had planned a fortress battle at Sylhet, with two brigades. The Indian Army's plans to capture Sylhet resulted in success only because the BUA was invested from multiple directions by lifting troops in helicopters, along with extensive bombing of the area by the IAF. One of the major lessons was that 'intelligence about the enemy' should be accorded the highest priority to succeed in such operations and to minimise own casualties.

IPKF Operations, Sri Lanka. The IPKF operated against the LTTE in Sri Lanka, both in the rural-cum-jungle terrains and urban areas, in 1987-89. Although the LTTE was a terrorist organisation, over a period, it had become a much stronger force—in both high and low intensity operational environments—with limited conventional capabilities, including an air force and naval vessels. It had acquired capabilities much beyond the hit-and-run tactics of guerrillas. The LTTE were predominantly urban guerrillas, comprising majorly middle class and educated youth who were armed with the most sophisticated weapons like AK-47s and the latest communication equipment. They had taken up proper defences in Jaffna, a prominent town with vast BUA. The LTTE gave a pitched fight to the IPKF in Jaffna, Achu Valley, Paranthan and Kondavil, to name a few. The battles in the urban terrains of Batticaloa, Vavuniya and Trincomalee are all too well known for the resistance offered by the LTTE, as the IPKF required large forces, resources and time to achieve their objectives/capture them. Tackling urban insurgency was a new phenomenon for the Indian Army, for which it was certainly not prepared. Operations in the BUA required clearance of one house at a time because of the LTTE's tactics and their adeptness in improvised explosive devices (IEDs) like claymore mines, grapeshot charges, mines, platter charges and booby traps.[16] From a military perspective, the IPKF's operations were a failure because it failed to achieve its objectives. Kalyanaraman summarises five main lessons of the IPKF (Operation Pawan) in Sri Lanka, but two lessons had a direct impact on the operations: command and control structures were ambiguous and ineffectiveness of the intelligence system. Indian forces deployed with the IPKF were deprived of useful information before undertaking military operations against the LTTE.[17]

Besides conventional wars, India has experienced many terrorist attacks in urban areas, which led to bloody fights between the security forces and the terrorists. While Islamist terror groups like the JeM attacked the highest seat of Indian democracy, the Indian Parliament on 13 December 2001, the LeT exploited India's maritime approach to carry out multiple terror attacks in the mega city of Mumbai in November 2008. Needless to say, Mumbai was highly ill-prepared to respond to such attacks in a dense urban area.[18]

In February 2016, in an operation against three Pakistan-based Lashkar-e-Taiba (LeT) terrorists who were operating from a government building (Entrepreneurship Development Institute) in Pampore in the Kashmir valley, the Indian Army lost six personnel (including two young captains). The buildings that were occupied by the terrorists were neither densely populated, nor were they in a congested area. Although the affected civilians were evacuated from the building, the army suffered heavy casualties. They had perhaps not visualised the modus operandi of the terrorists, the advantages enjoyed by the terrorists and the vulnerabilities of our own troops in a built-up area (BUA). Having learnt their lessons, the performance of the Indian Army and the supporting forces was much better against the terrorists holed up in the same BUA in Pampore during the latter part of the same year.

Wide Spectrum of Operations

Having briefly seen the nature and trend of operations in urban terrains across a wide spectrum, it is evident that warfare in the cities is 'highly destructive'. While these could encompass a wide range of operations, they are essentially of three types: one, high intensity operations (HIO) against conventional forces; two, low intensity operations (LIO) against insurgents, terrorists, guerrillas and violent non-state actors (VNSA); and third, the future remains uncertain with a combination of both low and high intensity operations against a blend of hybrid, asymmetric, cyber, space and nuclear weapons. The latter would be near similar to the operations in Mosul (Iraq) and Aleppo (Syria). Therefore, given the emerging geo-political and strategic landscape, and the significance of the cities, the aim of operations in cities would be to exploit the politico-economic-strategic-psychological advantages, as also to deny the same to the enemy.

Given the fact that we are operating against a backdrop of nuclear empowered-cum-nuclear capable states, the probability of a high intensity all-out war among the great powers is rather low. However, the probability of the HIO and LIO remains high, especially in the Indian subcontinent. These operations are likely to increase with the phenomenon of accelerated urbanisation, globalisation, information revolution, urban insurgencies, terrorism, and the role of transnational VNSA, who indulge in abetting insurgencies, violence and organised criminal activities to create instability in the region. Fighting in urban environments could also be in conditions such as peacekeeping or stabilisation operations under the United Nations' mandate; and humanitarian assistance and disaster relief operations, a few of which could escalate into conflict.[19]

Accelerated Urbanisation at Global Level

The Population Division of the UN Department of Economic and Social Affairs (UNDESA 2018) notes that Africa and Asia were home to nearly 90 per cent of the world's rural population in 2018. The salient features of the report are:

- The future increases in the size of the world's urban population are expected to be highly concentrated in just a few countries. Together, India, China and Nigeria will account for 35 per cent of the projected growth of the world's urban population between 2018 and 2050. By 2050, it is projected that India will have added 416 million urban dwellers, China 255 million and Nigeria 189 million.
- Out of the 36 fastest growing cities between 2000 and 2018, 28 cities (77 per cent) are in Asia.[20] The graph and the bar chart suggest that the population in urban areas in Asia has grown by 104 per cent between 1990 and 2015, and it continues to show an increase up to 2050.

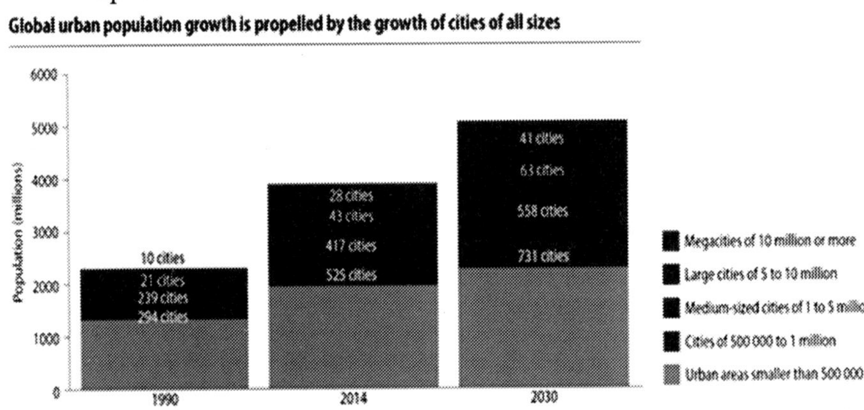

Source: 2018 Revision of the World Urbanization Prospects, Population Division (UN DESA)

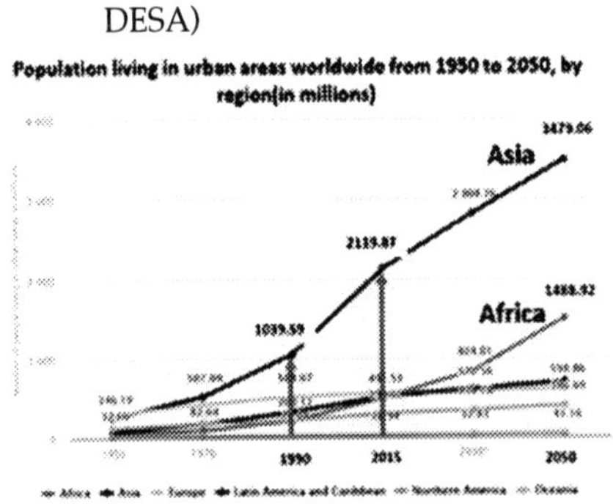

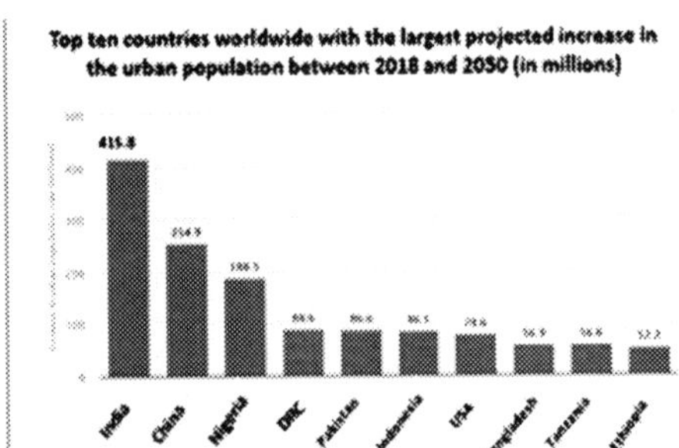

Source: *Statista,* May 2018 (Annotated by the Author), available at https://www.statista.com/statistics/672054/change-in-urbanization-worldwide-by-region/

India's Urbanisation and Implications

In India, urban population has increased by 74 per cent in 20 years between 1991 and 2011, from 217 million to 377 million. More than 60 million people (16 per cent) of the 377 million urban population that live in 429 cities are housed in slums and struggle for the most basic civic amenities.[21] Urbanisation is one of the most significant sociological and economic changes taking place in the world. With an uncontrolled increase in urbanisation, the probability of instability and conflicts within dense population centres would be very high. These areas form fertile breeding grounds for indoctrination, radicalisation and become hotbeds of insurgency and terrorism.

OPERATIONS IN URBAN TERRAIN

Categories and Peculiarities

Based on the density and strength of the population, and their spread, the BUAs in India can be broadly classified in four categories: one, villages and small towns; two, medium-sized cities, three, BUAs astride road axis or river/canal; four, large cities with high-rise buildings, along with industrial hubs and peripheral spread of residential complexes. The layout of BUAs in the western sector alone could be of four sub-types: **Satellite pattern,** i.e., one main hub and other small dependent urban areas; **Network pattern,** i.e., interlocking of primary hubs of satellite pattern, **Linear pattern,** i.e., along a road, body of water; **Segment pattern**, i.e., river or canal divides the urban area into segments. It is evident that the towns and cities are most complex, as each differs in its size, population base, and sources of water supply, surrounding areas and facilities available.

The intricate layout, shape, size and design of residential buildings, design of streets, houses and the nature of construction material used, are different in Jammu & Kashmir, in the North East, in the riverine terrain of Punjab, and in the deserts. Broadly speaking, there are wide patterns of constructions made of mud and predominantly stone and bricks in the deserts and Punjab, and houses made of bamboos and wood which are surrounded by thick vegetation of bamboo plantations and numerous fish ponds in the North East region. Houses in the Kashmir valley, being a cold region, have different architectural design with two to four storied houses made of concrete and wood, with tinned/tiled sloping roofs, and large low-lying areas filled with water (water bodies) and marshes. In the Kashmir valley, for instance, habitation has mushroomed astride the National Highways, district roads, major peripheral roads of Srinagar and major cities. As per the 2011 Census, J&K had a population of 12.54 million; out of which, 3.34 million (27.38 per cent) lived in urban areas (Master Plan 2035 Final Report).

Most of the big and medium-sized cities have an 'old town' with narrow streets and alleys in the inner core and a few well-spaced out residential complexes on the outer periphery. Most of the important cities have all-weather roads leading to them. The communication network in each region varies from an extensive network of roads to one-way metalled roads or animal tracks in rural areas. In cities, there are many important installations and institutions like electric power houses and fuel and water storage facilities, which offer lucrative targets to attackers. In the congested areas that are in the inner core of towns and cities, the alleys and streets are rather narrow. Not only are these suitable for barricading, booby trapping and placing IEDs, but they also restrict the movement of all types of vehicles including mechanised vehicles due to rubble of collapsed buildings or barricades established by the defenders. Obstacles in streets are far more effective than on open terrain roads.

Although there has been a varying degree of increase in urbanisation astride the borders with Pakistan and the neighbouring countries in the North East region, in that order, it is important to analyse the essential requirements of urban warfare. In the Indian context, we will continue to experience high and low intensity conflicts in urban terrains, though at relatively much lesser intensity in comparison to operations in Mosul (2017), Aleppo (2016) or Fallujah (2004). In future, there may be occasions when we may experience a combination of low-cum-high intensity operations, when regular forces with insurgents and terrorists have had enough time to prepare themselves to give a planned fight against the security forces (SF). The operations would depend upon whether the BUAs are heavily fortified or lightly held, the strength of the enemy or terrorists or NSAs, the degree of preparedness and their spread.

As each of these BUAs affect operations differently, they would require a different strategy, war fighting concept, force levels and its components to fight in them. Among many factors, the important ones that require brief examination are ISR, manoeuvrability, employment of various weapon systems, accessibility to BUAs, command and control, combat skills, and role of information and cyber warfare, and emerging-cum-disruptive technologies.

Conduct of Operations

"The battle always goes to the quickest."

—**General Erwin Rommel**[22]

Fundamental Shift. A study of the recent operations in cities by the Russians in Gronzy, the USA in Mogadishu, Baghdad, Fallujah and Sadr City, and against the ISIS in Mosul and Aleppo suggest the degree of difficulty and complexity involved. There is a fundamental shift in warfare in four areas: first, the new dimensions of warfare are information (cyber, electronic, psychological), AI, space, and the role of other emerging and disruptive technologies; second, an indirect approach to warfare; third, hybrid threats with an increasing role of non-state actors in a grey zone environment; and fourth, non-contact and non-kinetic warfare. With the use of emerging technologies to minimise casualties by direct confrontations, the traditional 'force on force' engagements have given way to multi-dimensional (multiple spheres and multiple types of forces) forms of warfare with added role of precision guided munitions (PGMs), surgical air strikes, unmanned aerial vehicles (UAVs), swarms of drones, stealth technologies, space-based enhanced ISR capabilities, non-contact warfare at long distances, with greater roles to airborne and special forces. In the current and future warfare, information systems will be the most critical asset of military operations. It may be vital to attack an opponent's information systems than to focus on physical destruction of forces. Simultaneously, greater reliance has been placed on information-age integrated forces. Also, the focus has shifted to 'Indirect Approach,' as advocated by Sun Tzu in his '*Art of War*' and Kautilya in his '*Artha Shastra*', to achieve political and/or military objectives. Hybrid threats in a grey zone environment also have information warfare as a major tool to achieve its objectives. The focus has shifted to non-contact warfare in different forms: the conflicts are revolutionised by the drone swarm technology that facilitates autonomous decisions by drones to engage select targets, and long-range vectors with PGMs to engage targets with pinpoint accuracy.

Armed Forces can better exploit the advantages of fire power, air power, mobility, communications, protection, intelligence and logistics, in a desert or in an open terrain in comparison to a BUA. The constraints of offensive operations in BUAs, with deliberate defences, are numerous: large spread of cities/BUAs with entrapped civilian population; limited availability of intelligence, surveillance and reconnaissance (ISR) capabilities; mobility and manoeuvring issues, difficulty of isolating large BUAs, and combating successive tiers of defences; communications, and command and control; large requirements of assaulting troops and reserves; limited effectiveness of heavy armoured fighting vehicles (AFVs), mechanised elements, artillery and air; monuments of cultural and heritage importance, religious places; and fuel and water storage facilities. The BUAs provide a huge advantage to the defender, including to the insurgents or irregulars in terms of camouflage and protection from buildings, hideouts and tunnels, better observation and domination of approaches to streets, and ability to lay obstacles and booby trap entrances to streets.

The conduct of operations, as envisaged on the Indian sub-continent, has been covered in four parts:

- First, Intelligence Preparation of Battle (IPB) and identification of the Centre of Gravity (CoG).
- Second, employment of various resources to gather intelligence, along with employment of a wide spectrum of weapon systems under varying conditions.
- Third, technology enabled operations: information, cyber, AI and air dominance, which may form part of the arsenal of the militaries on the Indian subcontinent in the near future.
- Centralised planning and decentralised execution: mission type orders.

Imaginative Thinking and Intelligence. Some of the difficulties can be overcome provided we give the highest priority to gathering intelligence and innovation. In Fallujah II, Gian Gentile et al mentioned three aspects: 'imaginative thinking and adaptation' proved equally important to succeed; manoeuvring by mechanised forces provided psychological advantage to facilitate close-quarter battle by the infantry; and intelligence preparation of the battle (IPB) was the most difficult task. In the urban battles in Mogadishu, Baghdad, Fallujah and Sadr City, the degree of success achieved by the US forces in IPB ranged from 'not successful to somewhat/eventually successful'. The combination of physical isolation and excellent IPB-facilitated operations in Sadr City in 2008.[23] Innovative means would be required to gather intelligence, to analyse and integrate to build an intelligence picture. General David Petraeus, Commander of Multi-national Force in Iraq, and other commanders gave huge credit to SIGINT, cyber warfare, imagery intelligence (IMINT) from UASs for the significant progress made by the US troops.[24] An accurate intelligence picture of the enemy's command, support and combat units is essential to initiate manoeuvres, to fight smart with minimum resources, time and casualties. With third-dimension systems in place, UAVs, swarm of drones, long range vectors and mechanised forces offer fair opportunities for manoeuvre warfare in urban terrains. But it requires a change in the mindset.

Centre of Gravity (CoG). Given the lessons of heavy casualties for an offensive force, it must be remembered that 'Force on Force' is not the solution. The aim should be to identify the enemy's CoG at strategic, operational and tactical levels—the critical vulnerability, the collapse of which will serve as a severe blow to his will to fight. The CoG at the three different levels could be: strategic, the seat of provincial or local power or hub of communications or transportation and logistical systems; operational, a joint operations control centre/communication centre/ command and control systems/fire control and air defence systems; and tactical, an operations room/a bottleneck/supply chain route/key terrain features, etc.,' which must be neutralised first. The CoG need not necessarily be his source of strength. It is practically impossible to physically isolate large cities; but it should be an attacker's endeavour to isolate the enemy, deny situational awareness, by information dominance and superiority; thus, achieving psychological advantage. If achieved, it would disrupt and paralyse his networks of command and control, fire control, air defence, surveillance systems, manoeuvre forces, target acquisition and logistics. The defender or the forces occupying BUAs would also endeavour to paralyse the attacker's systems.

One of the most difficult stages of attacking in a BUA against a 'well-prepared enemy with fortifications' or terrorists/irregular forces/NSAs is to achieve surprise, and to secure an initial foothold to progress the operations into the inner core. The aim should be to establish more than one foothold to progress operations. Mechanised forces can be employed for isolation of the city to prevent reinforcement, evacuation, logistics resupply from select directions, establish a foothold on periphery buildings by providing fire support role to the assaulting infantry, and AFVs can degrade the potential of fortified positions, destroy bunkers, metal barricades and any AFVs, using a wide variety of ammunition (HE, HESH, FSAPDS). With air dominance in place and where feasible, troops can be moved to rooftops by helicopters to progress operations from the roof tops and using Fin Stabilized Armour Piercing Discarding Sabot (FSAPDS) ammunition.

However, in 'lightly held BUAs', AFVs should preferably be employed in assault roles to provide a foothold on the periphery of the city's buildings, with mechanised infantry to dismount and assault. The good old principle of 'speed, surprise and shock' should be the guiding principle, supported by hi-tech systems and a swarm of armed drones. In the initial stages, armoured and mechanised infantry can be employed effectively in assault roles on scattered houses on the outskirts of the city to provide a foothold to the 'integrated infantry teams' to conduct block by block and house by house clearance. Considering the manoeuvrability space constraints in the outer and inner cores of a city, a mix of heavy and technology-enabled light AFVs would provide better flexibility and effectiveness to remain agile and quick to manoeuvre in a restricted space environment. The AFVs have a limitation of elevating their barrels to higher elevations to engage targets at closer ranges in BUAs. Depending upon the envisaged opposition, the mechanised elements can be employed to seize key terrain features or strong points, if any.

The Integrated Battle Groups (IBGs) are self-contained, agile, brigade-size combined arms units. Their composition should be based primarily on the threat and nature of urban terrain (wide open BUAs or narrow streets, dense and closed BUA), to achieve optimum results. Against the backdrop of nuclear armed states, and working simultaneously along with the holding corps, the IBGs, either with heavy AFVs or light AFVs and ICVs or a mix of both, can mobilise quickly, and launch shallow offensive operations across the border, which may involve clearing a select BUA.

Artillery, preferably self-propelled, can also be employed in direct firing roles. In Mosul, the ISIS is known to have dropped explosives and chemical-filled cluster bombs from rooftops against the Iraqi forces. The US Department of Defence estimates 40 per cent of the elite Iraqi Counter-Terrorism Service had become casualties in the battle for Mosul.[25] The Iraqi forces suffered more than 8,000 fatal casualties.[26] However, the movement by infantry, though slow, was feasible with due precautions against booby traps, IEDs and sniper fires. Due to unplanned and peculiar designs of constructions in different regions, the field of fire and observation gets restricted, with advantages to the defenders. Under such conditions, the infantry operates in small teams to clear house by house, in intense close combat, facing physical fatigue and psychological strain. Thus, the teams tend to get isolated. In several situations at the tactical level, split-second decisions are required to be taken. Therefore, these operations require 'centralised planning and decentralised execution', which thereby raises a need to improve situational awareness among the teams, and allow greater autonomy to take decisions in uncertain environments. Decentralisation would essentially mean 'mission type orders' to ensure mission accomplishment.

Given the nature of urban terrains and the advantages enjoyed by the forces/terrorists/insurgents operating from BUAs, the militaries would require weapon systems which ensure that the offensive troops or counter insurgents remain agile, light, protected with adequate fire power to neutralise or destroy the enemies. Besides effective training, troops must be provided with organic infantry weapons and combat support weapons with penetration capability, and portable flame throwers. The specific requirements are: lightweight assault rifles, sniper rifles, grenade launchers and RPGs; robust lightweight radio communication equipment with digital noiseless transmissions to ensure effective communications as also maintain situational awareness at the tactical and the dispersed small-teams level; portable flame throwers; equipment like light bullet-proof jackets and helmets with adequate lightweight protection of vital parts; respiratory systems to protect against poisonous gases and smoke in closed BUAs; and special equipment like grappling hooks, ropes, rope ladders, etc. UAVs and robotics using artificial intelligence should also be used to identify targets and engage. Plus, one of the prime requirements while fighting in a BUA in a decentralised manner is to maintain effective communications between the infantry small teams and the platoon commander. One of the systems being used by NATO forces is tactical VHF Combat Net Radio

(CNR) {Racal multiband inter/intra team radio (MBITR)} multispectral radio, which allows a rifleman a push-to-talk capability that does not require moving hands far from his weapon system.[27]

Technology-Enabled Operations: Information, Cyber and Air Dominance

In future conflicts, emerging technologies will play a predominant role in several ways: gathering detailed intelligence and analysis with data mining capabilities; digital mapping of the BUAs, every building and street, and the population pattern; precise engagement of targets with PGMs; extensive use of swarms of small drones and UAVs for multiple tasks; information warfare with special focus on cyber-attacks, psychological warfare, influence operations to target the cognitive domains of enemy/ NSAs/targeted population; space-based enhanced ISR capabilities; integration of robotics, lethal autonomous weapon systems and artificial intelligence; and non-contact warfare at long distances. High technology systems should be considered as force enablers and force multipliers. Thus, one of the prominent aims would be to make military operations more effective, with minimum casualties and destruction.

Intelligence preparation is one of the most important battle winning factors. In a dense BUA, the optical-cum-electronic equipment is unable to penetrate BUAs, to provide reasonable information of the enemy or the insurgents/terrorists/VNSA, who may also enjoy the support of the masses. Therefore, gathering information in BUAs poses far greater challenges to offensive forces than forces operating from within them. Besides basic information about observation, domination and strength of opposition, detailed information is required regarding design, shape, sizes and construction material of buildings, streets, avenues of approaches, and about sewer systems, mass transit routes, fuel, gas supply storage, and public facilities so as to build the intelligence picture. To gather intelligence, military, non-military and technology-enabled systems like the third dimension, satellites, stealth technologies, ELINT, SIGINT and UAVs must be used innovatively and imaginatively to link the dots, failing which troops could suffer heavy casualties. The aim should be to be precise in targeting select areas/buildings, to minimise destruction and collateral damage.

Due to excessive requirements of troops, resources, and command and control systems, it may be difficult to launch multi-directional attacks. With air dominance and air superiority, employment of unarmed and armed drones for ISR for intelligence preparation of battle in BUAs, delivery of explosives, IEDs, precision guided munitions into pinpointed openings should be exploited fully. Drones can also be employed to provide failsafe communications between all essential elements during critical phases of operations. Simultaneously, helicopters, armed with PGMs can manoeuvre to engage defiladed targets, and thus achieve psychological advantage against an enemy restricted in a confined space. Wall scaling robotics can be employed against holed-up enemy or terrorists. Similarly, robotic vehicles would serve a useful purpose against minefields, booby traps, IEDs and heaps of rubble.

Terrorism and Insurgency in Urban Areas: Only two contingencies have been discussed briefly:

In J&K, where two to four terrorists are known to occupy a single building or a cluster of two, which may be like the situation in Pampore in February 2016, and in Pulwama's BUA in end-February 2019, SF must not rush into operations. While clearing the BUA would be mandatory, it must not be done in a hurry which may expose own troops and result in avoidable casualties. Efforts should be made to isolate the terrorists by cutting off or jamming their communication networks, to physically and psychologically neutralise their effectiveness. After gaining adequate intelligence about the terrorists, location of local civilians, and effective cordoning of the BUA, protracted operations would be in order to avoid casualties to own troops.

In the future, we may face a contingency wherein insurgents, guerrillas, or terrorists may occupy BUAs in large numbers. Again, gaining intelligence in time would be most critical for conduct of operations against them. Insurgents, on the contrary, will maintain enhanced security measures by technology-enabled weapon systems, light personal protection gear, and non-contact communication systems, and also use information operations to maintain popular support. Counter insurgents should isolate them by attacking their communication networks by all information warfare tools available. Also, the endeavour should be to ascertain their aim, their capabilities and the modus operandi. The SF is likely to face difficulties to conduct ISR missions against terrorists and insurgents in dense urban areas due to advantages enjoyed by them. The endeavour of the SF should be to minimise casualties to the civilian population and own troops, and minimise collateral damage, in that order of priority. The more difficult part would be to establish the initial foothold, maintain situational awareness about the terrorists, and the progress of operations, and CI/CT forces to conduct clearance house by house. It would be expedient to have a rapidly deployable combined arms force, trained in urban warfare, that can respond quickly to the presence of insurgents or terrorists in BUAs. Depending upon the deployability, these integrated forces/teams must be supported by ISR elements, helicopters, UAVs, satellite imageries and medical and logistic teams. Precise intelligence would ensure minimum casualties to civilian population and collateral damage.

On balance, in the cities, the militaries must endeavour to minimise the effects of their operations on civilians, physical property, religious places, cultural and heritage property. Conceptually, the emerging technologies must innovate to make military operations in BUAs more effective, precise in its intelligence and, thus be less destructive.

Training

In such a complex urban warfare environment, a 'well-trained soldier and a unit' can overcome some of the inherent limitations. There is no substitute for four important aspects of training for both high intensity and low intensity operations: first, orientation training for urban warfare; second, gathering intelligence; third, fundamental urban combat skills; fourth, integrated training facilities and integrated exercises. Of course, the training modules would be different for both sets of operations.

- The scope of **orientation training** should be adjusted according to the level of the trainees. It includes principles of military operations in urban terrains and combat in a BUA, essential features of operations of the adversary(s), own concept of operations and role of units and sub-units. It also refers to awareness of basic features of BUAs, their characteristics and impact on military operations, nature of operations, and the likely BUA scenario.
- There is a need to train intelligence organisations and troops to use **innovative methods to gather intelligence** from open sources, civilian resources (police, fire departments, medical, essential

services), social media, SIGINT, IMINT, and satellite-based systems; and more importantly, analysis and creation of IPB.

- The fundamental **urban combat skills** to be acquired are tactical movement during various contingencies; methods of entry into a street, block and house (finding the elusive enemy) and their clearance drills; optimum use of weapons and suitable firing positions to be acquired; communications and situational awareness; methods to achieve cover and camouflage; and navigation and coordination with adjacent teams. Simultaneously, the concept of 'centralised planning and decentralised execution' must be practised during training exercises.
- The **integrated training facilities** should be large enough, with realistic depiction of varied urban terrains, to facilitate large size integrated arms units with their supporting elements to exercise and enhance their operational preparedness. One of the better-known urban warfare training facilities is in Israel's Negev desert on the Tze'elim army base.[28]

Legal Aspects

The rules of war, or international humanitarian law (IHL), are a set of international rules that regulate how armed conflicts are to be fought. It balances two significant aspects: weakening the enemy and maintaining some humanity by minimising suffering. These sets of rules are based on principles given in the Geneva Convention and pertain to wide-ranging issues: employment of lethal autonomous weapons, nuclear, biological, and chemical weapons, use of gases under Chemical Weapons Convention, etc. Militaries must be aware of them, as they operate under the watchful eyes of international bodies, IHL, media, and human rights activists.

'Transformation': The Way Forward

As urban areas are characterised by narrow streets, multi-storied buildings, alleys, blind spots, tunnels, sewers, holes in walls and floors, windows, it requires a large body of troops to clear them in close quarter battles (CQB), house-to-house and block-to-block type of fighting. Most militaries are not organised, trained, and equipped to operate in dense BUAs, with civilian populations in the midst of battle. Fighting in urban environments is becoming increasingly more complex and difficult due to structural changes in the landscape, immense strategic, tactical and psychological advantages enjoyed by the defender or the terrorists occupying BUAs, limited effectiveness of ISR capabilities, weapon systems, constraints of mobility and manoeuvring space, and requirement of additional troops, resources and time to secure or clear BUAs.

Challenges. On balance, there are wide ranging challenges to conduct operations in complex urban environments: mindset at all levels; innovative means of building intelligence picture in time; maintaining high degree of situational awareness at all levels; ensuring interoperability, integration and coordination among the forces; training and deployment of combined arms forces; ensuring uninterrupted communications during critical phases, command and control, and ISR inputs-cum-capabilities; management of casualties; minimising casualties to civilian populations, and collateral damages to infrastructure, property, religious places, cultural and heritage monuments.

Transformation. Therefore, urban warfare in an information age requires a 'transformation': to begin with, a change in the mindset at the political, strategic and tactical levels. Concurrently, based on the envisaged BUAs and opposition, it would require countries and armed forces to review their urban fighting doctrines, strategies, war-fighting concepts, role of technologies to gain intelligence (IPBs) and conduct operations, digital mapping of urban terrains, role of information warfare, reorientation of training doctrines, weapons and equipment profile, and logistics in urban environments. Conceptually, the emerging technologies must innovate to make military operations in BUAs more effective, precise in intelligence and engagements, and, thus be less destructive. It is undisputed that with accelerated urbanisation, conflicts in BUAs and cities would continue to increase. The earlier we fathom the magnitude of the envisaged threats and challenges of urban warfare, the better it would be.

> *"Whatever the time frame or location, urban operations are manpower intensive, time consuming and a lot of blood is spilled."*
>
> **—Ernesto Amador, Operations Officer**

NOTES

1. Sun Tzu, *Art of War.*
2. Lt Gen Dipender Singh, *'Indian Peacekeeping Force in Sri Lanka'*, 1987-89, Natraj Publisher, Dehradun, p. 80. He discusses the capture of Jaffna in Sri Lanka, a town that was

acknowledged as the symbol of power of the Liberation Tigers of Tamil Eelam (LTTE).

3. Sun Tzu, *Art of War*.
4. John J. Mahan, MOUT: The Quiet Imperative, *Military Review*, p. 49, July 1984.
5. United Nations, Department of Economic and Social Affairs, Population Division (2014). *World Urbanization Prospects: The 2014 Revision*, Highlights (ST/ESA/SER.A/352).
6. Sean M. Castilla, On the Likelihood of Large Urban Conflict in the 21st Century, *Small Wars Journal*.
7. D. Anderson, *Its Flames Will Blaze: The Battle of Fallujah, A History of Modern Urban Operations*, ISBN 978-3-030-27088-9_11, pp. 328-40.
8. Duncan Anderson, *Its Flames Will Blaze: The Battle of Fallujah*, 7-13 November 2004. Due to the international conventions, flame throwers were subsequently withdrawn.
9. Laub, Karin "Aleppo confronts vast destruction left by 4 years of war" *Washington Post*. Associated Press. (23 December 2016). Retrieved 29 December 2016.
10. "Syria death toll: UN envoy estimates 400,000 killed" www.aljazeera.com. Accessed on 12 January 2020.
11. Philip Smyth, The Shiite Jihad in Syria and Its Regional Effects (PDF) (Report). The Washington Institute for Near East Studies. p. 45. (February 2015).
12. Spencer, Richard, "Aleppo 'is becoming Syria's Stalingrad'", *The Telegraph*, 11 August 2012.
13. Shaken, Kareem (5 May 2015), "Syria war: 'unthinkable atrocities' documented in report on Aleppo". *The Guardian*.
14. Raphael S. Cohen, Five Lessons From Israel's Wars In Gaza, Commentary, War on the Rocks, 3 August, 2017, https://warontherocks.com/2017/08/five-lessons-from-israels-wars-in-gaza/
15. 165 government troops, 45 civilians, and practically all of the Abu Sayyaf fighters were killed. The damage to the city may be seen in this photo, essay: "Marawi in Ruins After Battle Against Pro-ISIL Fighters," Al Jazeera, Oct. 23, 2017, https://www.aljazeera.com/indepth/inpictures/2017/10/marawi-ruins-battle-pro-isil-fighters-171023071620271.htm
16. Ibid.
17. S. Kalyanaraman, Major Lessons from Operation Pawan for Future Regional Stability Operations, *Journal of Defence Studies Publication* details: http://www.idsa.in/journalofdefencestudies.
18. V.K. Ahluwalia, Terrorism and Successful Counterterrorism Strategies: *The Indian Chronicle*, Global Terrorism Index, 2017, Institute of Economics and Peace.
19. Gian Gentile, David E. Johnson, et al, Reimagining the Character of Urban Operations for the US Army, RAND Corporation, 2017, p. 1.
20. 2018 Revision of the World Urbanization Prospects, Population Division of the United Nations Department of Economic and Social Affairs (UN DESA). The World's Cities in 2018.
21. "Healing the Poor", *The Pioneer*, 13 December 2011 via http://www.dailypioneer.com/columnists/item/50661-healing-the-urban-poor.html, accessed on Feb. 23, 2012.
22. John Pilot, (ed). '*Rommel and His Art of War*', London: Wrens Park, 2003, p. 133.
23. Gian Gentile et al, Reimagining the Character of Urban Operations for the US Army, RAND Corporation, 2017, pp. 121-122, ISBN 978-0-8330-9607-4.
24. Ibid, pp. 140-41.

25. Euan Graham & Greg Colton, The 21st Century Will be a Battle on the Urban Front, Commentary, 15 August 2017, https://www.lowyinstitute.org/publications/21st-century-will-be-battle-urban-front.
26. Ibid.
27. Kira Wynne, Thales Launches New PRC6809V VHF Combat Net Radio System, October 6, 2017. Accessed on 20 March 2020, https://www.thalesdsi.com/2017/10/06/thales-launches-new-combat-net-radio-system.
28. "Preparing for More Urban Warfare," *The Economist*, January 25, 2018. (Nicknamed "Baladia," the Arabic word for "city," the training area was built in 2005 in part by the US Army Corps of Engineers at a cost of $45 million.

10

Imperatives for India for Dominating a Future Conflict (2030) in the Maritime Domain

Vice Admiral Satish Soni

ABSTRACT

The gateway to the Atlantic and the Pacific, the Indian Ocean has found renewed emphasis in the strategic political discourse of extant and emerging powers. Economic interdependence between littorals and extra regional powers is metamorphosing into strategic competition and impacting political inclinations. India is poised to play a pivotal role in shaping the destiny of this maritime landscape, which has now coalesced into the 'Indo-Pacific'. By 2030, Pakistan–China collusion is poised to become the most prominent threat on the maritime front. The outbreak of Covid-19 has underscored the importance of collaborative responses to non–traditional challenges. As a dominant economic and military power in the region, India would have to address key imperatives by building bilateral, regional and multilateral frameworks supported by a whole structure of government approach. Adoption of future technologies for development of strong naval capabilities deserves our utmost attention.

Historical Perspective

Centuries before Columbus sailed the Atlantic and Magellan and crossed the Pacific, the Indian Ocean had become an economic superhighway of the world and a thoroughfare of commercial and cultural traffic between the west coast of India and Babylon (modern Iraq) as well as the Levant (eastern Mediterranean). With trade to and from the Indian Ocean Region being lucrative, mariners from the littoral traded actively through the ages.

India has had a rich maritime heritage in ship-building and Buddhist missionaries sailed from our eastern shores to Sri Lanka, Myanmar, Indonesia and beyond to China; but we regrettably were never muscular at sea. The only exception to a passive maritime policy was Rajendra Chola in the 11th century, who looked east with an expeditionary intent. But for that brief period, India has been sea blind. Dynasties with pan-Indian footprints, which followed in the wake of the Cholas, remained pre-eminently continental in their outlook leaving the waters around the Indian peninsula for everyone to exploit. Sailors from distant lands including China used the monsoon winds to criss-cross the ocean for commerce and proselytizing coastal populations. No one enforced a maritime order at sea and there was a policy of live and let live. The landing of Vasco da Gama in Calicut in 1498 changed all that. The Portuguese wanted the waters to themselves and tax others for its use. An intense power struggle ensued between the Portuguese and home-grown Admirals of Kunjali lineage. Kunjali Marakkars were traders who lost business due to Portuguese interventions and took up arms, lasting just four generations.[1] Similarly, a century later, Khanoji Angre took to sea to resist the English and the Dutch. He was considered the first Maratha naval chief but was essentially a naval guerrilla fighter whose resistance lasted only two generations. The British Empire that drew power mainly from its naval fleet, emerged victorious and ruled the Indian Ocean well into the mid-20th century. After the Second World War, the Royal Navy withdrew and the Indian Ocean became a stage for power play between the USA and the Soviet Navy. The ending of the Cold War has witnessed an overwhelming US military presence in Saudi Arabia, United Arab Emirates and Afghanistan. The USA has a major naval base in Diego Garcia; the Fifth Fleet is headquartered in Bahrain and units of the US Africa Command are stationed in Seychelles and Djibouti. The USA is also spearheading international efforts for maintaining stability in the region; Task Forces 150 and 152 are stationed in the Gulf and Task Force 151 is stationed in the Horn of Africa. Naval ships from NATO countries are positioned for anti-piracy duties and the European Union. Naval Force (EURO-NAVFOR) in support of 'World Food Programme' missions are deployed off Somalia. At any time, over 120 foreign warships are present in this area. *In sum, our waters have for generations been dominated by extra-regional naval powers. Can India afford to continue outsourcing the security of these waters or is it time to take the lead in developing an organic response supported by the littorals of the Indian Ocean?*

Our Waters—An Arena of Contestation Due to Economic Interdependence

The Indian Ocean, with an area of 70.56 million square km, is the third largest water-body in the world covering approximately 20 per cent of the earth's surface. The littoral region covering 25 per cent of the world's landmass is inhabited by one third of the world's population, an agglomeration of diverse people of different religions from some of the richest and the poorest 51 nation-states. The unique feature of the Indian Ocean Region (IOR) is the abundance of its natural wealth and the sea lines of communication, which transport it to meet the requirements of industrialized, and developing countries. The region has 40 per cent of the world's oil and gas reserves, 60 per cent of the world's uranium, 98 per cent of diamonds and 80 per cent of the world's known gold reserves. The IOR abounds in 20 out of the 40 raw materials of strategic importance imported by the Western countries and 40 of the 54 types of imported raw materials used by American industry. The new 'Gold Rush' is in the rising demand for seabed minerals such as Polymetallic Nodules, Polymetallic Sulphides and Cobalt Crusts, which are in abundance in the South West Indian Ocean. Deep seabed polymetallic sulphides contain iron, copper, zinc, silver, gold and platinum in variable constitutions and have attracted worldwide attention for their long-term commercial as well as strategic value[2].

The sheer volume of merchandise carried across this region raises the stakes in the security of trade as over 100,000 ships transit its expanse annually. Since the mid-90s, trade between Indian Ocean littorals and China, Korea, Japan, Taiwan and the South East Asian countries has been increasing exponentially, primarily on account of rapid growth and consequent higher need for fossil fuels and resources. Over 70 per cent of the total traffic of petroleum products passes through the Indian Ocean on its way from the Middle East to the Pacific. About a fifth of the world's oil (crude, petroleum products, condensate, etc.), 26 per cent of the world's LNG, 90 per cent of the Gulf's oil exports, i.e., 17 mn barrels of oil per day transit through the Strait of Hormuz alone.[3] Since energy is critical in influencing the geo-political strategies of a nation, any disruption and consequent turbulence in its supply has serious security consequences. Given the spiralling demand for energy from India, China and Japan, the sea lines of communication (SLOCs) and choke points of the region have become strategically important for these countries. China, first became a net importer of oil in 1993 and economic interdependence with oil-exporting countries in the Persian Gulf has been increasing steadily with 44.1 per cent of its oil being sourced from nine Middle Eastern countries. The rise in China's share of global trade has been unprecedented. Since 2000, the African continent has also become economically interdependent on China with the quantum of trade increasing by nearly 400 times and overtaking the USA as their largest trading partner. Many of the continent's economies are sustained by natural resource exports and China, on account of its vast domestic manufacturing ecosystem and have served as the principal market for them. As of 2017, 54 per cent of Angola's total exports to the world comprised crude oil exports to China. The figures for the Republic of Congo stood at 44 per cent during the same year. Similarly, 32.7 per cent of Zambia's total exports consisted of copper exports to China. The same pattern is observed with respect to the Democratic Republic of Congo's cobalt exports. On 2 Sep 2018, at the summit meeting of the Forum on China-Africa Cooperation (FOCAC), President Xi announced a 60 billion USD commitment towards Africa and has repeatedly expressed China's commitment to align the Belt-and-Road Initiative (BRI) with the African Union Agenda 2063, an aspirational policy document that places a particularly strong emphasis on regional integration within the continent.[4] Closer home, China has committed 62 bn USD for the China Pakistan Economic Corridor. In the past few years, East Africa has emerged as one of the hottest natural gas fields in the world. The offshore region straddling north-east Mozambique and south-east Tanzania, known as the Rovuma Basin contains, on estimation, over 100 trillion cubic feet of recoverable natural gas, making it one of the largest gas finds in the world. Mozambique is expected to become one of the world's leading exporters of liquefied natural gas and both China and India have expressed interest in making investments in exploratory activities. Mega gas deals are being signed in Mozambique, each one bigger and more catalytic than the previous. In June 2017, the Italian oil and gas company ENI committed to investing $10-billion on the building of Coral South, a floating liquefied natural gas (FLNG) project off the Rovuma basin in Mozambique, the world's first ultra-deep-water FLNG facility. In June 2019, Mozambique LNG (led by US-based Anadarko) committed $20-billion on the development of integrated offshore and onshore gas fields, through LNG, in the Rovuma basin, east of Palma, and in December 2019, Rovuma LNG (led by ExxonMobil and ENI) is expected to commit $30 billion to develop the same.[5] Not very far from these approaches lies the South West ridge where reportedly, China's unmanned submersible Qianlong 2 has discovered polymetallic sulphide deposits[6]. *Economic inter dependencies have turned our waters into an arena of contestation—something India would ignore at its own peril.*

US-China Rivalry and India

Driven by competing visions of the future of international order, the USA and China are throwing up new security dilemmas and rekindling geopolitical rivalries reminiscent of the Cold War era. The South China Sea was the first to witness an intense game play with the Chinese developing military infrastructure on many artificial islands to dominate the first island chain. Under President Obama's leadership, the USA adopted a variety of initiatives including a rebalance to the East, aggressive freedom of navigation patrols and marshalling of international support through diplomatic and economic initiatives. After the initial hiatus under President Trump, the USA now appears to be more committed to the region. Rekindling of the QUAD initiative, with India as a possible bulwark against Chinese designs could see the US-China rivalry spilling over to the Indian Ocean. In June 2019, the USA released the Indo-Pacific Strategy Report (IPSR), a US vision on the Indo-Pacific based on the pillars of security, economics and governance and defined on four specific principles, viz., respect for sovereignty and independence, peaceful resolution of disputes, free and fair reciprocal trade and adherence to international rules and regulations. However, no red lines have been defined and there is no threat of the use of hard power. On the other hand, China has been the fastest to embrace the Indo-pacific by exhibiting sufficient resolve for using hard power. They seized the Paracel group of islands and the Johnson South Reef in the Spratlys from Vietnam in 1974 and 1988, respectively, the Mischief Reef in the Spratlys from the Philippines in 1994, established the Sansha City on the Woody Island in the Paracel group in 2012 and took over control of the Scarborough shoal from the Philippines in April 2012. Amidst vociferous objections in international fora, China speedily reclaimed 3,200 acres on seven features and made three airfields in the Spratly group of islands by 2015. The logistic facilities created there emboldened China into a long stand-off with Vietnam over the presence of their survey ships in Vietnam's EEZ and harassment of Philippines fishermen around the Thitu/Pagasa island and the Reed bank in 2019.

Whilst the world has been busy combating the Covid-19 pandemic, the PLA (Navy) continued to assert itself in the South China Sea by sinking a Vietnamese fishing boat in the Paracel islands and hindering Malaysian oil exploration efforts in their maritime zones. PLA(N) has also stepped up its activities in the Indian Ocean with the commissioning of a permanent presence in Djibouti and development of likely dual-use ports in Pakistan, Sri Lanka and Myanmar. Whilst the US naval presence in the Indian Ocean is much superior, both qualitatively and quantitatively, the Chinese may be expected to enhance their maritime engagement and consequent naval presence exponentially.

The Indian Ministry of External Affairs has reorganised the jurisdiction of its divisions to impart a sharper diplomatic focus to the Indo-Pacific region. The move is being interpreted as our intention to align with the USA to lay greater emphasis on the Indo-Pacific. The new division comprises the earlier divisions of the Indian Ocean Rim Association (IORA) and ASEAN sections and symbolises a shift in Indian strategic thinking from considering just the maritime arc from the Straits of Hormuz to the Straits of Malacca as its zone of influence to extending it to the Western Pacific. The combined division will be in a better position to coordinate India's efforts in increasing its footprint on the vast expanse of the Indo-Pacific on myriad issues ranging from an enhanced economic interface to addressing maritime security challenges. Whilst our intentions may not be to become part of an anti-China alliance, this reorganisation is a signal of a possible option we may consider to exercise in future. Geo-political realignments may only be expected to hasten in the wake of the Covid-19 pandemic. *The Indian establishment should enunciate its strategic thought in the form of a White Paper, formally, much like what other countries have been doing at regular intervals.*

India and the Quadrilateral Dialogue

President Obama's 'Pivot to Asia' followed by the current administration's advocacy of a 'Free and Open Indo-Pacific' rhymed with India's own 'Look East' and 'Act East' policies resulting in India becoming the linchpin of the rejuvenated Quadrilateral Security Dialogue (QSD). China interprets the grouping as an obstructive mechanism to oppose it in the South China Sea, a region it considers its sphere of influence. Notwithstanding some differences in perceptions, the QSD appears to be drawing India into the power play being enacted in the Western Pacific. It would be significant to note that the concept of the Indo-Pacific does not project India in a leadership role in the Indian Ocean, our backyard. Suspicion of the motives of a developing India-USA axis could catalyze strengthening of a China-Pakistan embrace and hasten a strategic encirclement by the PLA (Navy) by establishing a military presence in the many logistic bases under development. What are India's options? Do we join the US-led alliance that professes to shape a Free and Open Indo-Pacific or do we exercise our strategic autonomy and hedge our bets? The rather nebulous situation obtaining currently might afford an opportunity to encourage a grouping, more organic in nature and restricted in span, covering non-traditional areas of maritime security, which may elicit greater traction from the economically weaker but geographically more relevant littorals. The principle of grouping states together ought to be based on geographical proximity, commitment to international law, keenness on connectivity, focus on sustainable development, opposition to terrorism, commitment to open markets, free flow of trade/capital/technology and ideas, maritime and cyber security. The aim should be to evolve standard operating procedures for participating agencies for meeting these challenges without being under an umbrella of a strong political interface that could be misinterpreted. Such an inclusive grouping would also ameliorate adverse perceptions inherent in the initiatives led by extra-regional powers. It is for consideration that the foundation of such an initiative already exists in the Indian Ocean Rim Association and India could nurture it to have a wider applicability. A successful acceptance, especially by the ASEAN, Indonesia, Japan, France and South Korea with India in the lead may provide a sturdier bulwark (than the QSD) against an obdurate China that is less accepting of the concerns of the smaller and weaker nations of the Indo-Pacific littoral. *Finally, this mechanism would provide an insurance for the littorals against a possible rapprochement between China and the USA, which could leave the small and the weak out in the cold.*

CHALLENGES–2030

Pak-China Collusion

As the maritime domain regains prominence, traditional threats to India's maritime security emanate from states with organised military capability and resources, which harbour an adversarial posture and inimical intent towards India. India shares its maritime borders with seven countries of which Pakistan is assessed to be the most likely source of a traditional threat. China is not our maritime neighbour; however, the near continuous presence of seven to eight warships/research vessels in the IOR and development of permanent naval bases is indicative of their growing interest in our maritime neighbourhood. An aggressive posturing and dominance by PLA(N) in the South China Sea is likely to metamorphose into ambitions to have a strong naval presence in the Indian Ocean where they have economic dependencies. Whilst the Indian Navy, the most powerful of the navies in the region presently, may well be able to thwart any misadventure at sea by either Pakistan or China, a collusion between our two traditional adversaries could become a major challenge. By 2030, the PLA(N) would be in a fairly good position to deploy and sustain a major naval contingent in the Indian Ocean Region comprising a Carrier Battle Group including modern destroyers/frigates, two SSNs, one SSBN, two LPDs (075 class), three Tankers/COSCO logistic ships, one Intelligence ship and over 1000 big vessels of the fishing militia. PLA would also be able to spare up to four Long Range Maritime Patrol Aircraft for surveillance of the Indian Ocean Region. These would be able to operate from Djibouti, Turbat, Gwadar and Karachi. Whilst Gwadar may still not be able to be exploited as a naval base, warships would be able to do an operational turnaround at Djibouti, Hambantota or Karachi. All ships on deployment would be equipped with the most modern of machinery, weapons and sensors in the PLA's arsenal. These may not require as much periodic maintenance as the older versions. The naval contingent would therefore be able to sustain at sea for up to three months without the need for an operational turnaround. The total duration of deployment of any surface combatant would be up to six months with one/two operational turnarounds. Whilst the Pakistan Navy would remain somewhat a green water navy with new frigates replacing the older ones, a significant addition of up to three Yuan class submarines may be expected by 2025. They would claim operationalisation of a sea-based nuclear deterrent as these submarines could be capable of launching the Babur 3 short range cruise missile armed with a nuclear warhead. *Whilst our naval capabilities are pretty robust and would be able to raise the threshold of intervention by any naval power, a Pak-China collusion at sea could pose a formidable challenge by 2030.*

Increasing Importance of Non-traditional Threats

As countries look to the seas for economic prosperity, food security and social wellbeing of their people, there is a growing realisation that the emerging construct of Blue Economy holds great significance especially for the Indian Ocean Rim Region, which is home to many impoverished people with limited resources on land. On September 27, 2015, the global community announced commitment to Sustainable Development Goals 2030 in which Goal 14 is to 'Conserve and sustainably use the oceans, seas and marine resources for sustainable development'. There is a symbiotic relationship between Blue Economy, Sustainable Development Goals (SDG) and Security and therefore ocean governance has become critical to ensure the safety and security of economic assets and activities such as offshore oil platforms, protection of marine wealth, prevention of illegal fishing, and upholding national environmental regulations, thereby ensuring livelihoods of coastal populations as also enforcing national commitments to international agreements and initiatives such as SDG 2030. Human trafficking, illegal fishing and loss of bio-diversity of the oceans are affecting maritime economics and influencing Geo-Politics. An apt example is in the breakout of piracy off Somalia in the Gulf of Aden. The root cause lay in the lack of maritime governance, which resulted in exploitation of Somali waters by advanced nations. The impoverished Somalis retaliated and piracy was born. During 2008-12, 400 mn USD was paid to Somali pirates in ransom for 178 successful hijackings in 645 attempts. After spending 7 to 9 bn dollars a year, ironically by the countries who directly or indirectly gained from Somali exploitation, piracy has been brought under control but not before underscoring the lesson that lack of maritime governance affects the rich and poor alike.

Of particular importance is the threat of global warming which is affecting sea levels, coastlines, ocean acidification, ocean currents, marine life, tides, seawater salinity, sea water surface temperatures, etc., and can trigger several changes in ocean geo-chemistry, all of which affect the societies of the littoral states. A sea level rise of 3 mm per year (or 20 inches in 100 years) has been recorded on account of melting of glaciers and thermal expansion caused by increased temperatures. Such rises are likely to erode beaches, inundate lowlands and disrupt marine ecosystems on the coasts. Maldives, an archipelago of over 1,000 small islands with a maximum height above sea level not exceeding five metres and Bangladesh, which has a very low-lying coastline, are going to be the most affected in our region. The Covid-19 pandemic has further reinforced the importance of cooperative mechanisms for better governance to spearhead common non-traditional threats. *By 2030, it may be expected that the gravity of non-traditional challenges could well bring traditional foes on the same table for mutual benefit just as we witnessed whilst combating piracy when the USA, Iran, India, China, Pakistan and more than 35 international navies patrolled in support of a common aim to ensure safe passage to the world's merchant marine. Covid-19 may be the black swan event to alter the inter se priority between traditional and non-traditional threats.*

Improving Maritime Governance is the Key

Formal mechanisms, which could influence maritime governance in the Indo-Pacific, include the Indian Ocean Rim Association (IORA), Indian Ocean Naval Symposium (IONS), Western Pacific Naval Symposium (WPNS), Djibouti Code of Conduct and ASEAN Regional Forum amongst others. Numerous think tanks have sprung up and serve as an important medium for Track 2 interactions over and above the formal meetings, summits and conferences such as the Shangrila dialogue, Indian Ocean Conference, Galle Dialogue, etc. The Indian Ocean countries must however introspect that whilst they were unable to evolve a governance structure in response to the threat of piracy, the USA, NATO and the European Union orchestrated an effective riposte by a disparate group of more than 30 navies with diverse interests. A home-grown maritime order in the India Ocean has eluded us so far. It is of immense importance that India spearheads a collaborative effort to improve Maritime Domain Awareness (MDA) in the region for the benefit of the entire littoral. A reasonable success has been achieved in this regard by way of commissioning of the International Fusion Centre at Gurugram, installation of Coastal Radar and AIS stations along the Indian coast and on the many island nations in the Indian Ocean. *India must coordinate an organic response strategy to improve MDA, which would assist in maritime governance and address specific requirements of the littorals such as Humanitarian Assistance during disasters and other myriad challenges.*

Focussing on Non-traditional Threats

While combating piracy, the North Western Indian Ocean witnessed the coming together of an interesting coalition of disparate maritime forces from different and at times opposing political leanings. Their naval units started to communicate on a common channel 'Mercury' and exchange information to overcome a common threat; that of piracy. Interesting incidents came to be recorded when a US warship helped a merchant ship of its traditional foe, Iran, to thwart a hijack attempt. An Indian ship helped a Chinese merchant ship in an emergency and warships from all countries started to provide security to merchant ships irrespective of the flag under which they were flying. A very loose political convergence backed by a fairly rigid executive security mechanism had blossomed to address a common challenge. It is for us to introspect if such an approach is possible to counter the many other non-traditional challenges, viz., preservation of biodiversity, sustainable development, climate change, illegal fishing, etc. A coordinated approach at the executive level could perhaps change many a mindset at the political level in due course. *As an example, if all smaller countries of the region were to team up against Illegal, Unreported and Unregulated fishing, it would become apparent that the chief exploiter of their fishing zones is none other than their professed benefactor—China.*

The Navy—Most Important Constituent of Maritime Power

India's defence outlay has been steadily reducing in real terms and stands at under 2 per cent of GDP with the share of the naval budget cut sharply from 18 to 13 per cent of the defence allocations during the last decade. With the maritime front poised to gain more importance, it is imperative that the government considers an increase in defence expenditure and reprioritizes inter se importance of defence projects with an aim to strengthen capabilities at sea. The Indian Navy has around 130 odd ships and submarines. The time line to reach the 200 mark has been revised from 2027 to 2050. Given that only 20 ships have been commissioned during the last five years against the 24 decommissioned, it seems unlikely that we would be able to meet the timeframe of even the revised milepost. The Navy was allocated only 70 per cent of the total projected fund requirement in the XII plan period (2012-2017), which has precluded timely replacements of critical capabilities. Thirty-four ships and submarines are presently under construction and contracts for only 15 new ships have been concluded in the last five years. Capability gaps are slowly increasing and include conventional submarines, Unmanned Aerial Vehicles, Mine Countermeasures Vessels, Anti-Submarine Warfare and Naval Utility helicopters, torpedoes and medium calibre guns. The Indigenous Aircraft Carrier (IAC) project is progressing very slowly and it has taken us nearly

20 years to build this platform. We must not lose the acquired expertise and the government must accord an early approval to build the second Indigenous Aircraft Carrier (IAC 2) with enhanced capabilities. A monitoring structure akin to the Advanced Technology Vessel Project (ATV) may be considered so that the country does not lose on account of cost and time overruns like we have, for the IAC1. The Strategic Submarine Building Programme has been extremely successful and we must graduate to building bigger submarines with longer weapon delivery ranges to operationalize a 'Continuous at Sea Deterrence' capability. The recent announcement of the acquisition of 111 Naval Utility Helicopters and six submarines under the 75-I programme on a strategic partnership basis are extremely important for the Navy and both programmes must be pursued with alacrity. Similarly, the Navy needs replacements for the ageing Sea King multi-role helicopters and Mine Counter Measure Vessels and contracts for these must be concluded on a Strategic Partnership basis. The Navy would stand to gain by actively pursuing and developing asymmetric capabilities in the fields of Cyber, Space, Intelligence and Special Operations. The focus of such capabilities should be our ability to deliver a stinging blow in out-of-area scenarios in close neighbourhood to counter China's creeping influence. Navy's amphibious capabilities have served an important secondary role of providing a 'Strategic Lift' of Diaspora in case of unforeseen calamities such as the need to transport lakhs of Indians stranded on foreign shores in the aftermath of the Covid-19 pandemic. The acquisition of LPDs needs to be followed up urgently.

Technologies that would Influence a Future Conflict

Space-Based Capability. George Friedman, the founder and CEO of the think tank Stratfor till 2015, in his book *'The Next Hundred Years'*, published in 2010, predicts the first space war in 2050; a war in which pre-emptive strikes may be launched from lunar bases at the spatial Command and Control stations with an aim to achieve superiority in space. In this first space war, the author has visualized extensive use of unmanned hypersonic aircraft, Anti-Satellite missiles, High Energy lasers, Armoured infantry men, Robotic Logistics, Unmanned Air Vehicles, Precision guided missiles, etc. While the scenario is fictional, space is certainly the new dimension that aspiring powers are looking to exploit. The capability to use the ultimate 'high-ground' for strategic, operational and tactical advantage is crucial for the Indian Navy to evolve into a 'multi-dimensional, multi-spectrum force'. Space-based ELINT for near real-time surveillance of 'Emitters of Interest', to detect, locate, record and analyse intercepted data needs to be given impetus. There is also a need to vigorously pursue the acquisition of low-cost LEO micro/mini satellites. Space-based capabilities would also enhance communications, Position Navigation and Timing (PNT), Automatic Identification System, Command and Control, Cooperative Engagement and Network Centricity.

Unmanned Combat. Autonomous unmanned combat vehicles that can operate in the air, on the surface and under the surface are of great interest to all navies because of their ability to remain on task for extended periods of time and extend combat operations into the adversary's anti access/ area denial zone. Advancement in technologies would facilitate incorporating a greater degree of autonomy and 'Artificial Intelligence' in Unmanned Aerial Vehicles (UAVs) for combat/surveillance; developing swarm drones and manned or unmanned systems for surface and sub-surface tasks. The Indian Navy operates the Heron and Searcher class of Unmanned Air Vehicles (UAVs) and has a programme for arming the UAVs and developing a bigger and more capable platform, i.e., Rustom. The Defence Research and Development Organisation is also developing an Autonomous Sea Vehicle akin to a submarine drone. The pre-requisites for a successful system include precision guidance to avoid collateral damage, advanced Artificial Intelligence to enable decision making, a good collision avoidance system, exploitation of Internet of Everything (IOE) technology and better satellite coverage. We could explore the feasibility of co-developing with the USA in the research and development of technologies of their ongoing projects. Viz., Anti-Submarine Warfare Continuous Trail Unmanned Vessel (ACTUV) that looks for submarines in a given area and reports detection to the fleet, SHARK—an underwater submarine hunting probe, "Upward falling Loads" which remain dormant on the sea bed and rise on demand, X-47 unmanned aircraft and the vertical take-off and landing naval drone, the Tactically Exploited Reconnaissance Drone (TERN). Research on Boeing's Solar Eagle, a self-sustaining UAV, powered by solar energy with an endurance of five years has been stopped but we could expect development of such capabilities in the future.

Maritime Domain Awareness Capability. Development of MDA will be a key component of our strategy for conflict. It will help shape the battle space, enable disruption of the adversary's Information-Decision-Action

(IDA) cycle and contribute towards achieving Battle-Space Dominance. MDA will be developed using all sources, including aircraft—both manned and unmanned—ships, submarines, Special Forces (SF), ground and space-based assets and information and cyber systems.

Network-centric Warfare. The Indian Navy must aim to achieve full spectrum dominance at sea from peacetime operations to application of military power by having a credible Information superiority. This includes a real-time secure exchange of operational information between sensors, decision-makers and 'shooters', so as to enable rapid, accurate actions across wide areas and in all dimensions, thereby increasing mission effectiveness. Further, for next generation weapons, sensors and Command and Control (C2) systems, the primary criteria would be Cooperative Engagement Capability (CEC). Our efforts so far include putting a dedicated naval satellite 'Rukmani' in space, development of UHF, KU, C and S band transponders, indigenous development of Software Defined Radios, a common Combat Management System, commissioning of the Information Management and Analysis Centre (IMAC) and the IRNSS programme. Indigenous software defined radios will give us the ability to communicate over longer ranges in complete secrecy. Auto modulation and change of frequency will enable jam-proof communication. Exploitation of Multi Input Multi output (MIMO) technology will reduce requirement of more sets and antennae. But there are some technology gaps; we continue to depend on the GPS and have not been able to integrate information from all available sources for a perfect situational awareness on individual units at sea. Also, we need to have a global footprint. Launch of more satellites and early conclusion of our efforts at information integration is an impending need.

Cyber Warfare. Cyber warfare capability affords an inferior force with manifold advantages to confront a technologically superior and well networked adversary by disrupting the latter's information flow. Focused and well-coordinated tactical actions in cyberspace can lead to outcomes at the operational and strategic level. Along with espionage and data theft, disrupting or crippling an adversary's communication/IT networks, and strategically critical economic infrastructure, can accrue multifarious benefits. For an increasingly networked force, like the IN, it is imperative that we invest in technology to not only safeguard our assets, platforms, and sensor-weapon grids from cyber-attacks, but also develop the capability to carry out such attacks against our adversaries.

Aircraft Carrier Technology. There is certainly a need to build more and bigger aircraft carriers in quicker timeframes and the Navy must draw up plans to assimilate and integrate several advanced technologies such as the Electro Magnetic Launch System (EMALs), Advanced Arrester Gear (AAG) and Integrated Full Electrical Propulsion (IFEP)/Nuclear Propulsion.

Weapons and Sensors. Some major weapon and sensor technologies, possession of which would be relevant by 2030 would be Long Range Land Attack Cruise Missiles (LRLACMs) with the capability of striking targets at ranges greater than 1,000 km, Extended Range Anti-shipping Missiles (XRAShM) (>1,500 km) fired from Mobile Missile Coastal Batteries (MMCBs), Electro Magnetic Rail Guns, Directed Energy Weapons (DEW), Long Range Surface to Air Missiles (LRSAMs) of ranges greater than 250 km, Active Off-board Decoys, Ship-borne BMD capability networked with long range missile tracking radars, Synthetic Aperture Sonars (SAS) and associated integration technologies. The exponential surge in computational power and development of sophisticated Big Data Analytical (BDA) tools has facilitated incorporation of Artificial Intelligence (AI) into various facets of naval warfare and operations. AI enabled algorithms are capable of rapidly turning enormous volumes of gathered data into actionable intelligence, thereby boosting operational effectiveness and combat capability. AI-based applications that are being leveraged for naval use include Multi-Platform Multi-Sensor Data Fusion (MPMSDF) to achieve rapid data fusion for generating a Common Operating Picture (COP) and a Cooperative Engagement Capability (CEC); Inter-platform resource allocation; analysis of sensor data; Operational Level War Gaming (OLWG); Automatic Decision Support System (ADSS); Cognitive Radio and EW systems; and cyber security and physical security systems. AI would also be able to enable Predictive/Preventive Maintenance and supply chain management for cost optimisation. Underwater Autonomous Platforms/ Robots would in future facilitate hull inspections/maintenance thereby optimising manpower intensive jobs.

Draw up a Strategy for Developing a Maritime Industrial Base

Countries of the Indian Ocean littoral look up to India for ameliorating their maritime capabilities by improving connectivity, modernising their ports, building capacities to safeguard their Exclusive Economic Zones and implementation of measures for sustainable development of Blue Economy. They are striving to develop a maritime industrial base for exploration and exploitation of oil and natural gas along their coasts, cost effective mining of seabed minerals, building ecosystems for tapping renewable energy from wind, wave and tidal variations, giving impetus to the fishing industry, promoting cruise tourism, putting in place a safe ship recycling industry, promoting a culture for protection of marine environment, adoption of measures to tackle climate change and other avenues for using the seas for an economic turnaround. Greater cooperation across all these marine industries is feasible and a strategy needs to be spelt out to identify areas of commonalities that exist across some of these groups of industries. India needs to adopt a 'whole of government' approach to facilitate cooperation between myriad sectors. A strategy should be enunciated for identification of an export-oriented development by laying out a road map for skill development in specific areas. Investments could be prioritised and shared aims between different industries identified to benefit from economies of scale. Gains from such an initiative would help not only our maritime industrial complex but those of our neighbours as well. Indigenous capabilities to build warships by our shipyards have been developed and we are building destroyers, frigates, corvettes, missile vessels and offshore patrol vessels to world class standards. These shipbuilding lines must be kept alive by orders from the Indian Navy and those from our friendly neighbours.

Conclusion

India possesses excellent maritime geography, a long coastline, numerous island territories and a vast Exclusive Economic Zone. A modern Navy comprising big ships with long sea legs ensures constant surveillance of our maritime zones. We certainly have an edge over our adversaries and can influence and secure our maritime neighbourhood. However, by 2030 challenges at sea, both traditional and non-traditional are poised to escalate. An emergent collusion between a more capable Pakistan Navy and Chinese Navy with enhanced resident capacities in the Indian Ocean Region will raise the bargaining stakes for China and embolden Pakistan to pursue asymmetric warfare with greater vigour. Climate change and exploitation of the Oceans against the backdrop of the world's commitment towards

Sustainable Development Goals are likely to push all maritime nations on to a common platform to evolve cooperative responses. Whilst combating the Covid-19 pandemic, India has displayed an ability to provide leadership at the world stage. A similar resolve needs to be exhibited to shape the environment for better Maritime Governance of the Indian Ocean as also to build a strong Navy with advanced technological capabilities for providing robust maritime security.

REFERENCES

1. Dr. K.K.N. Kurup and Dr. K.M. Mathew, *Native Resistance against the Portuguese: The Saga of Kunjali Marakkars*, Calicut University Central Cooperative Stores Ltd., December 2000, pp. 54-104.
2. Strategic Importance of IOR. Vision IAS.www.visionias.in accessed on 25 March 2020.
3. Liam Denning, Bloomberg Opinion 14 June 2019, accessed on 29 Dec. 2019. 'Strait of Hormuz': The World's Most Important Oil Artery', *Reuters*, 21 July 2019, accessed on 25 March 2020.
4. Ministry of Commerce Peoples's Republic of China, Elaboration of the Eight major Initiatives of the FOCAC Beijing Summit, accessed on 25 March 2020.
5. Louis Bergeron. *"The Forgotten Choke Point: The Mozambique Channel's rich past and bright but insecure future,"* Centre for International Maritime Security, accessed on 25 March 2020; Sasha Planting, 'Gas in Mozambique—A 128-bn Opportunity', accessed on 25 March 2020.
6. *The Economic Times*, August 14 2018. China finds Poly Metallic Sulphide deposits in Indian Ocean. Accessed on 25 March 2020.

11

Relevance of Aerospace Power and Third Dimension Operations in Future Wars of India

Air Commodore (Dr.) Ashminder Singh Bahal

> *"There are experts of land, sea and air power, but as yet there are no experts of 'warfare', and warfare is a single entity, having a common purpose."*
>
> **—Giuilio Douhet**

Introduction

Aerospace power and technological advancements move in tandem and a minor innovation in technology produces out of proportion effects in aerospace powers' outcomes. Artificial Intelligence (AI), stealth, swiftness (towards hypersonic speeds), precision, extended reach, night vision, space and computing power provide improved accuracies, better integration and enhanced potency. The technologies that are likely to revolutionalize aerospace capabilities in future are AI, zero fuel aircraft, unmanned abilities, space propulsion systems, quantum computing, progression in material sciences, block chain, directed energy weapons (DEW) and 3D technologies.[1]

Formed in 1932, the Indian Air Force (IAF) played a crucial role in different conflicts. The only war in which the IAF was not utilised in anger (Sino-India conflict), cost India dearly. Currently, the IAF has developed into a potent strategic force with the induction of a wide variety of lethal fighters, long/medium range transporters and potent helicopters. Though the IAF's qualitative potential has improved significantly, its combat potential has declined to around 28 fighter squadrons.

21st Century Geo-Political Drivers in the Aerospace Domain

The global geo-political situation has become volatile by the rapidly growing Chinese power, its aggressive involvement in global affairs, its-Belt-and-Road initiative that has resulted in debt trap fears, trade wars, nuclearisation of the Korean subcontinent, spread of COVID-19 and radicalisation of Afghanistan, Iraq, Middle East and Syria. Globalisation has resulted in easier spread of deadly diseases such as corona and its subsequent impact on the economy, especially of developing countries, thereby facing difficulties in allocation of funds for defence acquisitions. This is compounded by the diminishing American influence and power, especially in the Indo-Pacific region where they are now looking at the formation of quadrilaterals to safeguard their interests. The current geo-political environment brings in its own dynamics as nations collate strengths to combat terrorism globally, fight diseases together and contain an aggressive China that creates doubts about its role in igniting bio-terrorism; either intentionally or by gross negligence. This is where the role of aerospace and naval power assumes significant importance. In future, integrated or even multi-nation forces may need to be projected regionally or globally, working in tandem with other countries, as the case may be, to protect Diasporas and global interests in the Indo-Pacific region.

The relevance of aerospace power in integrated operations has also seen a paradigm change. In the near future, no wars can be won without aerospace power providing an environment for the surface forces to operate freely with minimum loss of human life. This assumes enhanced relevance whilst fighting high intensity conflicts in a nuclear environment where conduct of wars for occupation of territory may become inappropriate to execute. This aspect would also become extremely important in multi-domain operations. Though this term is used by Westerners in all types of contingencies, its relevance becomes essential in coalition force application in areas distant from the homeland. In our context, multi-domain operations would be more applicable towards island territories and the Gujarat/Kutch areas or where forces are applied in theatre commands.

In other places, it would mostly relate to integrated application of aerospace and surface forces achieving national aims and objectives with naval power dominating the seas to affect the maritime domain and commercial trade, but not necessarily in integrated battle spaces. In addition, there is now limited demarcation between air and space power; therefore, air and space forces have now transcended into integrated aerospace domain. A slow shift is also taking place from manned to unmanned platforms and enhanced development of assets to control space. Winning or losing a war in future may also depend on perceptions and sensitivity to human losses. This is where the relevance of integrated aerospace operations becomes crucially important.

People's Liberation Army Air Force (PLAAF) and Aerospace Forces

PLAAF's Combat Potential. There are two key aerospace powers that impact India's security; PLAAF and Pakistan Air Force (PAF). PLAAF is the third largest air force in the world. Current evaluation of PLAAF's combat potential indicates 700-800 fourth-generation fighters comprising J-10, J-11, Su-27 and Su-30 MKK aircraft, which are comparable to IAF's Su-30 MKI. By 2023-2025, PLAAF is expected to deploy around 1300 4th/5th generation fighters[2]. PLAAF's quantitative strength may have declined in the last few decades, but its qualitative potential has improved significantly.

PLAAF considers stealth and unmanned platforms as key force enablers and has developed J-20 and S-37A fighters, to counter F-22 Raptor[3]. It is also developing H-20 and JH-XX stealth strategic bombers capable of carrying a large payload, range and nuclear weapons. Induction of J-20A low observable aircraft gives China the ability to undertake deep stealth strikes well inside India[4]. India's fifth-generation fighter aircraft (FGFA) project with Russia has received a crucial setback and the Advanced Medium Combat Aircraft (AMCA) project will take a long period of time to materialise. ***This increases China's stealth technology differential wrt IAF***.

The short-term goal of PLAAF is to develop into a fourth-generation plus aerospace force by 2030 and the long term (2049) is to possess global reach with aerospace dominance whilst building its unmanned capability significantly. Even in UAVs, stealth will make them less vulnerable. China is currently developing a stealth drone, Sharp Sword, which has already undergone initial flight testing. This drone has low observability characteristics[5].

PLAAF's Modernization Outcomes. PLAAF's modernization drive is likely to increase its qualitative strength by 2025 when its major projects bear fruit. It will then have significant superiority in terms of fourth/fifth generation aircraft, Directed Energy Weapons (DEW), space-based assets, anti-satellite weapons (ASAT), network centric warfare technology, anti-ship ballistic missiles (that target aircraft carriers to promote anti-access area denial strategy), Airborne Warning and Control Systems (AWACS) and strategic air lift assets. PLAAF's strength lies in its dense long-range integrated air defence (AD) network[6]. Added to this is the development of 16 airfields in Tibet that facilitates rapid force mobilization and could render the natural Himalayan barrier ineffective[7] in terms of integrated force dominance.

China's Aerospace Capability. China's aerospace plans include establishing space stations, manufacturing reusable space shuttles and developing potent anti-satellite capability leading to space control. China's satellite navigation system (Bideou) became operational in December 2011[8]. China's aerospace capability is supplemented with its robust surface-to-surface missiles (SSM) that include a variety of cruise and ballistic missiles with ranges between 180 km to 13,000 km. In 2017, China unveiled DF-31 ICBMs, which feature greater mobility. It has also developed DF-41, a road mobile ICBM capable of carrying multiple independently targetable re-entry vehicles (MIRVs) and hypersonic glide vehicles for strategic deterrence[9]. *It is gradually building such integration that exploits missile forces to paralyze the functioning of the adversary's command and control structures as well as his combat potential.*

China has progressively developed an array of counter-space weapons including ground-launched anti-satellite missiles, Directed Energy Weapons (DEW), satellite jammers and co-orbital systems[10]. The US military accused China of firing laser beams at their satellites[11]. This implies that not only can China target satellites in Low Earth Orbit (LEO), but is also attempting to develop capability to target Medium Earth and High Earth Orbit satellites. China's targeting LEO satellites implies that India's reconnaissance satellites would be at considerable risk; there is a need therefore to keep a number of satellites ready for launch at short notice including mini/micro satellites. India's ASAT weapon that destroyed the

Microsat-R satellite at 283 km altitude in March 2019 was a direct ascent kinetic kill weapon[12]. India is also developing a number of mini/micro satellites.

Operations in Tibetan Autonomous Region. The key game changers for China are its ASAT, BMD, SSM, Cyber and DEW capabilities; however, response by PLAAF across TAR in the near future requires dominant capability at all stages in their War Zone Campaign. This is where the IAF and India's Aerospace Power could prove to be a key spoiler in PLA's time critical operations. Furthermore, terrain friction due to peaks ranging between 4,300-5,400 m, imply that offensive ground operations from TAR would traverse difficult terrain and would require extensive logistics support. *Mountain operations inherently require pro-active sustained logistics systems; this is where the supply chain in difficult terrain and logistics dumps could easily be interdicted from air. The IAF could prove to be invaluable here.*

PLAAF would need to undertake extensive Counter Aerospace Operations before commencing extensive surface operations and obtain multi-domain dominance quickly. This is where India needs to operationalize its Defence Space Agency (DSA) and form it into an operational command soon. Simultaneously, there is a need to integrate all the AD elements belonging to the different services and form an integrated Aerospace Defence Command to counter the Chinese and Pakistani Aerospace threat. At the same time, *if the stealth differential is not reduced quickly, which is compounded with significant Chinese SSM, BMD, Cyber and DEW potential as well as their unmanned capability, post 2025, any Sino-India conflict could have perilous results for India.*

Pakistan Air Force and Aerospace Forces

PAF Combat Potential. PAF fighter strength presently includes 60 F-7PGs, 150 Mirage-IIIs/Mirage-Vs, 76 F-16s, 110 JF-17s and one reconnaissance squadron of 12 Mirage-IIIs. The first JF-17 squadron was made operational on 18 February 2010 with 14 aircraft at Kamra[13]. Currently, around 110 JF-17s are available in six fighter squadrons with the seventh squadron being established soon. Furthermore, 36 FC-20 aircraft were intended to be procured[14]. The FC-20s were planned to replace the F-7P/PG as well as Mirage-IIIs/Vs[15]. It is appreciated that acquisition of FC-20 is put on hold as it is only going to add another medium category fighter, which is in the same league as the F-16 C/D/JF-17 Block-3 aircraft, whereas, PAF is currently thinking of upgrading its stealth technology with JF-17.6 or another stealth aircraft. Acquiring stealth technology is where PAF will focus once it adds on more JF-17s. It would aim to keep the F-16 and JF-17 fighters as its main fourth-generation aircraft, while developing its stealth capability in manned platforms and enhancing its strength of unmanned elements.

PAF's Modernization Drive. In 2008, China and Pakistan agreed for joint development of ZDK-03 AWACS aircraft and currently PAF has four such aircraft and it is acquiring Chinese FT 2000 long-range missiles to deter Indian AWACS aircraft. Pakistan has also procured six Saab-2000 Airborne Early Warning (AEW) systems. In addition, Pakistan has acquired four IL-78 based Air-to-Air Refuelling aircraft and is procuring 10 batteries of SPADA 2000 integrated AD systems. Upgradation of the older version F-16s and Mirages, procurement of F-16C/D Block 50/52 fighters and acquisition of AWACS/AEW aircraft along with long-range AIM-120 BVRs (used by PAF after the Balakot strike against the IAF), give PAF enhanced BVR, EW and night attack capability.

With acquisition of R-27ER1 missiles for Su-30MKI, it still does not match the F-16C/D and AIM-120C combination. The IAF is therefore acquiring Meteor missiles integrated with Rafael to counter this key threat. Till 2030, PAF is likely to base its fighter acquisition strategy on enhancing the numbers of JF-17 and F-16 fighters and moving towards stealth technology instead of procuring other advanced aircraft to replace its Mir-111/V and F-7PG fleet that is likely to be phased out during 2020-2030. This is primarily due to the serious economic crisis that Pakistan is currently facing, which gives it limited flexibility to acquire modern aircraft that require high acquisition and maintenance cost.

PAF is also procuring 30 used Egyptian Mir-V aircraft to maintain and augment their current Mir-V fleet. These are upgraded aircraft with RC-400 radar, MAWS, mission pods and night strike capability. It intends to procure eight additional F-16C/D fighters to enhance their F-16 strength to 84 aircraft. If they get more F-16 C/D fighters at subsidized cost from the USA, then they may prefer increasing the strength of F-16 fighters to around 100. At the same time, their original F-16 A/B aircraft will start getting phased out from 2025-30. Whilst PAF's combat potential is improving, the IAF's has not grown at the same pace. The IAF is slowly losing its quantitative and qualitative edge with respect to PAF because of our failure to induct new systems in time and in sufficient quantities; this will start becoming critical by 2025 as a number of MiG-21 fighters and part of the Jaguar fleet will also be phased out after phasing out MiG-27s in December 2019 without finding suitable replacements in the desired numbers.[16]

By 2030, PAF is likely to have around 18 fighter squadrons with around three F-16, 10-12 JF-17 and two to three stealth or fifth-generation fighter aircraft along with a large number of Unmanned Combat Aerial Vehicles (UCAVs). Pakistan currently has more AWACS aircraft (ten) and China (around 30) to India's (05); whereas there is a requirement for 15 such aircraft for the IAF in a two-front scenario) as PAF would have more early warning aircraft with less area to cover on station wrt the IAF.

Pak Unmanned Capability. Pakistan operates a wide variety of Unmanned Aerial Vehicles (UAV) including armed UAVs such as Burraq (12), Satuma Bravo (45), Galileo, Falco (25), CH-4 (04), AAI (RQ-7) (12) and Shahpur (05)[17]. It is currently focusing on the development and production of armed UAVs as well as Medium Altitude Long Endurance (MALE) unmanned platforms. Pakistan has identified Project AZM for the development of its MALE UAVs and fifth-generation fighter aircraft.[18] Under Project AZM, UCAV manufacture will be carried out in Pakistan. The conceptual design phase of the armed drone is complete and it would go through three more cycles with high fidelity tools[19]. In May 2018, PAC signed a MoU with a Turkish company, Havelan, to collaborate with them on ground control stations, mission and weapon control computers and sensor integration. Pakistan and China have also been working on the production of Caihong-5 and Wing Loong UCAVs[20]. China is selling 48 advanced MALE Wing Loong-II UCAVs to Pakistan. This UCAV can carry 480 kg of ammunition with both bombs and air-to-surface missiles and has an endurance of around 20 hours.

Pak's Aerospace Capability. Pakistan's national space agency, the Space and Upper Atmosphere Research Commission (SUPARCO) is working in collaboration with China National Space Administration (CNSA). China has assisted Pakistan in the development of their space program including provision and launch of satellites. SUPARCO has multiple agreements with CNSA. In 2000, SUPARCO was brought under the National Command Authority. After successfully launching BADR series of experimental satellites (BADR-1 was launched with the help of China in 1991), SUPARCO plans include launching of high resolution remote sensing satellite system (RSSS).

Necessary infrastructure for ground control and image reception and processing has already been established in Pakistan. In 2011, China launched a Paksat-1R satellite in a geo-stationary orbit and on 9 July 2018, China also successfully launched two Pakistani remote sensing satellites, PRSS-1 and PakTES-1A, with a resolution of one metre. The PRSS-1 is China's first optical remote sensing satellite sold to Pakistan, while PakTES-1A is SUPARCO's indigenously developed experimental satellite.

Meanwhile, Pakistan has developed a wide array of ballistic and cruise missiles with ranges extending from 50 km to 2,750 km. Pakistan's thrust is mainly towards developing short- and medium-range ballistic missiles; however, it is also developing advanced cruise missiles and is researching on MIRVs. The short-range missiles include HATF1A & 1B (50-100 km), NASR (60-70 km), Abdali (180-200 km), Ghaznavi (240-300 km) and Shaheen-1 (750 km). The medium-range ballistic missiles include Ghauri-1 (1,250-1,500 km), Ghauri-II (1,800 km), Shaheen-II (1,500-2,000 km) and Shaheen-III (2,750 km). The cruise missiles include Babur-I (700 km), Babur-II (750 km), HATF-VIII Air Launched Cruise Missile (ALCM - 350-550 km) and Ababeel (MIRV 2,200 km; specifically designed to defeat the Indian BMD system). Pakistan is continuously improving its ALCM capability. This implies that while their aircraft remain within their territory, they can target crucial military and economic targets well inside Indian territory.

Pakistan Army Aviation Corps. Pakistan has around 20 operational Cobra attack helicopters The Cobra helicopter is old and uses dated technology and cannot operate at high altitudes. The Cobra is being replaced by 30 Turkish TAI T-129 attack helicopters, which are twin engine, tandem seating as well as have all-weather hot and high attack and reconnaissance capability. Pakistan's 10 T-129 helicopters will have Block-1 configuration and the balance 20, Block-II, which would possess advanced EW equipment with active radio jamming ability. There are 12 Bell AH-1Z Viper attack helicopters with Hellfire II missiles also on order (10 Viper helicopters have been delivered but stored at Arizona after the USA cancelled $ 300 m in military aid in August 2018; these could still land up in Pakistan in future like the F-16s).

Similarly, T-129 attack helicopters have many US components that require US approval and Turkey is likely to obtain it. If these acquisitions go through, it would give Pakistan reasonable attack helicopter capability in deserts and plain sectors against Indian armour. At the same time, the current Pakistani situation regarding attack helicopters is weak, especially considering their economic situation. With acquisition of around 22 AH64E Apache helicopters for the IAF and eight for the Indian Army and delivery of LCH, the Indian armed forces would be in a much better position by 2022-24. At the same time, *these attack helicopters are likely to be used during armour operations, for destroying radars and for Combat Search and Rescue (CSAR). They would need to be put under one functional command and control, preferably that of the Indian Army since the main role of anti-armour requires close integration with them,* but when used for radar busting or CSAR, they could be controlled by the IAF through the Integrated Aerospace Defence Command.

Balakot Operations. In retaliation to the Pulwama attack, the IAF carried out attacks by Mirage aircraft on JeM's terror training camp at Balakot during the early morning hours of 26 February 2019. Twelve Mirage 2000 jets carrying SPICE 2000 and Crystal Maze weapons and escorted by four Su-30MKI along with Netra and Phalcon AEW/AWAAC aircraft with two Il-78 air-to-air refuelling aircraft undertook the attack. Five Spice 2000 precision bombs were released. All the aircraft returned safely thereafter. Jaguars were also used as decoys to attack Bahawalpur. The Spice 2000 was pre-fed with GPS co-ordinates and target imagery[21]. Pakistan retaliated soon and one MiG-21 Bison on the Indian side and one F-16 C/D aircraft on the Pakistani side were reportedly lost. The Indian pilot was captured and interrogated and was returned after a few days.

Though there are questions asked as to the actual number of terror elements that were killed in this attack, the key outcome of the Balakot strike is that no other Pulwama type attack or a major terror strike has taken place since then. Furthermore, what was also signalled was the Indian resolve and willingness now to cross the border in case Pakistan continued to sponsor terror acts. This also implied that Pakistan could no longer consider India a soft state and there would be a cost involved, if Pakistan continued to nurture terror. In these issues, the IAF achieved India's aim. Furthermore, a number of urgent procurements that were pending for a very long time for the three services were acquired under emergency procurements. At the same time, shooting down of a Mig-21 Bison indicated that with AIM-120C adaptation on the F-16 C/D aircraft, currently, PAF has an edge in BVR air-to-air combat till the IAF acquires Meteor missiles on Rafale/Mir 2000 aircraft. Furthermore, shooting down of a Mi-17 helicopter due to fratricide indicates severe lacunae in our Air Defence process and procedures. *It is here that an integrated Air Defence and better still an integrated Aerospace Defence Command needs to be established soon.*

PAF and IAF. A comparison between the two air forces reveals that currently the IAF scores well over the PAF in terms of personnel (approx 2.6:1) and in terms of fighters (1.5:1). The ratio is also high when it comes to modern technology aircraft, of which the Indian Su-30MKI and the Mirage 2000 provide long-range strike and Air Defence capabilities. India has a large stock of specialist weapons, unmatched strategic reconnaissance and ASAT capability, better potent terminal defences and a much superior airlift capability. Furthermore, the IAF has the flexibility to operate in airfields located well in depth. Pakistan does not have the strategic depth to safeguard its crucial vulnerabilities. This weakness, if exploited correctly, could result in the IAF obtaining significant gains, especially in tackling Pakistan's AWACS/AEW and LRMP aircraft and attacking its crucial nodes. Pakistan cannot hide its key assets. In addition, due to India's superior satellite reconnaissance and ASAT capability, it could lead to information dominance, which would have a major force multiplier effect in any conflict.

India is currently developing a Hypersonic Technology Demonstrator Vehicle to attain Mach 6.5 speed at 32.5 km altitude. Shaurya is a hypersonic surface-to-surface missile being developed by the Defence Research and Development Organization (DRDO). It has a range of 750 to 1,900 km and is capable of carrying a one-ton payload, with a conventional/nuclear warhead. India is also developing Brahmos-2K (around 600 km range) that is likely to be fielded by 2022-24[22]. With Pakistan developing RAAD ALCM, that has ranges between 350 and 550 km, it would neutralise this advantage to some extent. The range of the air-launched Brahmos, which is a much better supersonic missile, needs to be enhanced to 550-600 km on priority. This would not only help in a high intensity conflict situation but also help during peacetime to respond to a Pulwama type attack. Furthermore, with Brahmos developing a range of around 600 km, no part of Pakistan would then be safe from an Indian attack, whilst the delivery aircraft remains well within the Indian territory.

The Pakistani Air Force earlier had a critical problem securing their airspace as their aircraft lacked long range BVR capability. While this gap has been filled with the acquisition of 500 AMRAAMs, it could still be overwhelmed by the numbers of upgraded MiG-29, Mirage 2000, Su-30 MKI, LCA and Rafale fighters that are likely to fly in the tactical airspace. The Indian aircraft too need long-range BVRs, which are being procured and then they are likely to have the ability to engage PAF aircraft at medium/long ranges, whilst operating under AWACS/Aerostat cover, thereby giving the IAF dynamic air dominance over the battlefield.

This would be further complimented with the acquisition of S-400 AD systems as well as additional procurement of Harop UAVs to target PAF AD radars, which, if effectively integrated could create serious problems for PAF aircraft to get airborne. This would be tackled by PAF by using their anti-radiation weapon systems. As compared to Pakistan's AWACS aircraft, the Indian Phalcon is much better, as it provides tactical surveillance of airborne and surface targets and helps gather signals intelligence. It is also capable of tracking fighters from a distance of 400 km[23]. However, PAF has more numbers of AEW aircraft and a better pilot-to-aircraft ratio, meaning it could sustain a greater sortie generation rate over a protracted conflict[24] with a better coverage of the area of interest and for a longer duration. This is where it is incumbent that the *IAF increase its strength of AWAACS aircraft initially to ten by 2030.*

While the IAF is likely to sustain aircraft losses to SAMs at low/ medium altitudes, Pakistan will suffer serious losses at all altitudes, whilst executing strike missions. The IAF also has the flexibility to operate in airfields located well in depth. Pakistan does not have the strategic depth to safeguard its vital assets and hence cannot hide its crucial vulnerabilities. *It is this critical weakness, if exploited correctly, that can give significant gains to the Indian armed forces, especially in tackling Pakistan's vital assets such as AEW&C, AAR and LRMP aircraft and attacking its crucial surface nodes.*

Defence Space Agency (DSA) and Defence Space Research Organization (DSRO)

In April 2019, India formed a tri-service Defence Space Agency with its HQ in Bengaluru. It is led by an Air Vice Marshal of the IAF with personnel from all the three services. It will command all the space assets of the Army, Navy and the Air Force including ASAT systems, Defence Imagery, Processing and Analysis Centre (DIPAC) and Defence Satellite Control Centre (DSCC)[25]. In June 2019, India established the Defence Space Research Organization (DSRO) for developing space warfare systems and technologies. India is also developing DEW, co-orbital systems, lasers and electromagnetic pulse (EMP) and ASAT weapons as well as creating the ability to protect space-based assets from hostile electronic and physical attacks[26].

Whilst DSRO develops systems and defence applications for all types of space technologies, the DSA is the agency that would evolve space warfare strategies and would control the technologies and systems that could be used for space control and defence. These organizations will be the primary means of developing as well as employing such systems and technologies in conflict situations as well as protect space-based assets during peace time as well as during conflict. They would be augmented with Space Situation Awareness information for monitoring and evaluation as well as for preventing the collision of space-based assets, thereby creating space debris. The DSA in time should transcend to become a tri-service Command led by an IAF professional.

Nuclear Environment and Aerospace Power

The nuclearisation of the sub-continent is bound to play an important role in any future conflict. It could be safely assumed that the nuclear threshold would be crossed only if a state's vital national interests are threatened; hence, there is conventional space available during conflict situations. At the same time, the possibility of hard line religious/asymmetric elements resorting to nuclear/dirty weapons cannot be ruled out. Due to our policy of "No First Use," there is a requirement to possess a potent second strike capability, which is based on a credible nuclear triad. Part of the nuclear triad is a strong air deliverance mechanism that has been tested during peace time. Survivability of nuclear assets and delivery mechanisms would be central to any "No First Use" doctrine; then only would second strike capability become meaningful. At the same time, India has said that it is open to review the nuclear doctrine, probably in relation to any Chinese aggression.

In a nuclearised environment where going to war needs to be avoided, when faced with a situation that is similar to the Pulwama attack,

Aerospace Power could be effectively employed in situations less than war to deliver a clear message. *The impact of selective and discriminate destruction of carefully identified targets located in depth increases the costs to the adversary*. With long-range precision weapons aboard fighter aircraft, the need to penetrate deep inside enemy territory may not arise. The adversary's options could then be to respond with aerial strikes and meet an equitable response or escalate the situation to a full-fledged war. The onus, however, would then be on the other side to escalate and the ability to escalate would be a major factor in the decision matrix. This is where the availability of a strong Aerospace Power in combat readiness provides powerful deterrence value discouraging any escalation in the conflict spectrum. In addition, aerospace power in our sub-continent provides an instrument to react whilst not occupying territory permanently. In addition, whilst the aircraft could venture inside the enemy territory to attack a target located deep; such operations may not be possible for the surface forces to undertake during a 'no peace no war' situation.

The negative effects of escalation in such a situation could be contained by maintaining the land, naval and air elements in a strong defensive posture. *Highly calibrated escalation in a nuclear environment as well as disengagement control is therefore possible with the employment of a superior aerospace power*. It is imperative that the IAF's capabilities need to be enhanced to cater to any eventuality. Furthermore, any combat operations in future would need to be fought in integrated battle spaces. Differentially strong localised rapid reaction potential both from the air and surface and inherently strong defensive capabilities need to be created to be able to successfully deter even a stronger opponent such as China.

Integrated Aerospace Defence Command. An analysis of the ballistic missile capability in the region indicates that China and Pakistan have the potential to strike at any vital asset of India accurately with limited warning. Coupled with nuclear weapons, this capability portends serious connotations. India's stated policy of no first use also makes it incumbent that an effective ballistic missile defence (BMD) against surface-to-surface missiles (SSMs) is put in place on priority. In the Indian context, flight times of Pakistani/Chinese missiles to targets located in India vary from six min to 30 min depending on the location of the launch site and that of the intended target. Quick detection and interception become essential to neutralise these missiles.

India is acquiring five S-400 systems and is currently developing a two-tier BMD system capable of tracking and destroying incoming missiles[27]. This system comprises long-range radars that pick missiles approximately 600 km away along with an interceptor surface-to-air missile[28]. However, *there is a need to acquire at least five more S-400 systems to cater to the island territories and other Vital Areas too*. As far as the indigenous systems are concerned, the first test of the Atmosphere Intercept System was carried out at 40-50 km altitude; the system is similar to the Arrow-2 BMD[29]. In December 2007, an endo-atmospheric interceptor successfully intercepted a Prithvi missile at 15 km altitude; akin to the PAC-3 system. Interception of missiles has now been carried out in exo and endo-atmospheric modes. The Prithvi Air Defence interceptor used at 75 km altitude indicates that India could engage Intermediate Range Ballistic Missiles (IRBM). In Phase-II, the BMD system would tackle 5,000 km-plus range missiles. Both the Indian Ballistic Missile Defence as well as S-400 systems need to be integrated in a systematic manner to plug any gaps that may occur in different terrains as well as to provide BMD to various crucial target systems located deep inside including political targets.

India is also planning to acquire American National Advanced Surface to Air Missile System (NASAMS). It is a distributed and networked medium to a long-range air defence system. The system in conjunction with S-400 and the indigenous Prithvi AD systems could create an effective missile defence shield. In addition, there is a wide variety of AD systems that are integral with the different services including those with the Indian Army and the Indian Navy. Furthermore, in multi-domain operations assets belonging to the different mediums and services would be participating in combat operations in integrated battle spaces. To prevent fratricide and losses due to friendly fire, there would be a need to impose significant restrictions in the effective use of all these AD systems. *It is vital that to prevent fratricide and to make effective use of all the AD and BMD systems that are with the different services, there is a need to evolve an Integrated AD Command under an IAF officer.*

It is also important that in future we need to move beyond the Integrated AD Command and what we require is an Integrated Aerospace Defence Command that integrates all the AD systems of the three services as well as the BMD and S-400 elements in a seamless environment that provides comprehensive Aerospace Defence against all attacks originating from or utilizing the air, space and sea environment. Furthermore, an integrated command could also provide a layered defence to all types of potential intruding systems in a multi-domain environment. This would assist in neutralizing threats comprehensively and well in time.

Relevance of Aerospace Power in Future Warfare and Integrated Operations

Integrated operations are promoted by two crucial elements; first, a ***seamless environment*** that promotes combined operations in integrated battle spaces, and second, ***'Flexible Mindsets'*** that allow Integrated Planning. The battlefields of the future are likely to be highly digitized, networked and seamlessly integrated. With a net centric environment, flatter and distributed tactical command and control structures are required that enhance speed of response whilst reducing sensor-to-shooter time; yet a centralized strategic command and control structure is required to facilitate joint planning between the three services for conducting integrated campaigns; especially in a theatre command environment.

Space based assets are likely to play a key role in enhancing the combat effectiveness of air, naval and surface operations. The distinction between air and space power would considerably reduce after integration takes place between ballistic missiles and hypersonic technology; aerospace term would then be more applicable. ***Aerospace power has today become the primary instrument of choice and would play a dominant role in emerging warfare in the subcontinent as it would provide a cost effective option at different stages of the multi-domain operations***. It would ideally provide such a favourable environment under which unhindered rapidly mobile surface operations can take place.

The aim in future conflicts would be ***to isolate the enemy's Command and Control structure, augment psychological warfare, paralyze his communication networks with the help of physical attacks and also with the help of cyber operations. Simultaneously, strike deep inside his territory in parallel on his crucial centre of gravity targets and vital nodes with precision. These concepts favour employment of aerospace power***. Aerospace Operations would therefore need to be intimately meshed with overall joint campaign plans. The focus should be on multi-domain dominance along with rapid surface operations providing such an effect that leads to attainment of political objectives cost effectively in shorter duration of time and with least bloodshed, at the same time not crossing nuclear thresholds.

Is the Day of the Fighter Aircraft Over? Today many strategic theorists are questioning the employment of expensive manned fighters and are asking whether Biggles' (war magazine hero) days are numbered. In September 2019, Russia released details of the first flight of the sixth-generation stealth Su-70/Hunter-B UAV flying alongside Su-57 fifth-generation fighter aircraft in a wingman role for manned-unmanned teaming missions. The low observable UAV is being developed by 2025 so as to have the ability to transmit radar and imaging data to the fighters that are flying in depth and that use long range air-launched weapons; the manned fighter remains well outside the coverage of the enemy's AD systems and attacks the vital targets after receiving the target inputs from unmanned platforms.

China too is undertaking development of Tian Ying, a similar class drone and the Americans are employing RQ-170 Sentinel (20) and are developing X-47B and X-45C drones. The American Valkyrie and the broader Skyborg programs are aimed at developing hardware and software to integrate manned aircraft with unmanned drones with the aim of separating the sensor from the shooter and flying mixed formations of stealthy UAVs with manned fighter aircraft[30]. It is a clear indication that modern aerospace forces are considering teaming manned with unmanned platforms to achieve common missions in the very near future.

Whilst aerospace technology has moved from UAVs towards UCAVs and smart drones that have the ability to locate, identify and destroy targets, the US Air Force has released details indicating ***how tiny drones will soon swarm hostile airspaces for undertaking surveillance, targeting and destruction activities and Boeing is creating a swarming system for larger drones***[31]. The future scenario could include a large number of small drones entering an adversary's air space with low observability characteristics. This would saturate the enemy's AD systems and simultaneously significant damage a large number of geographically dispersed high value targets. These drones would have interactive ability and would be able to transmit and exchange air and ground situation pictures between each other as well as with the manned fighters and simultaneously undertake multiple targeting.

The availability of unmanned combat drones may obviate the need to employ highly expensive manned fighters. This implies that slowly a shift will take place from manned combat and surveillance aircraft to small and highly manoeuvrable smart stealthy UCAVs that saturate hostile air defences and yet are significantly potent in destroying well defended targets with precision. The unmanned systems would interface intimately with their manned counterparts as Artificial Intelligence technology develops capability multiplication elements. This progress is expected to bring significant effectiveness in surveillance, navigation and direct combat action[32]. ***Initially, the transition would come with a combination of manned and unmanned elements operating in integrated battle spaces and working in tandem and subsequently, majority platforms in conflict spots would be unmanned with embedded AI systems both in drone technology as well as in Command and Control systems.***

Developments are taking place in unmanned rotor aircraft. China has developed a 500-km range V-750 unmanned helicopter that successfully test fired anti-tank missiles in June 2017[33]. These developments bring about a paradigm shift in the manner in which aerial warfare will be conducted in future. Drones enhance security in peace time in disputed areas by monitoring contested regions persistently at lower cost, leading to a reassurance that potential adversaries are not attempting to alter the status quo[34]. The UCAVs are likely to be used in combat operations initially for Suppression of Enemy Air Defence by pre-emptively attacking AD radars and other elements whilst providing continuous vigilance. They would also undertake high value time critical targeting on Centre of Gravity (CoG) targets. This may result in providing a "no win" tactical deterrence and also work towards attaining air superiority[35] at lower potential cost.

In the foreseeable future, that is up to 2035, a mix of manned and unmanned aerial platforms would participate in warfare with unmanned elements taking on high risk missions of locating and targeting Air Defence elements or/and heavily defended Centre of Gravity targets. They could also be used for relaying information to manned fighters operating in depth away from the lethal coverage of AD systems. This would reduce the risk on more expensive manned aerial platforms. In future, manned assets would mostly be used in situations where discrimination is required between targets, especially in a fast changing battle situation, act as an aerial command post, attack rapidly moving targets in close vicinity of friendly elements or be a shooter in the sensor-shooter chain where manned aircraft with long range air-to-air and air-to-surface weapon systems remain well away from the enemy's AD systems while the unmanned platform loiters closer to the target area. ***By 2035, the unmanned platforms***

would constitute a significant proportion of the combat forces and manned platforms would reduce in numbers. It is here that efforts are required by India to develop stealthy unmanned combat platforms quickly.

Way Forward for the Indian Air Force

The MiG-21 aircraft have been upgraded and AN-32 and MiG-29 aircraft are being upgraded[36]. The IAF has also upgraded 118 Jaguars with new engines, airframes, avionics, better communication systems, active electronically scanned array radars and airborne weapon systems; it gives the fleet an additional 20 years of life[37]. The IAF is also upgrading Mi-8, Mi-17/Mi-17-IV helicopters, 40 Su-30MKIs (to carry BrahMos missiles) and Mirage 2000H to Mirage 2000-5 Mk 2 variant that has new radar, weapons suite, missiles and electronic warfare equipment. The deal for the joint development of FGFA, however, has petered out. At the same time, the IAF Chief has announced that the IAF supports indigenous development of AMCA fifth-generation aircraft. Considering the track record of ADE/HAL, the aircraft is not likely to materialize in the next decade or so. There is a requirement to have a fifth-generation fighter aircraft by 2025-27 to counter the J-20 aircraft. ***The government needs to take a serious note of this vulnerability.***

In addition, the Request for Information to procure 114 medium weight fighter aircraft was made in April 2018[38]. It is a single engine non-stealth fighter and would be equivalent to the fourth generation plus LCA Mk II. There seems to be a dichotomy here. While the requirement is for a stealth fighter and that is not being met, the IAF is meanwhile trying to procure another aircraft in league with the LCA in large numbers, thereby, still remaining within the Fourth Generation plus regime and not going to the Fifth Generation stage. Simultaneously, it is also procuring 83 LCA Mk-IA fighters (fourth generation; the deliveries will start two to three years after signing the deal). This is in addition to the deal signed for 40 LCAs earlier. This would put the IAF in a significantly disadvantageous position wrt PLAAF by 2025 and wrt PAF by 2030, if no fifth-generation aircraft is available by then.

The decrease in IAF's fighter strength from 39½ to 28 squadrons was offset by the Su-30 induction that arrested the downslide, but the problem is that the ***IAF's retirement rate far outstrips its intake of new aircraft***[39]. If no new aircraft are acquired, then the IAF would be left with only 25 combat squadrons[40] by 2025-2027. Even if additional MiG-29 and Su-30 aircraft are procured, the squadron strength would still be around 27-28 squadrons. India needs to acquire another two squadrons of Rafales to tide over the short term. By 2030, Pakistan would have around 17-18 fourth to fourth generation plus combat squadrons "that could be brought to bear against us" with significant numbers of fourth generation plus aircraft in terms of JF-17 and F-16C/D and some fifth-generation aircraft. On the other hand, China would have approximately 1,200-1,300 fourth/fifth-generation fighter aircraft[41] and significant number of stealth aircraft; ***there is an urgent need therefore to enhance the IAF's stealth potential quickly***.

India therefore needs to advance the FGFA/AMCA program and instead of going in for more numbers of single/multi engine fourth-generation aircraft, it needs to acquire stealth aircraft akin to F-22/F-35 planes. Overall, they may be more cost effective, when survivability is factored. If 36 Rafale low observable fighters cost around $9-10bn, then probably an appropriate numbers of stealth aircraft (around 36) could be procured instead of 114 single/multi engine fighters. These procurements could be supplemented with additional LCA/Su-30 aircraft/force multipliers. Furthermore, there is a gradual shift taking place from manned fighters to unmanned elements, therefore ***to plug the combat potential degradation, six squadrons of UCAVs, preferably stealth, as force multipliers should be acquired on priority. This would help cross the fifth generation hurdle without losing combat edge and reach the sixth generation directly whilst simultaneously developing the AMCA***. Furthermore, the unmanned aerial elements along with manned aircraft should be maintained only by the IAF as in future wars will be fought in integrated battle spaces. All unmanned aerial platforms procurements should also be carried out centrally and thereafter maintained by the IAF.

The optimum force structure keeping in mind availability of funds could progressively move towards fourth/fifth generation 30-32 squadrons of fighters by 2030 along with additional five AWACS/AAR aircraft, Heavy Lift/METAC transporters, an additional five S-400 AD systems (or similar such systems whether indigenous or acquired from outside) and adequate numbers of armed/attack and heavy lift helicopters whilst developing stealth capability/AMCA. ***An ideal combination could include 10-12 Su-30 MKI, four Rafale, three stealth/FGFA, two upgraded Mir-2000, six LCA, two upgraded Jaguar and one Mig-29 squadron by 2030***. There should not be any additional multiplicity of types to prevent getting into a logistics nightmare. ***To supplement numbers, force multipliers such as UCAVs,***

preferably stealth, would be a cost effective option; therefore six squadrons of UCAVs each having 12 UCAVs need to be acquired by 2030. Meanwhile, development of small stealth UAVs should be progressed rapidly.

Even if we procure less fighter aircraft, it is more important to procure stealthy intelligent unmanned platforms to cross over to the sixth generation stage. More than transiting to the fifth generation, it is more important to reach the sixth generation so that the transition from manned to smart unmanned platforms is brought about. ***It is this change in mindset that must start coming in the research agencies today and also in the IAF and in our armed forces.*** In addition, these unmanned elements need to be supplemented with HAROP, Heron and other indigenous UCAVs including small stealth drones that should be developed in large numbers. The IAF too needs to have a number of small drones that could swarm into the adversary's territory. ***Furthermore, due to a slow shift from manned to unmanned elements and tests involving a combination of using manned and unmanned platforms in different tactical scenarios, there is a need to bring about changes in the operational concepts of force employment in multi-domain integrated warfare.***

If we are still looking at acquiring an additional 114 fourth-generation fighter aircraft and taking into account the time frames in which such acquisitions will take place, then we are not moving towards the future as by the time we acquire these fighters, they would be in the process of becoming dated technology.

Conclusion

In future, Aerospace Power will enhance its fundamentals of 'Reach, Accuracy, Lethality, Survivability and Command and Control'; more complex situations will witness increased employment of unmanned elements and aerospace power's peacetime employment will be interwoven into the fabric of homeland security for tackling asymmetric forces[42]. While Aerospace Power is likely to play a decisive role in any foreseeable conflicts in the Indian subcontinent, what is important is that the wars will become more joint with application of appropriately tailored integrated forces at the right time. ***While boots on the ground would continue to play a major role in both deterrence and maintaining a hold on the ground, acquisition of territory in a nuclearised environment and issues regarding loss of lives would become more sensitive.*** The Commanders' decisions would be questioned more and more in the future and too media would play its own key role in perception management.

Furthermore, there will be a slow shift from manned to unmanned platforms with the focus initially being on employing a combination of manned and unmanned elements to attain campaign objectives with minimum loss of manned aircraft. Manned platforms would become mostly stealthy to enhance survivability.

The optimum force structure, keeping in mind availability of funds, would be 30-32 squadrons of fighters by 2030 along with an additional five AWACS/AAR aircraft, suitable number of Heavy Lift/METAC transporters, an additional five S-400 AD systems (or similar such systems whether indigenous or acquired from outside) and adequate numbers of armed/attack and heavy lift helicopters whilst developing stealth capability/AMCA. ***An ideal combination could include 10-12 Su-30 MKI, four Rafale, three stealth/FGFA, two upgraded Mir-2000, six LCA, two upgraded Jaguar and one Mig-29 squadron by 2030. To supplement numbers, force multipliers such as six squadrons of stealth UCAVs need to be acquired by 2030***. Meanwhile, development of small stealthy UAVs needs to be progressed quickly.

Space would get interwoven in air operations and the term Aerospace Power would have greater meaning. ***There would be a need therefore to quickly form an integrated tri-service Aerospace Defence Command that integrates all the air and space assets of the three services for aerospace defence. This would also include Ballistic Missile Defence. There is also a need to move from Defence Space Agency to an Aerospace Command. Perhaps Aerospace Command should have an enmeshed Integrated Aerospace Defence organization. In uncertain times, bold initiatives and smart decisions are required.***

NOTES

1. Steven Brand, 6 Emerging Technologies You Will Want To Know All About, accessed from the site https://www. cmtc.com/blog/emerging-aerospace-technologies on 23 Feb 2018.
2. Information updated from Group Captain Ravinder Singh Chhatwal, China's Military Modernization and PLAAF Capabilities against India, accessed from the site http://www.icsin.org/uploads/2015/04/20/ c98446766d8b4e19cd3be6770fc0a604.pdf on 22 Jul 2018.
3. Robert Henson, "China Boosts its air assets with Ilyushin aircraft", Jane's Defence Weekly, 21 Sep 2005, pp 16; Richard Fisher, Jr, "Chinese Dimensions of the 2005 Moscow aerospace Show", International Assessment and Strategy Centre, 12 Sep 2005, information obtained from web site http://www.strategycenter.net on 14 Jan 2011.

4. ORF online, Indian Defence News, accessed from the site http://www.defencenews.in/article/The-widening-gap-between-Indian-and-Chinese-Air-Power-557939 on 19 Jul 2018.
5. By Kelsey D. Atherton, How The Next Generation Of Drones Could Reshape Future War, accessed from the site, https://www.popsci.com/how-next-generation-drones-could-reshape-future-war on 24 Feb 2018.
6. Kartik Bommakanti, China's Military Modernisation Recent Trends, accessed from the site https://www.orfonline.org/research/china-military-modernisation-recent-trends/ on 22 July 2018.
7. Cdr. Kamlesh K. Agnihotri, Modernisation of the Chinese Air Force and its Implications for India, accessed from the site https://www.tandfonline.com/doi/abs/10.1080/09733159.2011.641394? scroll=top&needAccess=true&journalCode=rnmf20 on 22 Jul 2018.
8. China launches two satellites to enlarge its own global positioning system. Accessed from the site beidou-2-beidou-system-xichang-satellite-launch-center on 22 Sep 2012.
9. Michael S. Chase, PLA Rocket Force Modernization and China's Military Reforms, accessed from the site https://www.rand.org/content/dam/rand/pubs/testimonies/CT400/CT489/RAND_CT489.pdf on 22 Jul 2018.
10. Joe Pappalardo, Could a Chinese Junk Laser double as an anti satellite weapon, accessed from the site https://www.popularmechanics.com/military/weapons/a15338238/china-space-junk-laser-weapon-potential/ on 21 Feb 2018.
11. Loro Horta, The Dragon's Spear: China's Asymmetric Strategy Thursday, October 17, 2013 Yale, Global Online, accessed from the site https://yaleglobal.yale.edu/ content/dragons-spear-chinas-asymmetric-strategy on 14 Feb 2018.
12. Rajat Pandit, DRDO also aims to build shield for space assets, India planning star wars arsenal, Times of India, 07 Apr 2019.
13. "First Squadron of JF-17 Thunder inducted in PAF | Air Force News at DefenseTalk". Defencetalk.com. 18 Feb 2010. http://www.defencetalk.com/first-squadron-jf-17-thunder-inducted-in-pakistan-airforce-24275/. Accessed on 10 Aug 2010.
14. "Asia-Pacific - Pakistan in Chinese fighter jet deal" Ft.com. 2009-11-10. http://www.ft.com/ cms/s/0/c42d66b0-cdd0-11de-95e7-00144feabdc0.html?nclick_check=1. Retrieved on 2010-08-10.
15. defpro.com, Pakistan buys military jets, The Muslim Observer, 21 Jan 2010, accessed from the site http://muslimmedianetwork.com/mmn/?tag=indian-air-force on 28 Jan 2011.
16. Gp Capt B Menon, Pakistan Air Force Today, Implications For India, Military and Aerospace, Vpl 30.4, Oct-Dec 2015, Apr 2016, accessed from the site http://www.indiandefencereview.com/news/pakistan-air-force-today-implications-for-india/ on 23 Dec 2018.
17. List of Pakistani Air Force Aircraft, accessed from the site https://en.wikipedia.org/wiki/List_of_active_ Pakistan_Air_Force_aircraft on 15 Sep 2019.
18. Update: Pakistan Unmanned Aerial Vehicles, Quwa, September 15, 2019, accessed from the site https://quwa.org/2018/08/03/update-pakistan-unmanned-aerial-vehicle-uav-program-2/ on 15 Sep 2019.
19. Usman Ansari, Government report reveals Pakistan progress on military acquisitions and financial woes, Asia Pacific, accessed from the site https://www.defensenews.com/global/asia-pacific/2019/09/19/government-report-

reveals-pakistans-progress-on-military-acquisitions-amid-financial-woes/ on 12 Jan 2019.

20. Ambuj Sahu, Analysing the trends in China-Pakistan arms transfer, 14 Jun 2019, accessed from the site https://www.orfonline.org/expert-speak/analysing-trends-arms-transfer-china-pakistan/ on 10 Sep 2019.
21. Snehesh H Phillip, Inside Story of Attack on Balakot, From IAF Officer Who Planned and Executed it, accessed from the site https://theprint.in/defence/inside-story-of-attack-on-balakot-from-iaf-officer-who-planned-and-executed-it/370972/ on 19 Mar 2020.
22. Satyajeet Kumar, Can Superpowers deny India Hypersonic missiles, accessed from the site http:// idrw.org/can-superpowers-deny-india-hypersonic-missiles/ on 02 Mar 2018.
23. Note 13.
24. Meinhaj Hussain, Analysis of the PAF Vs IAF-Air Combat over the sub-continent, accessed from the site http://www.grandestrategy.com/2009/01/48392928192analysis-of-paf-vs-iaf-air.html on 28 Jan 2011.
25. Vivek Raghuvanshi. India to Launch A Defense-Based Space Research Agency, accessed from the site https://www.defensenews.com/space/2019/06/12/india-to-launch-a-defense-based-space-research-agency/ on 22 Feb 2020.
26. The information is accessed from the site Wikipedia https://en.wikipedia.org/wiki/Defence_Space_Agency Wikipedia on 22 Feb 2020.
27. India-USA, Will US Extend the Ballistic Missile shield to India? The Times of India, 09 Jan 2009, Nuclear Security: A Fortnightly News letter From CAPS Vol: 3, No.6 Jan 15, 2009, pp19.
28. "Missile shield heading for completion," The Statesman (India), 12 February 2005; in Lexis-Nexis Academic Universe, 12 February 2005, web.lexis-nexis.com.
29. "India unveils new indigenous anti-.missile system", "India acquires anti-missile capability," PTI News Agency (New Delhi), 27 November 2006; in Lexis-Nexis Academic Universe, web. lexis-nexis.com on 12 Jan 2010.
30. David Axe, America's Stealth Drone Fighter is Back:XQ-58 Valkyrie Makes a Second Test Flight accessed from the site https://nationalinterest.org/blog/buzz/americas-stealthy-drone-fighter-back-xq-58-valkyrie-makes-2nd-test-flight-66321 on 29 Sep 2019.
31. Michael Abrams, Top 5 Aerospace Trends of Now and the Future, accessed from the site http://www.asme.org/ engineering-topics/articles/aerospace-defense/top-5-aerospace-trends-now-future on 24 Feb 2018.
32. Engineeringpro, The top 5 Aerospace Trends to Watch, accessed from the site https://www.fircroft.com/blogs/ the-top-5-aerospace-trends-to-watch-71011112263 on 24 Feb 2018.
33. Gp Capt AK Sachdev, "Advances in Technology", *Indian Defence Review*, Lancer Publishers, New Delhi, Jul-Sep 2017, Vol 32(3), pp 16.
34. Lorenzo J. Burleson, X-47b Hoisted Onto The USS Truman, Accessed From The Site https://Www.Popsci.Com/ How-Next-Generation-Drones-Could-Reshape-Future-War On 24 Feb 2018.
35. X-45 Unmanned Combat Aerial Vehicle, accessed from the site https://fas.org/man/dod-101/sys/ac/ucav.htm on 24 Feb 2018.
36. This information is obtained from a site http://indianairforce.nic.in/

show_page.php?pg_id=13 on 30 Aug 2012. Title of the article is Indian Air Force Today.

37. Vivek Raghuvanshi, Indian Air Force launches new effort to ramp up Jaguar Fleet, accessed from the site https://www.defensenews.com/air/2018/07/26/indian-air-force-launches-new-effort-to-revamp-jaguar-fleet/ on 26 Dec 2018.
38. This information has been based on the RFI issued by the Indian Air Force to procure 110 single/twin engine aircraft accessed from the site http://indianairforce.nic.in/sites/default/files/RFI_Fighter_Aircraft.pdf on 28 Dec 2018.
39. Air Marshal VK Bhatia (Retd), IAF's Modernisation A review (2015-2017), accessed from the site http://www.indiastrategic.in/2017/03/05/iafs-modernisation-a-review-2015-17/ on 26 Dec 2018.
40. Sanjay Bhadri Maharaj, The Indian Air Forces' Declinging Squadron – Options and Challenges, accessed from the site https://idsa.in/issuebrief/the-indian-air-force-declining-squadron-strength_sbmaharaj_031117 on 27 Dec 2018
41. Rafale, S-400 missiles necessary to boost India's defence capabilities: Air Force Chief BSDhanoa, HT Correspondent, accessed from the site https://www.hindustantimes.com/india-news/rafale-s-400-missiles-necessary-to-boost-india-s-defence-capabilities-air-force-chief-bs-dhanoa/story-mrAoW2iRLbJap9Jw ESX0mJ.html on 19 Dec 2018.
42. Air Chief Marshal PV Naik, Indian Air Force, Future of Aerospace Power, accessed from the site https://www.indiastrategic.in/topstories3546_Future_of_Aerospace_Power.htm on 26 Feb 2020.

12

The Two-Front Dilemma

Lieutenant General AK Singh and Lieutenant General DS Hooda

General

The classic two-front war was last fought during World War II, with Germany taking on its adversaries both on the eastern and western fronts, as also in out of area theatres like North Africa, etc. The overall German strategy was to deal with one adversary at a time, and in the initial stages, this strategy worked to plan. Later, with the entry of the USA and the great resilience shown by the Soviet Union and the UK, the Germans were forced to fight on both fronts, which led to their ultimate defeat. Soon after its birth, Israel was also faced with a 360 degree challenge, but the scope and intensity were confined. However, over the decades, Israel was able to deal with this challenge using a combination of force and diplomacy, secure with the unqualified backing of the USA.

Today India is faced with two neighbours, Pakistan (Pak) in the west and China in the north and east, with whom there are border disputes. While India has faced three major and one limited conflict with Pak, apart from an ongoing proxy war, it has fought a major war with China in 1962 and faced numerous border provocations/incidents, some of them being major confrontations like the Nathu La incident of 1967 and the ongoing confrontation in Ladakh in 2020. In none of these conflicts did we face a two-front dilemma, though this was a major consideration for choosing the timing of the 1971 war with Pak, which resulted in the creation of Bangladesh.

So, why has the two-front dilemma become relevant and come to the fore in the 21st Century? One reason for this is the increasing danger of a military conflict with a resurgent China, which could then lead to a wider conflagration along both borders. The Indian military has looked towards China as the bigger military threat, while considering the chances of a war with China as being comparatively low. Although the border was unsettled, various agreements ensured calm along the borders, and deep economic and political engagement kept tensions at bay. It is not as though the two-front dilemma has emerged out of the blue and has only been realized now. Over a decade ago in 2008, both the authors (posted in Perspective Planning & Military Operations Directorates of Army HQ, respectively) were primarily responsible for highlighting this emerging challenge and threat very candidly to the hierarchy. In a high-powered and detailed presentation where the Raksha Mantri, the Service Chiefs, and the Foreign Secretary were present, the likelihood of a two-front threat manifesting within a decade was clearly highlighted and accepted. This formed the basis for the sanction and raising of additional forces for the China Front, including the Mountain Strike Corps, which was later truncated. Unfortunately, instead of turning our focus towards China, we continued to find comfort in dealing with Pak, with serious ramifications as are evident today.

With the massive Chinese intrusions into Eastern Ladakh in May 2020, all established agreements and protocols have been brought to naught, and a conventional conflict with China is now looking like a real possibility. Even if the current India-China crisis on the border is resolved peacefully, the Chinese threat will remain a clear danger and occupy greater attention of Indian military planners. This comes at a time when the situation along the Line of Control (LC) with Pakistan has been deteriorating over the past few years. Between 2017 and 2019, there has been an almost four-fold increase in ceasefire violations.[1] Some media reports had indicated that Pakistan had moved 20,000 troops into Gilgit-Baltistan, matching the Chinese deployments in Eastern Ladakh.[2]

In such an environment, it would be pragmatic and desirable to carry out an objective analysis of the two-front challenge, its likely manifestation, and thereafter outline a philosophy for combating this threat. This would also provide clarity for devising a capability development strategy for a focused and optimised utilisation of scarce financial resources.

Likely Two-Front Scenarios

Though India is a peace-loving nation, it has to be prepared to face possible military contingencies in the future. An India-Pakistan conflict would most probably be the result of a major act of terrorism in India that has the direct imprint of Pakistan-based groups. The conflict would unfold with a series of escalatory actions following the Indian military response to the terror attack and Pak's counteractions. This could ultimately lead to a limited or full-scale war.

In this scenario, India would have international opinion on its side, and it is unlikely that China, conscious of its image as a responsible power, will initiate active military hostilities in support of Pakistan. However, we could see an increase in LAC intrusions, induction of additional ground and air assets in Tibet, increased PLA Navy presence in the Indian Ocean, as also supply of urgently needed military hardware to Pak. This could tie down some Indian military assets from moving to the Pak front, but with India's conventional edge, there would not be a significant impact on the final outcome of the conflict. India has the requisite superiority in force capabilities and other critical tangibles and intangibles to achieve its politico-military objectives against Pak, whilst holding a robust defensive posture against China. The problem with most analysts is that whilst focusing on India's shortfalls, they tend to grant optimum preparation and capabilities to the adversary.

A war between India and China will, in most cases, be initiated by China, and its strategic aim will shape the character of the conflict. If the idea is to teach India a sharp lesson, the conflict could be geographically limited to a specific area or sector. If there is a larger geopolitical objective, the PLA could launch a more extensive air, land, and sea campaign.

In case of a major India-China conflict, Pakistan could be tempted to take advantage of the Indian military's commitment along the northern borders. It could undertake limited operations along the disputed Line of Control in Jammu and Kashmir (J&K) and Ladakh to improve its positions and bring international attention to Kashmir.

Thus, a two-front dilemma is a possibility that cannot be dismissed lightly; therefore, prudence demands that we have at least the minimum safeguards against such a collusive threat. This would be the best way to deter and prevent such a threat from taking shape. Three other issues are also relevant:

- It is generally understood that diplomacy is the art of possibilities and probabilities; it would always be our endeavour to contain one front diplomatically, but it cannot be guaranteed. No nation can depend entirely on diplomacy alone to safeguard its vital security interests and must have the hard power to fall back on.
- India is currently not a part of any military alliance/grouping and hence has to possess independent capabilities to meet its security requirements. This is a clear lesson from history, which we can ignore only at our own peril.
- The growing collaboration of China and Pak, reflected in arms supplies, China Pakistan Economic Corridor (CPEC), and Gwadar port point to a de-facto military alliance status between the two countries.

The Additional Half Front

While the other two Services refer to a two-front threat, the army often talks of a two-and-a-half front war.[3] The additional half front refers to the army's commitments in the ongoing internal security operations in J&K and the North Eastern states. It must be clearly stated here that the primary task of the army is to deal with external threats, and in the contingency of a war on either or both fronts, the responsibility for internal security will be completely handed over to the Central Armed Police Force. The deployment of the army in depth areas, if at all, will only be to secure and protect important road axes for unhindered movement of reserves and logistics.

A realistic assessment of the current state of insurgencies indicates that a temporary pull out of the army from internal security is unlikely to result in any significant rise in militancy or violence. It is perhaps time that we stop talking of the half front as a threat that would require allocation of resources that are in addition to those fighting along the border. Not only would this be a drain on the existing capability, but it would also weaken the single-minded focus on the external enemy.

Threat Manifestation from China

The India–China standoff at Dokala in 2017 was a strong wake-up call to Indian strategic planners to change tack vis-à-vis its policy of dealing with China. The recent transgressions and clashes (in fact, a silent Chinese aggression) in Eastern Ladakh should have removed any remaining doubts of Chinese duplicity and aggressive intent towards India. It is now more than obvious that in geostrategic terms, while Pak may continue to be an immediate irritant, China is the major long-term challenge and threat to not only India's security but also to India's rise in Asia and in world affairs. The "Two-front challenge" in our view is already an existing reality, whether or not it manifests in an all-out conflict.

What about the nature of the contest with China? Will China risk its ascendance on the global stage by resorting to a major conflict with India, especially after being surprised by the tough Indian posture and reaction, after some initial hesitation, in Ladakh. The Indian Armed Forces have come a long way from 1962, and even though China may have a technological edge, the contest will be fierce, and the outcome uncertain.

A more likely scenario is of China deftly weaving force into its statecraft to aggressively pursue its interests and constrict India's geostrategic space,[4] through skilful leveraging, particularly in the non-kinetic and non-contact domains, a glimpse of which we saw in Dokala in 2017, and a more brazen manifestation in Ladakh in 2020.

The Chinese challenge is an all-encompassing one, covering the geostrategic, economic, diplomatic, technological, informational and, most important, the military realm, coalescing into a very formidable threat. This needs a whole—of-nation approach to checkmate it. As this chapter is focused on the military challenge, some pointers are discussed below. The professional ethos and ethics of the Indian military drive it towards delivery and excellence in the kinetic domain. However, any future conflict with China is more likely to encompass allied domains such as the non-contact, non-kinetic, informational, cyber, and space, optimized by innovation in emerging and disruptive technologies like artificial intelligence and unmanned weapon systems, especially swarm drones and directed energy weapons. Quantum technology leadership will give China an advantage in offensive Intelligence operations and encryption. China thus seems poised to seize the initiative of technological innovation in the military domain.[5]

With the character of conflict changing so rapidly, we need to be prepared for this challenge and build our capacities in these domains to a level where we are not disadvantaged or surprised. There are other posers, too, that demand answers. Are we prepared for tackling the Chinese Anti-Access Area Denial (A2AD) strategy or their large number of non-nuclear missiles, which in combination with a massive cyber attack, could cripple military infrastructure and facilities up to a great depth? In the absence of a viable response option in the non-kinetic, non-contact domain, will a ground and air escalation be our only answer?

Therefore, developing layered intertwined military response options within a carefully thought out escalatory frame is something that we need to attend with dispatch.[6]

Collusive and Collaborative Threat

'Collusive threat' from China and Pakistan to India implies both countries are acting covertly to achieve a fraudulent, illegal, or deceitful goal. 'Collaborative threat' implies a joint threat, covering both overt and covert actions against India.[7] It can be summarised, therefore, that India faces both a collusive and a collaborative threat from China and Pak.

China and Pakistan have close collaboration in multiple projects in Gilgit–Baltistan and POK under the ambit of CPEC, and most of these projects have military usability. There is also a high degree of interoperability between the two defence forces based on the large commonality of equipment, shared infrastructure, communications, frequent joint training, and shared interests. This is the edifice on which the collaborative threat is built against India.

In a China-led scenario, Pakistan is likely to take advantage of India's focus on its northern borders. While many options are open for Pakistan, the collusive and collaborative threat is optimally manifested across the LC in J&K. In contemplating a J&K and Ladakh-centric two-front war, with two diverse but colluding adversaries, strategic geography matters immensely in addition to the intent, war fighting capabilities, and military strategy. The strategic geography has vast variations from rivers, low hills, high altitude mountains, glacial regions, and the super high-altitude cold desert of Eastern Ladakh.

In Ladakh, India retains a strong wedge of the Saltoro range–Siachen glacier and the sub-sector north of Eastern Ladakh (the Shyok river valley and the super high-altitude reaches of the Karakoram range and the Depsang plains) that deny a direct connect between China and Pak. While war fighting has transcended to domains of cyber, space, precision-guided long-range missiles, and unmanned aerial vehicles, territorial contests have and will always remain contingent upon diktats of geography, vagaries of the terrain, and of course, military capabilities adapted to such an area of conflict.

Though a collaborative threat can take place in diverse areas in J&K and Ladakh, Siachen and the Shaksgam Valley are the two places where the territories of our adversaries converge. If a shooting match starts between India and China, the Pakistanis will be greatly tempted to jump into the fray, probably goaded by China, hoping to catch India in a pincer and make territorial gains.

The Indian Armed Forces have a vast and unmatched experience of operating in such hostile terrain, including the Siachen glacier. The tiered defensive layout, quantum of direct and indirect firepower available, the adequacy of reserves for defensive and offensive plans, and integrated air operations have been well-honed for such a two-front contingency. Without unnecessary bravado, in matters of territorial wars in J&K and Ladakh, the Indian Armed Forces have the requisite capabilities and the resolve to prosecute war fighting to their adversaries' detriment. However, the Indian strategy must not become completely defensive and be capable of selective offensives across the border. The Indian Armed Forces also have to focus on improving their capabilities in the emerging technological and allied domains, which are beginning to dominate war fighting in the 21st century.

Philosophy for Combating a Two-Front Scenario

The best way to deter war is to be prepared for it. However, if deterrence fails and war is thrust upon us, the Nation must have the requisite force capabilities for favourable outcomes. Before we start talking about capability, it must be clearly understood that a war is fought for political outcomes. The absence of a political aim in the military's strategic planning will result in a doctrine that may not stand scrutiny when the political leadership has to actually issue directions for employment of military force in pursuit of its political aims.

As an example, it would be instructive to look at the official strategy of the Israel Defence Forces (IDF) issued in 2015, which states:

"When the political echelon finds it must use the army it should draft the guidelines as follows:

- What are the goals and strategic conditions necessary to end the conflict?

- What is the role of the IDF and how is it integrated into achieving these goals?
- In what contingencies would force be employed?
- Defining the additional efforts (political, economic, media, social) and IDF's role in relation to them."

War is not the business of the Armed Forces alone but will always be a national effort of multiple instruments of the state and support of the people. Diplomacy would play a crucial role in not only preventing a two-front threat manifestation but also shaping world opinion in our favour. The military and diplomacy should work in unison to create a favourable climate. The government must be fully involved in the strategic planning so that a comprehensive politico-military strategy can be adopted. A good start can be made if the government sheds its reticence and comes out with a comprehensive National Security Strategy.

In crafting its strategy, the military must maintain a strategically balanced posture on both fronts, i.e., an offensive posture on the western front and an offensive-defence stance on the northern front, with suitably located reserve formations. The Air Force and Navy may feel that with their advantages, an offensive strategy can also be adopted against China. However, the reason that an offensive-defence stance has been suggested is that in most contingencies, India would not be the initiator of a full-scale war with China.

Once the manifestation of threat is clear, the military must decide on a primary front and a secondary front. Thereafter, refocus the combat capabilities on the primary front as per a pre-planned strategy and mobilisation plan. The military strategy should be to seek the desired favourable outcome on the primary front whilst effectively containing the secondary front. Inter-theatre flexibility will be the key to achieve success, based on a well-planned and rehearsed mobilisation matrix. With China's aggressive designs on display, it is also time for an ab initio rebalancing of forces that presently have a strong Pak bias. It is not just boots on the ground but other force multipliers that need rebalancing.

When we talk of a two-front threat, we are not advocating powerful, independent capabilities for each front, but what we require is a capability to fight a decisive war on the chosen primary front whilst holding the secondary front in a defensive posture. It also implies that in a conflict on the eastern/western front, the Armed Forces should be able to move a percentage of combat power from the west to the east or vice versa through the move of dual tasked reserves, which have been trained and are equipped for such a dual tasked role.

While fighting on the primary front, the military strategy and operational plans for the secondary front will have to be harmonized within the remaining combat capability available on that front. For example, if dual tasked formations are moved from west to east, military strategy for the western front will have to change from offensive to offensive defence. An entirely defensive posture on the western front could encourage Pakistan to continue and perhaps increase its attacks in J&K, and the Indian Army must retain an offensive posture in the desert, based on its superiority in mechanised forces. The above philosophy will also hold true for the Indian Air Force and Navy, each Service focusing a majority of aircraft/vessels on the primary front whilst retaining minimum required forces for the secondary front. The Air Force will, of course, be advantaged with the flexibility to switch forces as per the unfolding operational scenario, in an effective time frame, a luxury not available to the army and navy in most contingencies.

The maritime domain offers some interesting possibilities, both against Pak and China, whose Achilles' Heel lies in the Andaman Sea and the Malacca Straits. Despite the large growth of the PLA Navy, the Indian Navy has a dominant advantage both on the eastern and western seaboards. With the Andaman & Nicobar Islands akin to an unsinkable aircraft carrier, the sea lanes of communication can be disrupted, and the Malacca Straits blocked for hostile shipping. Such a course will have to be part of a well-thought out politico-military strategy, keeping in view various international norms and laws of the seas. However, in the case of an all-out conflict, India's strength in the maritime domain will play a vital role.

What Capability should India Possess

If a two-front threat is a reality, the Government needs to ensure that the military is equipped for it. A simple solution would be to state that greater military resources are required. Some experts estimate that the Indian Air Force needs 60 combat squadrons to deal with a serious two-front threat,[8] though a realistic estimate would be around 40 squadrons. The Indian Navy's perspective plan calls for a 200-ship navy by 2027; here again, a more realistic figure would be near about a 175-ship combat fleet. The

Indian Army needs a massive infusion of capital to modernize its vintage equipment,[9] and induct modern force multipliers. However, the reality is that military funding to support these highly ambitious plans has so far not been forthcoming. It defies logic as to how the defence budget has been on a continuous downslide as a percentage of our GDP, despite such a hostile environment around India. Each time there is a serious crisis, we are scurrying for emergent defence purchases. This is, in fact, a matter of serious intellectual and strategic concern.

The military must bluntly inform the political leadership that with the current levels of the budget, it would be extremely difficult to build capabilities to counter a two-front threat. However, whatever demands are made must be on the basis of a tri-service capability development plan and not some fixed percentage of the GDP. Now that the Chief of Defence Staff (CDS) is in place, a tri-service capability development plan covering the next 15 years must be drawn up. This plan must have the sanction of the Government, and matching funds should be provided. The current capability development process suffers from a mismatch between the perspective plans of the three Services and the availability of funds. If these two aspects can be aligned by the Government, it will provide a clear future path.

It is incumbent on the military leadership to do a deep introspection on the force structures, doctrines, and types of capabilities required to fight a two-front war. These capabilities must be focused on combating the more potent threat from China and would automatically enhance our war fighting ability against Pakistan.

Developing a military force development strategy to combat the PLA in a future war will require a certain realignment in the type of capabilities required. While we would prefer to fight a conventional battle along the Himalayan watershed and in the Indian Ocean, the PLA would exploit its advantages in the non-kinetic, non-contact domains. They will engage in war from afar, employing long-range missiles to target strategic locations in India's hinterland, electronic warfare to degrade the command and control networks, cyber attacks on critical infrastructure, and focus on achieving information dominance. Physical battles on land and sea, and in the air would be fought for control of territory/domain, but these could be limited in scope.

After the Chinese intrusions in Ladakh, there are calls to recommence the raising of the Mountain Strike Corps.[10] However, we need to balance the cost of adding more manpower along the LAC against the building of other essential capabilities.

The CDS, of course, as per mandate, will have a major say in inter-Services prioritization of the defence budget for capital acquisition. The best way is to scrutinize all big-ticket items and see how they fit into the joint war fighting doctrine/plans while keeping in view the effect it will have on prolonged committed liabilities. The CDS has his task cut out. [11]

Organisational Restructuring

The CDS has put in motion a plan for creating joint structures and ensuring integration in defence strategy. The raising of integrated theatre commands must be carried out after a thorough review and as part of an overall plan for restructuring in the three Services. Piecemeal raisings, starting with those that appear to be a "low-hanging fruit", could prevent or delay the adoption of a holistic restructuring plan. Some suggestions for restructuring (including five integrated theatres) based on the military threat that India is confronted with are enumerated below:

Create two integrated theatres, one each for the Northern and Eastern borders. There have been some suggestions to have a single theatre to deal with China, but with our current state of surveillance and command and control networks, exercising battle control over the entire Northern and Eastern borders by one theatre may not be feasible. The Northern Theatre should cover the LC along the Pak border in the hills and mountains and the China border in Ladakh, Himachal Pradesh and Uttarakhand, with reserves suitably located to react in an acceptable time frame. The Eastern Theatre should cover Sikkim and Arunachal Pradesh along with a Bhutan contingency. The Indian Air Force (IAF) can integrate an air command with each of the theatres, the Western Theatre covering the riverine terrain and the semi-desert and desert areas should focus on Pak, supported by an air command. There is a strong case to restructure the three army commands facing Pak across the international border into two, with suitable readjustment with some restructuring in the existing air commands.

- A Maritime Theatre covering both Western and Eastern Naval Commands, as also Andaman Nicobar Command (ANC), suitably supported by an air command and amphibious forces from the army will greatly optimise our maritime capability. Two separate maritime theatres for the eastern and western seaboards could also be considered, keeping in view the vast span of control.

- Similarly, an Aerospace and Air Defence (AD) Theatre, with the bulk of the AD assets of the Air Force and the Army under it, should assume overall responsibility for the air defence of the country. A portion of aircraft assets should also be grouped under it as reserves to provide the requisite flexibility. For out-of-area contingencies, both the above theatres should be mandated.
- Enhance the Defence Cyber Agency to a full-fledged Cyber Command capable of deterrence and offensive operations in the field of cyber and information warfare.
- Carry out a review of the role of Special Forces with a focus on operations across our borders. The simmering discontent in Tibet can be exploited in war, provided preparations are made in advance. A similar situation also exists in many areas across the border in Pakistan.

Capability Development

Our disproportionate reliance on manpower and major weapon platforms should be replaced by capabilities that maximise our geographical advantage and neutralise China's technological superiority in non-contact warfare.

- All the three Services must look at technology enhancement in the area of robotics, networked unmanned systems (including armed ones), artificial intelligence, surveillance, and command and control.
- There must be greater investment in electronic warfare, cyber, and space as these are the realms in which future wars will be fought. If we are unable to neutralise our adversary's advantages in these areas, the battle will become very challenging.
- India's Intelligence shortfalls are well known. There must be a strengthening of both technical and human intelligence capability across both borders. Turf considerations should be ruthlessly curbed.
- Maritime domain awareness in the Indian Ocean must be further improved, coupled with long-range precision strikes capability by air and naval assets along with anti-submarine warfare capability.

- The Indian Navy should also carry out a realistic debate on whether it wants to invest more in an undersea capability rather than surface vessels, including carrier groups. Cost-effectiveness would be an important criterion.
- The requirement of the IAF to build up to a strength of 40 fighter quadrons could be reviewed in the light of the acquisition of sophisticated aircraft and air defence systems. Unmanned aerial platforms are likely to revolutionise future warfare, that too at a fraction of the cost of $4^{th}/5^{th}$ generation aircraft. A deeper analysis is necessary to find the right mix.[12]
- Strategic and tactical lift capability must be enhanced. The ability to quickly move troops between theatres could lessen the requirement to ab initio deploy a large number of forces on the ground. This could ultimately lead to an overall reduction of manpower in the Indian Army without compromising on the ability to fight a two-front war.
- The Indian Army should improve its battle awareness and lethality by downsizing and diverting the funds saved towards up-gradation and modernization of existing platforms vis a vis new purchases. The Army must retain its edge in fighting a manoeuvre battle in the plains and deserts along the western front.
- The military should also develop the capability to counter China's conventional missile threat. This will require a building of both missile defence and an offensive arsenal comprising short and medium-range ballistic missiles. The Strategic Forces Command could be suitably reorganised and tasked for this purpose, in addition to its existing charter.

Nuclear Stance

There is also a view that in case faced with a two-front threat, India should jettison its "No First Use" doctrine to thus deter the adversaries from colluding and exploiting the situation. Such a postulation is debatable since nuclear weapons have not proven to be a fail-safe deterrence against limited conventional/sub-conventional threat. This aspect requires greater debate and deliberation and will have grave risks if adopted as an alternative to conventional capabilities.

It is also a fact that India's war fighting doctrine appears to completely ignore the fact that a two-front war will be fought between three nuclear-armed countries. There should be a deeper study of nuclear deterrence and escalation control, as also its impact on military strategy.

Conclusion

The Indian Armed Forces are neither eager nor planning to fight a two-front war, i.e., major conflicts on both our flanks simultaneously. But being the last resort of the nation, they have to be prepared for even this worst-case remote possibility. The three Services are conscious of this, and contingency plans would exist in case the nation is faced with such an extreme threat. The operational preparedness of the Armed Forces is an ongoing process, based on long term integrated perspective plans of the Services. Whilst shortfalls would always exist, it should be the endeavour of each Service always to maintain the minimum levels, while they strive to build the optimum. Requisite planning and operational preparedness, along with tri-service synergy, will be the key to success and victory. However, there will be a need to review doctrine and capability development strategy, supported by an adequate defence budget.

The Nation can surely rely on its Armed Forces to deliver when the call comes.

NOTES

1. Mint. "3,200 Ceasefire Violations: LoC Hostilities with Pak Doubled in 2019 from 2018," December 28, 2019. https://www.livemint.com/news/india/3-200-ceasefire-violations-loc-hostilities-with-pak-doubled-in-2019-from-2018-11577475445771.html
2. https://economictimes.indiatimes.com/news/defence/pakistan-moves-20000-soldiers-to-gilgit-baltistan-loc/articleshow/76718059.cms
3. "Army Prepared for Two and a Half Front War: Gen Rawat." *The Hindu*, June 8, 2017, sec. National. https://www.thehindu.com/news/national/army-prepared-for-two-and-a-half-front-war-gen-rawat/article18867921.ece
4. Changing Nature of conflict in the 21st Century by Lt Gen A. K. Singh and Lt Gen Raj Shukla, pg 32 in the book, *Military Strategy for India in the 21st Century*, KW Publishers Pvt Ltd., New Delhi, 2019.
5. www.canada.ca; Chinese military innovation in emerging technologies.
6. *Military Strategy for India in the 21st Century*, p. 36.
7. 30th USI National Security lecture by Gen V. P. Malik, delivered at USI, New Delhi on 3, December, 2014.
8. Tellis, Ashley J. "Troubles, They Come in Battalions: The Manifold Travails of the IAF - Carnegie Endowment for International Peace." Accessed March 28, 2020. https://carnegieendowment.org/2016/03/28/troubles-they-come-in-battalions-manifold-travails-of-indian-air-force-pub-63123.
9. "68 per Cent of Army's Equipment Is in Vintage Category - Rediff.Com India News." Accessed March 29, 2020. https://www.rediff.com/news/report/sixty-eight-per-cent-

of-armys-equipment-is-in-vintage-category/20180313.htm.

10. Bhatia, Vinod, and Ahuja, Anil. "Revisiting Mountain Corps to Deter China." Tribune India News Service. Accessed August 16, 2020. https://www.tribuneindia.com/news/comment/revisiting-mountain-corps-to-deter-china-100707
11. Appointment of Chief of Defence Staff.....A Game Changer, *CLAWS Journal*, Summer 2020.
12. Ibid.

13

Ever-increasing Span of Intelligence Operations

Lieutenant General Dushyant Singh Chauhan

"We stand at the cusp of a new era in military operations in which the speed of information, advancements in technology, networking of our organizations and mind-set of our people will directly shape the success or failure of our intelligence and military operations. These technologies and challenges have trumped the buffer of geography that historically afforded us the luxury of time to think and act, demanding that we alter our farmer-culture mind-set and begin to act more like hunters."[1]

—Lt Gen David A. Deptula, USAF

ABSTRACT

It is perceived that Intelligence retains a degree of mystique, if not a sense of surrealism. It is not just the story of spies and sources that often appear to be a jigsaw puzzle. It is the sum total of knowledge about geo-political, economic and military trends about our adversaries and has relevance all across the world. Future conflicts would be dynamic in nature and military operations will be executed in cyber, aero and maritime space, including land, air and the information spectrum. The wars will be fought in strategic, operational and tactical domains simultaneously or near simultaneously. The intelligence operations will be shifting to electronic, AI, big data and, last but not the least, human resource. Intelligence requirement for all the above domains is different in nature and scope. The response time is reducing and the speed of operations is increasing, hence the need to provide timely and actionable intelligence. Thus, the concept and doctrine of intelligence operations for the future will be quite different from the current methodology. The focus would be on integration of technology with the human resource. The future threat scenarios will be network-centric and hybrid in nature which will pose challenges to national security, such that which have never been experienced in the past. The access to improved surveillance platforms and space-based technology as also AI and robotics has opened new avenues and areas of research. This has led us to believe that organisational reforms of Intelligence architecture could be undertaken in the near future. This chapter analyses the ever-increasing span of intelligence operations and the potential to harness the latest technology in planning and executing intelligence challenges.

Broad Overview. Future conflicts are dynamic in nature and military operations will be undertaken in cyber, space, maritime, land, air and information domain. The war will be fought in strategic, operational and tactical domains simultaneously or near simultaneously. The intelligence operations will be shifting to electronic, Artificial Intelligence (AI), big data and, last but not the least, human resource. The Intelligence requirement for all seven domains is different in nature and scope. Response time is reducing and speed of operations is increasing, hence the need to provide timely and actionable intelligence.

Intelligence Dilemma. Today, the intelligence problem is that you may not know you are under attack, who is attacking, what he is attacking and how he is attacking. To decipher such attacks, you require intelligence of a different nature. The OODA loop of the classical intelligence process comprising collection, analysis, processing and dissemination has been shortened and become more complex. Intelligence Inputs and Critical Vulnerabilities are still processed and analysed; however, the fusion of technologies like surveillance, use of satellites and AI has led to a transformation in the development of capabilities, thereby delivering information swiftly.

The process of the synthesis, analysis and collation of intelligence is cumbersome, long and tedious. The introduction of planning processes like the Joint Operational Planning Process (JOPP)[2] provides a platform for integration of all services and agencies to achieve better synergy at the tactical and operational levels and simultaneously work on synthesis of intelligence. The Mission Analysis Step lays down the 'Joint Intelligence Preparation of the Operational Environment' (JIPOE). Decision-makers are able to identify critical information requirements and the Essential Elements of Information, which are key to the planning of the operation and are updated throughout the planning process.

Doctrinal Changes

Doctrine and Concept of Intelligence for Future Conflict. There is a desperate need of doctrinal clarity amongst the decision-makers of any country. They need to be sensitized about the type and variety of threats that may emerge which the country may have to face in the future and the role that Intelligence will play in mitigation of these threats. Thus, the concept and doctrine of intelligence operations for future conflicts will be completely different from the current requirement. The focus would be on integration of technology with human resource (digital, cyber, AI and big data mining). In order however, to harness technology, one has to develop capabilities. Let us take the example of China. It has the best possible SIGINT capability in the Asia-Pacific with the country having access to a wide range of satellites for imagery and surveillance, amongst many other uses. Recently, China has launched the Yaogan Military Satellites for remote sensing and electromagnetic environment detection, primarily known to be for intelligence-gathering purposes. At any time, China has in place at least 16 satellites which are together able to monitor military activities in any part of the world in near real time. China is fielding these satellites with sensors that have capabilities of Electro Optical (EO), Synthetic Aperture Radar (SAR), Electronic Intelligence (ELINT) and also provide imagery.

India presently has very few military satellites, which is grossly inadequate as compared to the 40 or so civilian ones and needs to be upgraded. Our first military satellite was launched in 2013,[3] and hence it is time to rethink our approach in this field. In addition to satellite imagery, high-quality Image Intelligence (IMINT) would be required for target identification or Post-Strike Damage Assessment, as was the need after the surgical strikes and the Balakot raid. There is also a need for better aerial surveillance by UAVs or drones that have a greater endurance and provide better battlefield transparency. The integration of surveillance resources and all-weather electro-optical sensors need to be state-of-the-art for any modern defence force. Further, in order to effectively transmit info from the sensors, the communication infrastructure needs to be improved with advanced media, greater bandwidth and faster data transmission. India also has to develop capabilities of AI and Robotics, which at present is at the research stage. India is accelerating plans to develop air launched swarm drones system designed to attack enemy air defence systems.

Intelligence, Surveillance, and Reconnaissance (ISR). Conceptually, unless there is a wider understanding of intelligence as a function of ISR, the seamless transmission of real-time intelligence will be a challenge. A nation needs to address the issue of ISR as a whole and not consider it as just a tactical or sub-tactical requirement of the armed forces. Effective employment of resources in today's complex and time-dominated operating environment is more critical than ever before. The US Department of Defence defines ISR[4] as, *"an activity that synchronizes and integrates the planning and operations of sensors, assets, processing, exploitation, and dissemination systems in direct support of current and future operations. It is an integrated intelligence operations function."*

Strategic Intelligence.[5] Strategic Intelligence is required for formation of policy and creating requisite capability to guard against dents in national interests. Such intelligence would encompass political assessments and intentions of hostile states, inclusive of their stated or hidden agenda and hence indulgence in proxy wars and utilisation of non-state actors as an instrument of state policy. It would guard against damage to economic interests (The drone attack on the Saudi oil facility is a case in point). It would include intelligence on scientific, technical, spatial and military capability in all four dimensions, with geographical and demographic or religious aspects being factored in, in addition to industrial capability/ capacity. It would also include relationships and support for the enemy state from other countries and the likelihood of their tacit support in capability enhancement and a favourable stance in international forums. ***In the war against Iraq, in 2003 (Operation Iraqi Freedom), the US Strategic Intelligence was extremely poor. Knowledge of the true picture of Iraq's state of weapons of mass destruction proved to be off the mark and the subsequent post invasion phase had devastating consequences.***

At the operational level, deployment of sensors, sharing of intelligence across all services and the transmission of real-time intelligence continues to be an area of concern. The recent Balakot Operation and the subsequent escalation led us to witness the importance of ISR and an intelligence mechanism in the escalatory continuum. Two incidents took place recently; The Mi-17 helicopter crash on 27 February 2019 and an AN-32 that went missing in Arunachal Pradesh and was not located for 8 days. These incidents tell the story for the need of an integrated battle space picture and better Intelligence Surveillance, Target Acquisition and Reconnaissance

(ISTAR). The deployment of drones by the adversary into our air space is a new challenge, which requires anti-Drone Technology (response).

Intelligence Reforms. In order to understand the functioning of intelligence agencies, certain principles need to be followed such as a formal act of legislation, working as per a charter and accountability and performance judgement by an oversight committee. After the Kargil War, on 23 February 2000, the Kargil Review Committee (KRC) laid down recommendations for the intelligence set-up in India, post the Kargil conflict that led to some valuable lessons. Some of these have been discussed later. In 1996, the US Government published the Les Aspen and Brown Commission[6] on US Intelligence reforms that brought in various regulations and recommendations for funding, control, covert operations and precautions against agents being compromised by the KGB. The commission laid down mechanisms for collecting intelligence in a cost-effective manner, operational security (OPSEC), checks and balances for agents and reporting. Intelligence the world over struggled with the civil vs military divide, balance between strategic vs tactical intelligence and assessment vs policy-making decisions.

Nature and Character of Intelligence

Domain Specific Intelligence. Each domain would require different or diverse intelligence. A cyber war would require AI and more of machine tools. The world's first digital weapon such as Stuxnet[7] to disable and disrupt the Iranian nuclear enrichment process will be unleashed more often. Intelligence requirement to employ Stuxnet was different from employment of long-range missiles or any other strategic weapon.

Multi-domain operations would require intelligence to execute disruptive, disabling and destruction of military and non-military targets. Similarly, intelligence for defensive and offensive operations will be completely different from the current milieu. The nature of intelligence would range from surveillance of targets to/post-strike capture of videos or pictures. The next gen precision-guided munitions like the Israeli Spice-2000[8] have inbuilt cameras to capture a precision strike with the ability to relay live streaming of attacks. Let us analyse the changing perspective in each domain and the scope for the future.

Maritime Domain Awareness (MDA). Sea Power as explained by Geoffrey Till in his book *'Sea Power–A Guide for the 21st Century'*[9] brings out that 'Sea Power' constitutes primarily four attributes of the sea which are resources, medium of transport, information, and seas as a medium of dominion. The control of seas would only be possible for a nation with a modern navy and with assets to dominate the strategic Sea Lines of Communication (SLOCs), important choke points and straits like the 'Strait of Mallaca'. The rise of India in the Indian Ocean Region (IOR) has an increasing commercial, cultural and strategic role for the region as a whole. The vast threat of piracy, trafficking, narcotics, gun-running and illegal fishing as also the threat to the coast from terrorism requires an effective intelligence grid. Surveillance of the high seas and the EEZ has to be done concurrently from space with Maritime Surveillance (MR) aircraft like the P-8I or P-3C Orion, drones, coastal and offshore radars. Post 26/11, various tracking mechanisms like Vessel Traffic Movement system (VTMS), AIS, and GPS aided–trackers, are being coordinated by the Joint Operations Centre (JOC), which has been set up across the country to monitor the coastal threat in India. India has also set up the Information Fusion Centre–Indian Ocean Region[10] (IFC-IOR) to monitor the Indian Ocean coastline by a single-point mechanism for interlinking all coastal radar chains to generate a seamless real-time picture of 7,500 km of coastline. In addition to the above, Information Management and Analysis Centres (IMAC) have been established for coastal surveillance and security against a 26/11 type terror attack. There is however wide scope to address the voids in the existing system and improve the MDA.

Aerospace Domain. Recent conflicts have demonstrated that aerospace power plays an important role in building the ISR for undertaking any kind of mission. Induction of Force Multipliers (FMs) like Airborne Warning and Control Systems (AWAACS), Intelligence Surveillance Targeting and Reconnaissance (ISTAR), Airborne Early Warning (AEW), S-400 AD missiles, UAVs, Reconnaissance Helicopters, all provide key intelligence for operations. Induction of Rafael with Beyond Visual Range (BVR) missiles and Active Electronically Scanned Array (AESA) radar are game changers. These FMs can be exploited if responders are well connected by a robust communication system with network-centric capability. The recent standoff between India and Pakistan witnessed the importance of the intelligence grid and ISR to detect any aerial threat.

Network Centric Capability. Network Centric Warfare (NCW) capability will be the key for a coordinated intelligence grid and a swift response for any situation for future conflicts to develop a near real-time information and data flow of all agencies, sensors and platforms. There is a need to exploit the NCW[11] capability from terrestrial, airborne and space-based networks. The terrestrial network with OFC and sitcom overlays needs to be integrated for tri service operations. The presence of one common network like Defence Communication Network (DCN) will enhance net centricity in the future.

Special Forces. The Special Forces have always been a part of intelligence operations. In future, India could also re-organise their special forces like the US Navy Seals Team that executed OP GERONIMO to neutralize Osama Bin Laden. The Special Forces could operate directly under the NSA closely integrated with DIA, RAW, NTRO and the IB.

Information Operations. Information or Influence Operations have now become major tools by nations to execute intelligence operations. The war in Chechnya is replete with examples of psychological operations, deception, perception management and EW. The Chechens reduced the effectiveness of Russian air mobile and bombardment by jamming Russian radio transmissions and hunting down their Forward Air Controllers[12] (FACs). The Pak DGISPR has dedicated staff who are experts with specific portfolios and staffing to work on certain domain areas of specialization. Influence operations can be used to gather intelligence and exploit information technology for national interests.

Hybrid Warfare. Intelligence for contact war will differ from intelligence operations in hybrid, grey zone and asymmetric war. The violent conflict between Russia and Ukraine, which broke out in 2014, is a classical example of hybrid conflict, where kinetic operations were shadowed by information warfare. During the Russia–Georgia war, botnets were used to deface websites and conduct Distributed Denial of Services (DDoS) attacks and make them inaccessible. Today social media is used for disinformation on a wide scale with misleading photographs, possibly with state involvement.

Covert Operations and Counter Intelligence. Covert Action has been defined as a clandestine, deniable action undertaken by an intelligence agency in a foreign country to achieve a national security objective. Kulbushan Jadhav had been captured by the Taliban in Iran and shown as having been arrested in Pakistan for espionage. However, India has denied any such charges and has maintained that he was there in Iran for business. In its report in 1996, the Les Aspen and Brown Commission strongly underlined the need for a continuing covert action capability even after the Cold War. Counter-Intelligence relates to preventing external elements, foreign intelligence organisations, their surrogates or private individuals or groups, including corporate houses from collecting intelligence about the government or any sensitive department. This has both human and technical aspects where a penetration can take place. Aldrich Ames, a CIA officer in the 1990s, compromised several CIA operations and got many agents executed in Russia over 9 years for $2 million. In India, the CIA successfully penetrated the R&AW and IB[13] in the 90s at a very senior level. Many Intelligence agencies have been called the 'Deep State'. CIA, KGB and other agencies have all operated in this manner, says ISI Chief Asad Durrani. As per him, Kulbushan Jadhav, a retired Indian naval officer, who was accused of espionage activities, is an example. Durrani says, "Post the Pathankot attack when India was looking for links of Pakistan's involvement, Pakistan had a big catch and said that India has been involved in Balochistan too.... So it is a game of one-upmanship."[14]

Intelligence Operations for Attack Assessment. Iranian and Yemeni militias had mapped the US and Saudi Air Defence grid to the last detail including electronic/digital footprints. The target profile was monitored and mapped with pinpoint accuracy. Therefore, the Intelligence requirement to detect and attack was completely different. Even if drones/ missiles were picked up by ground forces, it was difficult to assess the target to which they were heading. Recent drone attacks[15] on the Saudi oil facilities of Khurais and Buqyaq operated by ARAMCO have confirmed a new level of unprecedented attack of an asymmetric nature based on specific intelligence.

Intelligence operations can be planned as standalone military operations for disruption and disabling capabilities with the employment of autonomous weapon systems such as drone attacks and Unmanned Combat Aerial Vehicles (UCAVs) such as MQ-Reaper or Raven. In March to April 2019, post the Balakot surgical strike a number of drones entered Indian air space as deep as 12-15 km. Two of these drones[16] were brought down by the Indian armed forces. The recent war between Armenia and Azerbaijan witnessed the use of drones such as Turkish Bayraktar and the Israeli Harops by Azerbaijan to conduct intelligence based attack operations.[17]

Role of Technology in Intelligence Collection and Assessment

There is a need to look at the way intelligence agencies are exploiting the latest technological advancements. Some of these are AI, Satellite/Drones, Information and Electronic Warfare. Quantum technologies promise a vast increase in processing capabilities and secure communication, particularly for encoding and deciphering sensitive messages and signals analysis. This may also lead to improvements in precision sensing, allowing the visualisation of objects and voids in subterranean locations or behind obstructions. This will drive changes to stealth technology thereby directly impacting intelligence operations.

Information and Communications Technology. By 2035, computers will be able to connect, collect and share data with other devices effortlessly without any human intervention—the so-called 'Internet of Things'. Unlimited data storage will be available on micro-scale devices, driven by the growing volume of digital data. Agencies will need to continue to monitor to understand the impact on privacy, assurance, jurisdiction and security of data stored on any foreign-based servers. The growing volume of data will increase, opportunities as will the risk levels. Big Data analytics (the ability to collect and analyse a vast amount of information quickly) will become increasingly important and sophisticated in future.

Surveillance. Recently, General Qassem Sulimani of Iran's Qud's Force along with Abu Mahdial-Muhandis, Iraqi leader of the Iranian-backed Shia militia, Kata'ib Hezbollah, were tracked by an American MQ-9 Reaper[18] drone transmitting directly to the Pentagon and the CIA and eventually launching an attack with precision missiles to target them. In future, the persistent real-time, multi-sensor surveillance capabilities will be ubiquitous, cheap and passive, offering considerable advantages. This will have substantial implications for operational security and counter-surveillance techniques. The sensors will be integrated with weapon delivery systems that track multiple targets in near real time.

AI and Robotics. Artificial Intelligence is the ability of a machine/

computer program to think and learn and execute a task, or simply the effort to automate intellectual tasks, normally performed by humans. There are many other definitions of AI; however, it is the applications for defence that many countries have identified as the future technology. Machine Learning, Big Data Analytics, Pattern Recognition and Natural Language Processing are few examples of how AI can learn and mimic the way the human brain can think and function. A few other applications such as identifying a more agile OODA loop, Strategic decision making, ISR, Big Data Analysis, Multi-lingual recognition of speech, Target recognition by video and audio analysis, Infer a building's function by pattern of life analysis are all very interesting defence applications. Robotics has a future in intelligence too. US Army Robotics and Autonomous Systems Strategy, 2017 has started making smart drones for surveillance. Russia is developing an autonomous drone that will be able to take off, accomplish its mission and land without human interference. "Nerehta," an unmanned Russian ground vehicle has outperformed combat vehicles. So, has India missed the bus? Well not so...India has launched the National Strategy for AI in June 2018, which lays down the roadmap for strategic implementation of the same.

Cyberspace. As military systems become increasingly dependent on information networks (particularly to integrate sensors, weapons and command and control), cyber safeguard and resistance will be essential. Cyberspace will continue to be contested and challenges to information and infrastructure security will be enhanced. Countries will employ adaptive technologies to develop intelligence operations and malicious cyber effects that strike at strategic, operational and tactical levels against various targets. Recently, the USA has put Cyber Warfare, EW and SIGINT all in one place under the concept of Cyber Electro-Magnetic Activities (CEMA). In 2014, it came out with its first doctrine FM3-38[19] on CEMA. In Operation Orchard, Israel used cyber tools to support an air strike on a Syrian nuclear reactor.

Electronic Warfare. By 2035, advanced electronic warfare capabilities will have become ubiquitous. In order to survive, our information systems and platforms will need to have electromagnetic protection to be resistant to electronic attacks and have the ability to penetrate passive and active protection measures and systems for cyber-intelligence through the electromagnetic environment.

Space. There is a need to coordinate the use of space-based applications for Intelligence agencies such as Signal Intelligence, Defence Image Processing and Analysis Centre (DIPAC), Aviation Research Centre (ARC), and National Technical Research Organisation (NTRO). These agencies can exploit SIGINT, which constitutes COMINT and ELINT for recording radio traffic, electronic signals and deployment of payload on a satellite for better results to monitor various activities. ISRO has launched dedicated military communication satellites, GSAT–7 and GSAT-6 in 2013 and 2015 respectively for defence use.[20] France has identified use of nano satellites for a wide range of military roles for space-based ISR, 2019-25 defence spending by France included $4.1 billion for electro-optical reconnaissance satellites–CERES and a communication satellite SYRACUSE–4.

Threat and Type of Attacks

The Future. The future structure of intelligence has to support integrated multi-domain operations. The nature of threats to a nation ranges from a simple cyber attack like data mining on employees of a company like Sony International in 2009 or a more devastating drone strike like the one on Gen. Qassem Suleimani or a suicide bomb attack akin to the one in Pulwama by JeM, which killed 44 CRPF soldiers in India. The spectrum of conflict has widened with 'Grey Zone' and 'Hybrid Threats' being a reality. Likewise, Intelligence operations have to cover a plethora of operations and threats to a nation.

Threats in the Realm of Modern-Day Dynamics. There has been a paradigm shift in the threats of the 21st century. The hostile nation-states or rogue elements as also non-state actors need not necessarily inflict threats in the physical or geographical dimension and yet achieve very disproportionate results. Some of these threats could be conventional in nature or be like some of the attacks in recent history such as Influence/ Intelligence operations by Russia (Crimea 2014), Hybrid War (Hezbollah 2006), Attacks by non-state actors (26/11 Mumbai Attacks), Uri Attack (2016), Cyber Attacks, Asymmetric Threat such as the attack on an oil tanker in the Persian Gulf (2019), 9/11, Yellow Revolution (2017), and Hongkong protests (2019-20). Amid rising tensions and face offs on the LAC between India and china, there are reports that indicated a systematic build up and mobilisation by the PLA under the garb of an exercise and some training. As per reports India is rightly planning to acquire Israeli

Heron drones[21] and further build up its ISR capabilities as also upgrade its existing UAVs under Project Cheetah. Its is evident from the recent stand off that there is a need to be vigilant and acquire state of the art intelligence equipment to provide timely intelligence about any misadventure by the adversaries.

Cyber Attacks. Recent attacks in the cyber security plane have affected countries, corporate organisations and even individuals more than ever. The Stuxnet attack on Iranian nuclear systems in 2009, the Adobe Cyber Breach that affected 2.9 million people, who lost their banking data and more recently the Ransomware, Wannacry and the NotPetya Cyber attacks affected millions. Seventy per cent of organisations the world over have experienced a security breach in the last two years. Sensitive installations in our country are also vulnerable. The USA was the first country to formally declare Cyber Space as the fifth domain of warfare after land, sea, air and space. It has also formally classified the use of cyberspace as a "force," a euphemism for offensive capability.[22] The Chinese adopted the concept of "informationalisation" in the mid-1990s and have relentlessly built up structures and operations in this domain. Consequent to the raising of the US Cyber Command (USCYBERCOM), South Korea followed with the creation of a Cyber Warfare Command in December 2009. This was also in response to North Korea's creation of cyber warfare units. In 2010, China overtly introduced its first department dedicated to defensive cyber warfare and information security in response to the creation of USCYBERCOM. The race is thus on.

Data Management and Protection. One of the most serious and relevant concerns of various establishments, banking institutions and systems as also government departments is data protection. Counter measures have to be brought in and at the same time, the vulnerability of the enemy can be exploited. Other vulnerabilities include threats from Artificial Intelligence, Telemetric Domain, Augmented Reality, Biometric and Threat to Intellectual Property.

Vulnerability of Critical Infrastructure. The Railways, aviation sector and many institutions or organisations can be brought to a standstill. The NTPC having shut down in North India is an example and hence the threat has to be guarded against. Imagine aircraft of VVIPs vulnerable because of radar and control systems in airports being crippled by the enemy or his agents.

Identification of Threats. While considering threats, so as to focus on Intelligence capability building, it is pertinent to see them in the Immediate Term, Mid Term and in the Long Term. If threats from a maritime power in the Indian Ocean, from where two-thirds of the world's oil flows, are to be analysed, the concerned power has to create maritime capabilities, establish an effective Maritime Domination Network, establish bases and collaborate with allies to know the footprint in the IOR. There is a need to know a nation's aspirations and, above all, what is its economic strength, in addition to its geopolitical interests and its signature in the geo-strategic spectrum. Similarly, if threats to the border states (e.g. J&K) and the North Eastern states of India are to be analysed, the role of rogue states and their support to non-state Actors or in promoting proxy war will need to be factored in and accordingly intelligence-gathering capability will need to be created. The threat could be in the economic spectrum, misleading of a given population (minority community), damage to infrastructure or threat to human lives, apart from threat to military Installations and strategic assets. The threat could also be claiming of real estate (eg. J&K), territorial ambitions of the adversary or any other type of asymmetric threat.

COVID-19. An unprecedented spread of the virus has dislocated many nations across the world after it was initially detected in China. The USA has accused China of not informing the world in advance and perhaps risking the exit of the virus from Wuhan. The need for intelligence agencies to monitor threats like the corona virus and take suitable decisions is possibly one of the biggest lessons from the present pandemic. Nations have equated this catastrophe, parallel to if not greater in measure to the World Wars or the Great Depression of 1929. While there is suspicion that a biological weapon has been mishandled or the theory that the leak was deliberate to defeat the USA as written in a book by two Chinese Generals in 1993, the last word on the subject will be written well after Covid-19 is controlled.

Intelligence Failures, Lessons and Voids

Intelligence Failures. Kargil was not only due to lack of intelligence inputs from agencies but in equal measure due to the inability of the assessment machinery to decipher the inputs. This would be evident from the report of the Kargil Review Committee (KRC). In July 1998, IB reported 'laying of mines by the Pak Army in Kargil Sector'.[23] RAW reported in the same month that 8 NLI and 69 Baluch were deployed at Hamziqund and Olthingthang, where 15 to 20 per cent soldiers from each company of NLI and 69 Baluch had been imparted commando training and were in forward deployment, which should have rung a bell. Let us take the example of the Indian intelligence structure. Presently, it has 14 intelligence agencies in operation, with some involved in intelligence collection and a few having investigative roles. Most of them however work with undefined boundaries[24] and indulge in turf wars over their mandates. Additionally, the absence of a single unified supervisory mechanism has affected the coordination of intelligence acquisition and intelligence assessments at the apex levels. In 1999, India failed to detect the Kargil incursions where Pakistan Army regulars from the Northern Light Infantry (NLI) infiltrated deep into Indian territory and occupied key heights that dominated the Kargil–Leh highway. Recently, various terrorist attacks in India either directly by Pakistani players, or their Indian proxies, Mumbai attack of 26/11, Pathankot Air Force Base, Uri and the Pulwama attacks have questioned our intelligence.

Many breaches of national security have occurred in the past and continue to occur today, not for want of intelligence, but because of the faulty analysis of available intelligence and inadequate follow-up action thereon, and/or co-ordination of inputs.

Analysis of Existing Intelligence Structures and Recommended Changes

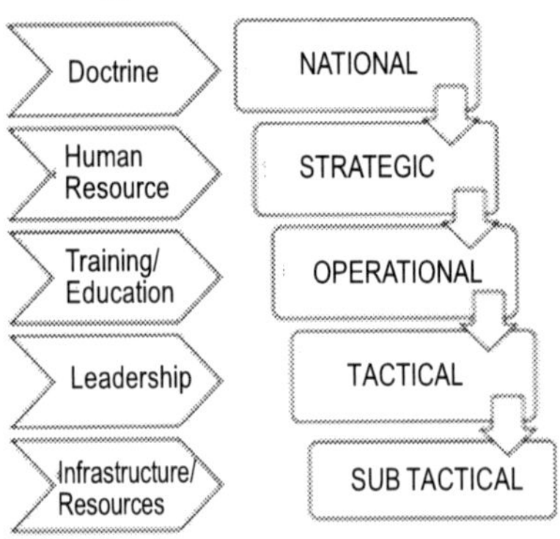

The approach to restructure the Intelligence architecture has to be multi-pronged and multi-tiered. This would include aspects of doctrine, personnel, training, leadership, infrastructural upgrades, organisational structures and tech systems. Whereas, the multi-tiered setup would encompass the aspects of collection, collation and dissemination at all levels based on operational requirements rather than hierarchical control. The key focus areas of this recommended strategy are: Doctrinal, Organisational, Technological and Communication (DOTC).

Issue of Strategic vs Operational /Tactical Intelligence policy vs military intelligence. While the intelligence agencies in India report to different ministries, there is a lack of coordination. It stands to logic that the concerned intelligence agency must report to the ministry under which it falls. At the same time, a central authority coordinates the activities of all the intelligence agencies, as also carries out specific tasking. This, in our context, is being achieved very successfully, with the Joint Intelligence Committee[25] and the National Security Advisor (NSA), as the coordination authority. The NSA chairs regular meetings and gives out specific tasking. The NSA most judiciously addresses the Short Term, Medium Term and Long Term requirements. For each intelligence agency the concerned ministry is the main stake holder, for instance, for urgent matters related to internal intelligence, the Director IB must immediately sensitize the Ministry of Home Affairs, which in turn will take necessary steps to task or advise the Home Department of the concerned state as also assign Central Police forces, or the National Security Guard (NSG), depending on the type of action to be taken. If the IB were functioning under a central authority, tasking would be based on lateral requests from the Ministry of Home Affairs and at the same time consequent to availability of actionable intelligence, there would be delays in inter-ministry sharing of information. It goes without saying that the present arrangement is highly practical. Since the NSA coordinates the functioning, he also sensitizes the Prime Minister's Office (PMO). In any case, the PMO would also receive the relevant inputs from the Ministry of Home Affairs. The CIA could not for certain predict the invasion of Kuwait by Iraq. Similarly, Israel could not predict the Yom Kippur war of 1973, when Egypt breached the Suez Canal. The USA could not predict 9/11 either. There were inputs, perhaps, but all inputs and leads do not necessarily result in an occurrence or an event. It is however, understandable that we must learn lessons and continue to improve upon our way of functioning.

A classic example of this has been the establishment of Multi-Agency Centres at the state and national levels, where representatives of all intelligence agencies meet every morning and pass down relevant information. This helps in ensuring that lateral sharing takes place. The HUMINT voids in the target country like Pakistan or China are quite evident. The 21st century threats will range from non-kinetic influence operations like social media campaign or a hard cyber attack, and at the extreme end, a kinetic attack on land, sea or air under the nuclear overhang.

We have not been able to detect the terrorist intrusions in 26/11 or the Uri attack and therefore need to review the resources, reporting, coordination and response of our sources in all dimensions.

Cyber Security. It is appreciated that, in keeping with current needs, the Defence forces, DRDO, NTRO, CERT-In, RAW, IB, C-DAC, Ministries, NIC, NASSCOM and private industry, all have to work in concert. The impact of this on every aspect of electronic media requires a coordinated and integrated approach. Given its all-encompassing nature, it also follows that control of all cyber and IW activities at the national level must fall under the purview of the NSC and controlled by its Secretariat, i.e., the NSCS as mentioned. Within this, lead agencies for executing offensive cyber operations inter alia could be the NTRO, CIDS and the DRDO.

The US Model. It is pertinent to study the US Model of intelligence Agencies. The USA has 16 intelligence agencies that are divided into the National Intelligence Programme (NIP) and the Military Intelligence Programme (MIP). The main agencies of the NIP are the Central Intelligence Agency (CIA) and the Federal Bureau of Investigation (FBI). While the CIA deals with external Intelligence, the FBI deals with internal intelligence and counter intelligence. Similarly, the MIP has Air Force Intelligence, Surveillance and Reconnaissance Agency, Marine Corps Intelligence, etc. A combination of the NIP and MIP has the National Security Agency (NSA), the Defence Intelligence Agency (DIA) and the National Geo-spatial Intelligence Agency. The NIP budget has been in the range of approximately US $ 58 billion, whereas the MIP budget has been approximately US $ 21 billion. After 9/11, US $ 500 billion were spent on intelligence. The US model works extremely well and its relevance is well known. Apart from seeking various kinds of intelligence, the CIA also has covert assignments.

Russian Intelligence Agencies. The erstwhile Soviet Union had an agenda encompassing a huge network to counter NATO. The situation has however changed after the breakup of the Soviet Union and Russia having become an independent State. Russia has the following Intelligence agencies:

(a) Foreign Intelligence Service (SVR). It is responsible for External Intelligence. It collects intelligence outside the Commonwealth of

Independent States and directly reports to the President. It is also known to undertake covert operations.

(b) Main Intelligence Directorate (GU). It was previously known as GRU. It is the Intelligence Service of the Russian Armed Forces.

(c) Federal Security Service (F&B). It is responsible for Counter Intelligence and other aspects of State security as also for Intelligence gathering of CIS. It also reports directly to the President.

Note: SVR and F&B are the successors of the KGB. They are independent of each other.

Mossad (Israel). Mossad is considered the No. 1 intelligence agency in the world. Formed on 13 December 1949, it is the main Intelligence agency of Israel. Its main role is external intelligence but is also assigned tasks, some of which are covert in nature. It is also responsible for Counter Terrorism. Aman is responsible for Military Intelligence and Shin Bet is responsible for Internal Security.

NATO. Communications and Information Agency (NCI Agency). Intelligence agencies of different NATO countries are not being discussed. However, the NCI Agency is NATO's technical and cyber hub. Basically, it provides C4 ISR (Command, Control, Communications and Computers, Intelligence, Surveillance and Reconnaissance).

Tasking of Intelligence Agencies. Tasking of intelligence agencies must correspond with the needs of the national leadership, based on the threat assessment and national objectives. Information requirements at the strategic level may be related to likely enemy intentions in the economic spectrum, Nuclear capability, means of delivery, preparation for clandestine threats, training of non-state actors and sponsorship of terrorism and proxy wars, etc. When, however, it comes to Military Operations, the tasking may be more specific relating to military capability, military installations and capability of arsenal, including air and naval assets. Similarly, tasking for operational and tactical requirements may be more specific.

Conclusion

The intelligence architecture of India needs reforms for addressing the voids as also integration of modern sensors with futuristic technology. The drawbacks as experienced and analysed by various think-tanks and research committees that were instituted by the government also recommend the same. The major aspects that require immediate attention are integration and obsolescence of equipment in the ISR architecture and the development of future technologies in space, AI, cyber, robotics, aerospace and many other emerging fields. The integration of various agencies operating on deviating lines of operations is the most critical which needs to be addressed. The future threat scenarios will be network-centric and hybrid in nature, which will pose challenges to national security, such as has never been experienced in the past. The signatures of such threats can be confirmed in the form of drone attacks on the ARAMCO oil fields in Saudi Arabia on 14 September 2019 or the Mumbai terrorist attack of 26/11 in 2008. The nature of conflict with respect to traditional adversaries is also going to transform rapidly as witnessed in the recent escalations in Ladakh and post the Balakot air strike and the unprecedented effect of COVID-19 which emanated from China and has impacted the whole world.

The aspirations of our country in future to grow economically and emerge as a regional superpower and eventually strive to be a global force to be reckoned with, requires a secure environment. The aspect of organisational reforms of the intelligence architecture dwell on integrating the existing ISR set-up. The infrastructural developments mandated by futuristic force structuring will be driven by heavy expenditure which will require a deliberate need-based cost benefit analysis. A long-term action plan up to 2030 is required in order to systematically achieve these up-gradations. The future will be a mix of multi-domain, multi-spectrum technologies and India needs to focus on all these for a secure environment.

NOTES

1. Young, Adam B, Employing intelligence, surveillance, and reconnaissance: organizing, training, and equipping to get it right, *Air & Space Power Journal* (Vol. 28, Issue 1), Air Force Research Institute, p, 1, Accessed on 13 Oct 2019.
2. http://US Planners Handbook for Joint Operational Planning Process Workbook, Naval War College.
3. Nitin Pai, What it would take for India to become a space power, 23 June 2019, Accessed on 20 Mar 20.
4. JP 1-02, Department of Defence (DOD) Dictionary of Military and Associated Terms, pp. 268-272, p. 525, p. 453.
5. Joint Operational Warfare, Theory and Practice, Milan Vego, Vol II, pp. VIII-25, Operational Intelligence.
6. B. Raman, Intelligence – Past, Present and the Future, Chapter 1, pp. 16-17.

7. http://few.com/articles/2009//feat'dod-cyber-timeline.aspx, Amber Corrin, "Some key events in the history of Cyber Warfare", 2009 accessed on 18 Mar 20.
8. http://www.theprint.in/Spice-2000 bombs hit Jem Camp in Balakot, 19 Mar 2019, accessed on 17 Mar 20.
9. Geoffrey Till, Sea Power-A guide to the 21st century, pp. 6, 32.
10. http://www.Indiannavy.nic.in/RakshaMantri inaugurates IMAC centre and IFC-IOR a Navy and CG joint Operations Centre which networks 51 Naval and coast guard stations.
11. A.K. Singh and B.S. Nagal, *Military Strategy for India in the 21st Century*, Chapter 7, pp. 112-115.
12. John Arquilla and Theodore Karasik, 'Chechnya: A Glimpse of Future Conflict' Paper in Conflict and Terrorism, accessed from Internet on 20 Mar 20.
13. B. Raman, ibid, p, 287.
14. A.S. Dulat, Asad Durrani and Aditya Sinha, *Spy Chronicles, RAW, ISI and Illusion of Peace*, Chapter 22, p. 151.
15. http://www.indiatoday.in/story on Yemen rebels claim drone attacks on Saudi Aramco facility, 21 Mar 20.
16. http://www.indiatoday.in/story/ IAF shoots down Pakistani drone Rajasthan on 04 Mar 2019. Accessed on 21 Mar 20.
17. https://www.timesnownews.com/india/article/how-drone-warfare-helped-azerbaijan-vanquish-armenia-and-the-lessons-for-india/684508#:~:text= Drone%20 strikes%20destroyed%20artillery%20and,edge%20over%20its%20old%20foe. Accessed on 21 Mar 2020
18. http/www.theguardian.com/world/2020/Jan 20/ The making of a martyr: How Gen Qassem Suleimani was targeted, 19 Mar 2020.
19. US Army Field Manual FM 3-38, FM 3-12.
20. Technology perspective and capability roadmap (TPCR), HQ IDS, MoD, April 2013, http:/mod-gov-in/TPCR-13.pdf, accessed 13 Mar 20.
21. Indian forces to acquire Heron drones, Spike anti-tank guided missiles from Israel. *The economic Times*, 14 July 2020. Accessed at https://economictimes. indiatimes.com/news/defence/indian-forces-to-acquire-heron-drones-spike-anti-tank-guided-missiles-from-israel/articleshow/76959494.cms. Accessed on 18 July 2020
22. IDSA Task Force Report on India's Cyber Security Challenge, Section 3.2.1, pp. 28-32.
23. B. Raman, ibid, pp. 349-350.
24. Re-Energising Indian Intelligence: A National Imperative – USI, accessed in January 2020 at https://usiondia.org/publication/usi-journal/re-energising-indian-intelligence-a-national-imperative.
25. Ibid.

14

Artificial Intelligence and Cyber in Future Conflicts

Air Commodore (Dr.) Ashminder Singh Bahal

The role of AI, big data and block chain technologies have already revolutionized the existing paradigm of war fighting. The defence industry too is undergoing a churning to cope and employ these technologies, in order to safeguard the safety and security of critical infrastructure.

—Rajnath Singh, Defence Minister, Nov 04, 2019

To win one hundred victories in one hundred battles is not the acme of skill: To subdue the enemy without fighting is the acme of skill.

—Sun Tzu

Introduction

Artificial intelligence (AI), dubbed as Industrial Revolution 4.0, is the simulation of human intelligence in machines that are programmed to think like humans, mimic their actions and exhibit traits normally associated with a human such as learning, reasoning and problem solving.[1] There are two key characteristics of AI; first, the ability to use data to facilitate decision making and second, being autonomous; implying that they do not need human intervention. An artificially intelligent system learns on its own and includes neural networks, which can make connections and reach meanings without relying on pre-defined behavioural algorithms.[2] The sheer impact of AI on the battlefield is being considered as the next revolution in warfare after gunpowder and nuclear weapons that took place in the twentieth century and all major military powers are working hard and fast today to build cutting-edge systems for AI and autonomous weapons.[3]

In future, AI applications would increasingly be incorporated in military systems, operational processes, target recognition sensors, homing devices, autonomous weapons, decision support elements, training and simulation systems, reconnaissance and surveillance platforms and offensive and defensive weapons. AI may also develop robots that could attain superior intellect than humans and operate under the control of another AI.[4] AI integration would then significantly affect nuclear, conventional, asymmetric and hybrid warfare. Meanwhile, cyber operations too are considerably affecting the use or corruption of networks and digital systems. They too would play a key role at the commencement of an armed conflict. There is therefore a need to evaluate the effect of AI and cyber operations on force employment in conventional wars, multi-domain operations and hybrid warfare, especially in our subcontinent.

AI Development in Subcontinent

President Xi Jinping intends China to become a world leader in AI by 2030 and has placed military innovation at the centre of its program. China's vision is to create a $150-bn AI industry by then. Commercial giants such as SenseTime, Megvii and Yitu have developed smart cameras, voice recognition capabilities and big data services. Such technology has also been used to police the Xinjiang[5] province. The future of AI in military is directly related to the ability of scientists to design autonomous systems that demonstrate an independent capacity for knowledge and expert-based reasoning that relies on coupling the perception—cognition—action loop, which effectively means that actions typically come within seconds of a stimulus.[6] China believes in this concept.

Chinese AI strategy integrates the government, academia, domestic and public sector companies and commercial applications. This is encouraged in their institutions of higher learning too. China has already established the importance of long-range precision strike capabilities with the integration of AI and cyber capabilities.[7] In order to leverage the advantages of AI in an intelligent military, they believe that AI needs to go beyond robotics and be based on Human Machine Interface.[8] China has made significant advances in unmanned platforms that include Wing

Loong Unmanned Combat Aerial Vehicles (UCAV), remotely controlled tanks, autonomous amphibious landing vehicles and helicopter drones such as Blowfish 2. The Chinese dominance on 5G technology will help them progress the development of their AI technologies much faster.

They have now moved their operational concept of 'Informationalised warfare' to 'Intelligentized warfare'. 'Intelligentization' is a uniquely Chinese concept of applying AI's machine speed and processing power to military planning, operational command and decision support.[9] Intelligentization has become their guiding principle for future military modernization and they do not intend to merely integrate AI into their war fighting functions; rather they are going to use it to shape a new cognitive domain that would lead to a new approach to war fighting.[10]

The Indian Armed Forces meanwhile integrated AI by inducting unmanned elements and increasing the precision of guided weapons, accuracy of ballistic and cruise missiles and accuracy of smart ammunition. The Indian defence services are currently employing indigenously designed the Remotely Operated Vehicle, Daksh, for Bomb Disposal and Unmanned Aerial Vehicles (UAVs) such as Netra, Rustom, Heron and Searcher.[11] Yet, there are critical gaps in the current AI framework in the Army. The possibility of human error is very high when it comes to weapons and decision support systems. To minimize these limitations, a plan is being drawn up to engage with the industry and have a platform for artificial talent intelligence.[12] In 2018, the NITI Ayog came out with a discussion paper on National Strategy for Artificial Intelligence. It discusses skilling, ethics and actions for the government and undertakes a global strategy review. Recently, the MoD too has taken a number of steps to enhance AI integration with the Indian Armed Forces.

The MoD created a multi-stakeholder task force for Strategic Implementation of AI for defence, which submitted its report in June 2018. Based on its recommendations, it has been decided to create an institutional framework for AI policy implementation with guidelines for India's defence forces.[13] In Feb 2019, the MoD established a Defence AI Council (DAIC) under the chairmanship of the Defence Minister that will guide the partnership between the government and the industry. It will be assigned with the task of providing strategic direction towards adoption of AI in defence and envisions formation of the Defence AI Project Agency (DAIPA).[14] The Indian Army has also planned to induct constructive (decision support systems) and destructive AI technologies in the next few years, especially in the mechanized forces.[15]

Currently, the Indian Armed Forces are closely working with the Centre for Artificial Intelligence and Robotics (CAIR) on projects dealing with Multi Agent Robotics Framework (MARF). This development jointly focuses on Image interpretation for target identification and classification as well as in systems for missiles that focus on trajectory analysis for prediction of kill zones.[16] At the same time, extensive research on AI is taking place in the commercial sector. Currently, we are considerably lagging behind China in integration of AI technologies for defence purposes. It is for this reason that one cannot completely rely on the DRDO or government research organizations to be able to develop niche technologies in the requisite timeframes. There is therefore a need to combine commercial applications with defence use by bringing in collaboration between the public and private sectors, both to share the costs of development as well as to gain expertise in the development of AI technologies.

AI Applications in Military

There are numerous AI applications that can be used for military purposes including in Command and Control Support systems, enhancing accuracy of weapon systems, target identification, autonomous weapons or robots, unmanned platforms, training and simulation as well as in operational logistics and maintenance.

Command and Control Systems. The first and foremost application of AI could be in Command and Control and decision support systems. Currently, it has become extremely difficult to plan air, land, sea and space missions jointly in an integrated battlefield. Imagine the multitude of aircraft, drones, ballistic and cruise missiles, air defence weapons, armoured vehicles, artillery guns, class B/C vehicles, troops, neutral elements and anti tank/anti artillery systems that would use the same battle space with elements being both friendly and hostile. It is here that machine learning would need to be applied. The air defence (AD) concept too now needs to transcend towards integrated aerospace defence and the command and control of the air, surface, sea and space elements would need to be integrated and made part of an integrated war situational awareness board that displays integrated pictures of all different elements and platforms utilizing all the domains. Currently, it is becoming extremely difficult as well as humanly impossible to centrally plan and task missions of all platforms in an integrated battle space. This can only be made possible with the employment of AI-based systems; maybe with an element of human intervention to choose the option/s.

The AI technologies provide intelligent computer systems with embedded software applications (data possibly held on a secure cloud server) to facilitate command and control architecture to enhance speed and effectiveness of decision-making processes. AI also helps in strategic campaign planning and operational tasking, which in turn is linked with identification of real-time battle tactics. AI integration could also seamlessly provide intelligent interface to tri-service networks of command, control and communication structures to collate, analyze and transmit data, pictures and imageries. The benefit of AI technologies is that it can provide critical decision support when time is short or/and when the number of choices are too large for the planners to analyze the voluminous data and different alternatives quickly. The side that successfully implements AI can become the best and fastest at analyzing information and as a result choose the right options quickly and thereafter gain operational advantage faster over opponents.[17]

AI can also help forecast enemy behaviour, monitor battlefield conditions and increase situation awareness.[18] It is extremely important that the friendly side operates within the Observe Orient Decide Act (OODA) loop of the adversary and this can only happen if AI technologies are integrated in the Command and Control decision support architecture. Combat operations are dynamic and fast paced; therefore, the need to operate within the OODA loop becomes more and more essential in a technologically advanced battlefield. It is here that an Identification of Friend and Foe (IFF) system linked with large accurate data and deep learning AI could provide a significant edge to friendly elements and enhance their speed and mobility in the dynamic battlefield. The emerging opportunities in a fast-moving campaign would be fleeting and transitory. AI could help in targeting the adversary's elements quickly while reducing the probability of fratricide, especially in close combat.

AI could assist in carrying out rapid terrain analysis to ascertain the options available with own surface forces and the choice of an appropriate combination of forces or weapon systems to use, taking into account the location of adversary elements and the offensive and defensive weapons deployed there. AI inherently collates data obtained from different types of sensors, carries out data fusion, undertakes threat assessments, assists in target identification, carries out effective analyses, prioritizes targets, assigns forces and undertakes mission planning, monitoring and execution.[19] It filters and fuses the information to provide integrated situational pictures, thereby facilitating the decision making process while shortening the targeting cycle and continuously updating the operational planning process.

In campaign planning, AI technologies could considerably assist in rapidly analyzing the data streamed by different reconnaissance and surveillance platforms, correlating it with the available characteristics of each element, discerning the friendly elements from those of the enemy and choosing the ideal and appropriate weapon systems to target the enemy's systems and forces with minimum collateral damage. Thereafter, it can predict the enemy's reaction options with own tactical and operational solutions so as to arrive at appropriate decisions while operating within the enemy's OODA loop. This would provide a significant advantage to the forces that use AI in operations ranging from high intensity to low intensity conflict situations.

AI Technologies in Weapon Systems. Weapons controlled by AI will appear on the battlefields of the future. A cheap, fully automated system that can detect, track and engage a human with lethal fire can be made today even in a home garage.[20] These systems will continue to get refined and become more potent. In future, there would be cheaper, smaller, more powerful processors that are integrated into an individual soldier's equipment and fielded in large numbers. This will enable the "internet of things," which will soon become the internet of battlefield things.[21] These advances not only provide enhanced ability to the weapon systems in the hands of manned elements but would also lead to developing robots that could be effectively employed in asymmetric warfare as well as in high intensity conflicts. Furthermore, recently developed Lethal Autonomous Weapon Systems (LAWS) search and engage targets based on programmed constraints and operate in different domains; examples include active automated protection systems, such as radar-guided Close in Weapon System (CIWS) to defend ships, similar systems for tanks and stationary sentry guns actually used in South Korea and Israel.[22]

There are sea systems too that are autonomous and unmanned. The

Sea Hunter is designed to travel in oceans for months with no crew aboard to search for enemy submarines; it recently completed its trip from San Diego to Pearl Harbour. Swarms of such unmanned elements could be deployed worldwide, capable of attacking submarines or surface vessels in accordance with sophisticated algorithms.[23] China deployed around 12 Sea Wing underwater drones in 2019-20 from its research vessel in the Indian Ocean region ostensibly to undertake hydrographical survey, oceanic research and gather naval intelligence for deep-sea mining operations as well as to aid in future for submarine and anti-submarine warfare. There are certain key advantages of using such systems; first, the long endurance that they offer where no crew is involved; second, no loss of life can take place, especially when the system is lost; third, ability to maintain high alert status for extended duration of time and fourth, incredibly high speed of autonomous decision making and action.

An AI-based target recognition system plays an important role in discriminating between different target systems in ballistic/cruise missiles, especially at the terminal stage and in different long-range weapon systems to enhance targeting and precision. This ensures greater success with the ability to distinguish between friendly and elements of an adversary as well as between different target systems of the adversary; either by visual recognition/IR discrimination or by discriminating radar imageries with the help of pre-fed data. AI-enabled recognition systems could also take into account enemy behaviour and weather such as different contrasts of the target system due to cloud cover.

AI and Military Robots. Military robots are autonomous or remotely controlled objects that are designed to undertake specific tasks. The types of military robots include transportation, search and rescue, bomb disposal, mine clearance, armed and fire fighting robots. One of the American PackBot robots was deployed to trawl the remains after 9/11 attacks and in 2002, it was used in Afghanistan to deal with improvised explosive devices (IEDs).[24] In 2005, the Special Weapons Observation Remote Reconnaissance Direct Action System (SWORDS) became the first ground robots to see action when the US forces used them in Iraq; these robots were equipped with light machine guns and were mobile, but officials opted to keep them at fixed locations, where they were used to defend perimeters.[25]

Controlled by tablets and utilizing deep learning, future robots will proceed ahead of troops to identify IEDs and ambushes and also forward detailed data on targets.[26] These robots will also be able to handle a wide range of combat tasks that include picking off snipers and carrying out target acquisition. They can be deployed in dangerous situations with the robots providing backup during heavy artillery fire, thereby reducing the number of casualties; they can also map a potentially large hostile area by accurately detecting a variety of threats.[27] The key advantages of using robots besides reducing risks to soldiers as well as executing tasks more efficiently are that robots do not get tired, have phenomenal memory, do not sense fear and are able to process battlefield information quickly. Hence, their use in the military in conventional warfare to defend outposts during peacetime as well as in sub-conventional warfare both in rural and urban areas would only increase in the future.

AI in Drones/Unmanned Aerial Vehicles. Aerospace technologies have moved from Unmanned Combat Aerial Vehicles (UCAV) to smart drones that have the ability to locate, identify and destroy targets[28] with accuracy. In future, a large number of stealthy small drones would swarm an adversary's air space/AD systems whilst causing significant damage to a number of crucial target systems. These cheap drones obviate the need to employ expensive manned fighters thus bringing in a progressive shift from manned aircraft to smart drones that are highly potent in destroying well-defended targets with precision. China has progressed extensively in developing stealthy UCAVs; India, meanwhile, is developing AURA, though its pace of development is extremely slow. By 2035, the number of unmanned platforms would be high and employment of a combination of manned and unmanned platforms would be the norm.

The drones undertake persistent extended duration monitoring of contested areas relatively inexpensively. AI technologies not only make drones smart and provide techniques to control them effectively, but also help in identifying hostile elements, prioritizing them and then targeting them. A high degree of situational awareness can be achieved by employing a number of smart drones that fly over a wide geographically dispersed contested territory. The large amount of data that is gathered over a period of time needs to be stored securely, processed quickly and analyzed accurately. Subsequently, meaningful conclusions need to be drawn to facilitate quick decision making and accelerate the targeting process; this can only happen if AI is intimately meshed with drone technology. The drones gather intelligence through electro-optical, radar and thermographic Infra Red (IR) sensors as well as Communication and Electronic Intelligence sensors. This process when integrated with AI is akin to machine learning that includes algorithms that help drone-AI combinations to learn and improve.

This technology progresses to the next stage of deep and super learning when artificial neural networks are connected in such a manner that the system becomes superior to the functioning of a human brain as it gathers, collates and processes large amounts of data obtained from a number of different drones and sensors (something that will happen when swarms of drones enter enemy territory simultaneously) and these neural networks operate much faster than a human brain can ever while simultaneously learning and upgrading itself by interpreting data patterns and the experience that it obtains in the process. Neural networks have algorithms that search for patterns inside the data and whose code could have thousands of lines.[29]

Integrating AI technologies completes the detection-identification-targeting-destruction-Battle Damage Assessment loop in a much faster timeframe. As technology evolves quickly and computing speed and big data analytics improves, the size of the drones too reduces resulting in their becoming stealthier, lighter and more effective. The drones' tasks would be undertaken while linked with distant command and control centres that are seamlessly presented with integrated air, land, sea and space situation pictures, thereby facilitating efficient and effective decision making and targeting.

Being unmanned, there are no pilots to get captured in case drones get shot down in hostile territory whilst undertaking operational tasks. This would reduce the media pressure and perception management constraints as happened after the Balakot operation. The advantages of using AI with drone technology are significant. Supervised learning process could train the drones to discriminate between objects and the algorithms would identify objects, filter them and thereafter the drones could move to other areas to locate more objects.[30] True autonomy would remove the human element, with the unmanned vehicles operating on their own, reporting to humans on what it has found and if armed, could act on their own in a hunter/killer mode; but current international understanding prohibits armed attacks without a human "pulling the trigger."[31]

Training and Simulation. Perhaps, the most significant impact AI can make is in simulation and training. Most predictive models developed for simulating battle conditions and outcomes rely heavily on AI-based systems and technologies. The effectiveness of such simulation depends on the reliability of data and probabilities that are fed into the simulation models. In military simulations, there are so many variables from the use of tanks, infantry, artillery, aircraft, helicopters, ballistic/cruise missiles and satellites to ships and submarines, which utilize different as well as common battle environments in situations varying from asymmetric to high intensity conflicts that the use of AI technology becomes essential to derive meaningful learning.

Many military tasks can be performed more smartly when soldiers practise with realistic role players, implement potential solutions and freely experiment with new tactics, procedures and materials; behaviour of entities in such simulations is based on the artificial intelligence and machine learning algorithms fed to resolve intricate puzzles and to forecast fuzzy situations.[32] An AI-based simulation model typically mimics human intelligence that deals with reasoning, learning, perception, planning, language comprehension, problem-solving and decision making.[33] Deep learning components can replace rule-based models and can be used to reflect the real system by generating the data sets necessary for neural network training.[34]

American university researchers today are developing a number of AI tools that would significantly assist in the conduct of training exercises as well as in deriving meaningful lessons while enhancing the safety of the soldiers. One such tool focuses on developing a deep learning model assessing team-level communication, which is critical for mission success and the second tool focuses on identifying effective ways to provide feedback to trainees in near real time.[35] Project Maven of the USA uses computer vision, which is a combination of machine and deep learning, to independently find objects of interest,[36] which could give significant training value.

AI in Logistics and Maintenance. In modern warfare, logistics and maintenance would play a key role in achieving success as high intensity battles are highly resource intensive and would require efficient sustenance of operational effort. Large amounts of data would therefore need to be sifted and analyzed to take decisions regarding supply, transport and communications of logistics and armament support depending on the field requirement and battle conditions. Using artificial intelligence and machine learning for logistics and maintenance purposes could speed up that process and make it significantly agile.[37] Transportation-integrated AI lowers costs and simultaneously reduces human effort. AI technologies enable military fleets, ammunition supplies and ordinance depots to identify requirements and predict component failures. Recently, the US Army collaborated with IBM to use its artificial intelligence platform to pre-identify maintenance issues in Stryker combat vehicles.[38] AI systems could also be used for predictive aircraft maintenance; the USAF is testing AI-enabled systems that tailor maintenance schedules to the needs of an individual aircraft. Similarly, the Army could also use AI-based fleet maintenance systems.[39]

Cyber Warfare and Military

Cyber warfare is computer or network-based conflict involving politically motivated attacks by a nation-state on another nation and in these types of attacks, nation-state actors attempt to disrupt the activities of the organizations/nation-states through computer virus or denial of services, especially for strategic or military purposes that also includes cyber espionage.[40] Attacks by terrorists or hacker groups aimed at furthering the goals of particular nations[41] also form part of cyber warfare. There are a number of examples of cyber operations including those by Estonia, Georgia and Iran and the first instance of kinetic action used in response to a cyber-attack was seen on May 5, 2019, when the Israelis destroyed a building associated with an on-going cyber-attack.[42] The USA, Russia, China, Iran and Vietnam have developed offensive/defensive cyber security operations and capabilities.[43]

The Indian Computer Emergency Response Team (CERT-In) was formed in 2004 to prevent cyber attacks. After numerous cyber intrusions, India established the National Critical Information Infrastructure Protection Centre (NCIIPC) to prevent attacks against energy, transport, banking, telecom, defence, space and other sensitive areas.[44] Currently, India has formed the Defence Cyber Agency (DCA) as a tri-service organization commanded by a two-star naval officer, which will handle cyber security threats and control and co-ordinate joint cyber operations. All the three services had earlier established Cyber Emergency Response Teams. In future, DCA would have the capability to hack into networks, mount surveillance operations, recover deleted data from hard disks and mobile phones and break into encrypted communication networks.

A unique feature of cyber operations is that it can be carried out any time, including during peacetime, for intelligence purposes or to disrupt an adversary's critical infrastructure as a retaliatory measure while remaining within the deniability regime. In cyber warfare, it is difficult to identify who launched/sponsored attacks and usually nobody claims responsibility; while it is possible to speculate, there never are clear answers, especially because states easily cover their tracks.[45] There are numerous ways in which cyber attacks can be planned and carried out. One could employ worms, Trojans, virus or bots as part of malware to disrupt, destroy, steal or damage data or harm computers or networks. It can also be undertaken to obtain an adversary's vital information as well as to get into his command, control and communication network so that during actual operations, the same can be disrupted or degraded. The botnets can cause distributed denial of services (DDoS) to cause widespread disruptions to critical services and social engineering and by spear phishing, introduce an attacker into the adversary's system.[46] This can result in extracting critical information from the systems or disrupting the system for vital use or even cause misinformation that can lead to disastrous results. A combination of Artificial Intelligence and cyber warfare can wreak havoc in the way warfare is conducted in future.

Cyber weapons can infiltrate networks, infect individual computers, confuse enemy signals, negate military attacks before they occur, and disrupt communication systems; they may rely on software vulnerabilities and poor cyber hygiene.[47] In 2011, Stuxnet, the American-Israeli cyber-attack on an Iranian nuclear facility, disabled thousands of centrifuges. In response, the Iranians targeted multiple US institutions including the New York Stock Exchange, JP Morgan Chase, and Wells Fargo.[48] A US secret cyber attack against Iran in June 2019 cleaned out an important database that was used by Iran's paramilitary forces to undertake attacks against oil tankers. It also degraded Iran's ability to covertly target shipping traffic. Cyber attacks are powerful because today all of us are controlled by data. A cyber attack can impact systems throughout the country, knock out emergency services, disrupt the economy and weaken military responsiveness. Cyber-attacks can also be launched instantly, without any evidence, making them hard to predict or counter.[49] Currently, international laws are weak to effectively counter cyber warfare.

Civilians do involve themselves in hacking, but it is more for personal interest or to flaunt their hacking skills or for profit. Effective targeting of sensitive sites requires preparation in the form of mapping out an adversary's networks far in advance, and is one of the hallmarks of cyber warfare professionals,[50] not civilians. Sometimes, however, civilians are able to hack through sensitive sites and are able to glean through classified information, thereby, compromising their value. However, for resource-constrained defences where skills are weak, knowledgeable civilians may be able to offer services in the event of an attack.[51] Their worth needs to be recognized and a data bank of such civilians should be identified and maintained. In future, cyber weapons could be used at the beginning of combat operations or even during peacetime. It is here that they may target our computer systems, communication networks/nodes, campaign planning computers and command and control systems. This is where a number of protective measures need to be taken and firewalls created with a large number of cyber warriors prepared for offensive and defensive operations.

Fusion of AI and Cyber Operations in Integrated Battle Spaces For Multi-Domain Operations in Indian Subcontinent

The presence of nuclear weapons in the subcontinent is likely to play an important role in any future conflict. It is here that undertaking numerous shallow penetrations by surface forces in different terrains and rapid response during contingency situations becomes more prudent as deep ground thrusts may not be appropriate in a nuclear environment. The Indian Army is in the process of establishing around 12 Integrated Battle Groups (IBG) in the next few years. These battle groups would be larger than a brigade, but smaller than a division and would integrate elements of infantry, armour, artillery, air defence, engineers and signals. Creation of such lean, agile and tailor-made structures increases the rapidity of response to achieve operational objectives closer to the border/LoC in diverse terrains depending on the perceived threat. IBGs would provide significant flexibility and mobility to control the surface battle space quickly, both in offensive and defensive operations.

In future, *IBGs of the advanced countries such as the USA, would employ organic long, mid and short range weapon systems to create operational and tactical standoffs with the adversary that would lead to gaining operational advantage or attaining strong deterrence value. They may focus on attacking functions more than physical elements (though physical assets too would be targeted) so as to deny the enemy his ability to function effectively*. It is here that the importance of AI technologies and offensive and defensive cyber operations play an important role while undertaking multi-domain operations (MDO) in integrated battle spaces.

Future wars fought in integrated battle spaces with MDO strategy would move forward from the post World War concepts of air-land battles to attaining 21st century multi-domain superiority. This fighting construct integrates different systems, which belong to the three services, regardless of where they reside, whether on surface, in air, in space or under water and also includes the electromagnetic spectrum and the cyber domain. The MDO is still a developing concept that links platforms and systems belonging to different domains into a strong interconnected system of systems to fight integrated conflicts.

The US armed forces now profess MDO as a critical capability to defeat near peer adversaries by following tactical concepts of compete, penetrate, disintegrate and exploit, especially to defeat the Chinese Anti Access Area Denial (A2AD strategy). From platform centric, the operational philosophy would gravitate towards fusing platforms over interconnected systems. The effectiveness of the armed forces would depend on how well all the three services and all the systems belonging to the different domains can be integrated seamlessly to exploit the capability of multi-domain operations, thereby creating a significantly large effect. This multi domain integration cannot take place without the use of AI technologies and bringing in significant interoperability in the command, control and communication networks of the three services. The forces need to integrate, synergize and synchronize command, control and secure communication networks with the help of AI platforms and cyber technology.

The integrated aerospace and naval forces must have the resilience and coherence to operate across the multiple domains without facing fratricide and friendly fire and the surface forces must have the ability to conduct fast-paced manoeuvres by applying cross-domain fires and maximizing the potential of windows of opportunity. The operational environment would then become increasingly lethal and hyper active. It is expected that in future combat operations in the Indian subcontinent could take place in a challenged operational environment. More than space and physical degradation, functional paralysis would then become extremely important. To achieve this, the focus, besides being on the physical targeting of command, control and communication nodes by manned and unmanned platforms, would also be on targeting the adversary's AI technologies with the help of cyber warfare.

Remote devices such as laptops, wireless and mobile devices, and IoT sensors are highly vulnerable to cyber attacks and machine learning can identify and analyze unknown files and detect cyber threats such as malware.[52] AI technologies and systems could therefore be both vulnerable to cyber operations as well as be the enablers that provide protection from cyber warfare. This would bring in important changes in the way warfare would be conducted in the future and the operational concepts would include working towards obtaining multi-domain dominance quickly, which would also imply dominating the cyber dimension at the commencement of conflict. *The focus here would be on targeting 'the will' of the enemy by neutralizing his ability to function.* Currently, the Indian armed forces are at least a decade away from this type of integration; even if we commence the integration process today.

The conduct of warfare essentially hinges on the speed of decision-making. This in turn depends on the ability of a side to collate large amounts of voluminous data originating from different systems and sensors. This is where AI comes in. AI will have a significant effect in the way integrated battle spaces are controlled. It would enhance the ability to collate and analyze large amounts of data collected through different types of sensors, whether electro-optical, radar and electromagnetic, through satellites, unmanned platforms, fighter aircraft and HUMINT. No human would be able to collate and analyze actionable knowledge from diverse systems so quickly as AI technologies would be able to do. Subsequently, AI systems would be able to analyze the collated data swiftly, fuse it as one picture on the multi-domain situational boards, identify the appropriate target systems from the maze of information collected, determine its threat potential, facilitate quick decision-making and subsequently complete the operational action including the targeting loop.

AI will thus enable dynamic and swift planning, provide flexible operational options, reduce time of response, minimize focus on analyses and shift to execution of actions while minimizing the gap between identification of opportunities and initiation of response. It will also significantly assist in converging diverse capabilities while rapidly disseminating actionable information at a speed and scale that is humanly impossible. The growth in operative speed implies that the reaction time with the enemy would be lesser. The enhanced speed of action ensures that the side that is able to generate multi-domain capability based on AI technologies will have a significant advantage in maintaining an upward spiral of combat operations as they would be operating within the OODA loop of the adversary. In fact, the operational outcomes will continue to become considerably larger with every phase of operations as the adversary would be fighting a losing battle from the very beginning and would be unable to co-ordinate its operations while continuously losing vital capabilities.

The only thing that can disrupt this synergy, synchronization and integration is the adversary's cyber warfare capabilities as cyber weapons can infiltrate networks, infect computers and command and control architecture, dislocate signals and break down encrypted communication systems. There are many ways to bring about such disruptions; the botnets can cause distributed denial of service that can cause widespread interference with critical infrastructure. This could include disrupting satellite command and control and crippling vital communication networks. Both defensive and offensive cyber operations would be essential to be conducted at the preparatory stage itself.

At the outset, however, the importance of cyber space being a separate dimension of warfare would need to be appreciated by all military planners by bringing in a cultural shift in the rigid mindsets of those that still perceive it as an enabler. There would be a need to have a proper understanding of the adversary's and own cyber capabilities by preparing accurate cyberspace situational awareness knowledge, identify an adversary's and own cyber limitations, undertake predictive modelling and evolve dynamic cyberspace operational mission plans. These mission plans should ensure that, in a time-bound manner, the cyberspace is shaped in our favour and that cyber plans are meshed with the integrated multi-domain operational plans. In defensive cyber operations, signature masking and stealth measures too need to be adopted.

AI and Cyber Operations in Grey Zone/Hybrid Warfare

In hybrid warfare, data could be leveraged effectively to achieve distinct advantages, yet remain below the threshold of conventional warfare. Though kinetic effect may still remain relevant, however, utilizing AI, big data and cloud computing could play an important role in distinguishing, tracking and neutralizing asymmetric elements. Computer vision powered by AI and machine learning is rapidly improving and could help the armed forces and intelligence agencies to accelerate the screening and scouring of vast amounts of data.[53] With social media and other online platforms offering mountains of data on virtually every citizen, AI can be used to detect influence operations and identify terrorist plots.[54] AI-based communication technology and data analytics could assist in locating and tracking such elements and thereafter help in either preventing terror attacks or in neutralizing such elements. Profiling and tracking of non-state actors, terror elements and their handlers along with their behaviour quirks would be much easier with the help of AI technologies based on predictive software and use of cyber domain to penetrate their communication networks.

The US Defence Advanced Research Project Agency's (DARPA) program "Collection and Monitoring via Planning for Active Situational Scenarios (COMPASS)," aims to develop software that gauges an adversary's response to stimuli and then discerns the adversary's intentions that give commanders intelligence on how to respond.[55] It uses a mix of game theory, modelling and AI technologies to provide options using decision support tools. The ultimate goal of the program is to provide theatre-level operations and planning staffs with robust analytics and decision-support tools that reduce ambiguity of adversarial actors and develop simulations to test and understand various potential actions and possible reactions by an adversary employing grey-zone activity.[56] It is apparent that AI is likely to play a key role in operations less than war and in hybrid warfare. This would include identification of hostile elements, profiling them, tracking their communications, building a database, identifying options and eventually neutralizing such elements.

Challenges with AI Systems and Ethical Issues

While AI would have a significant impact on the weapon systems and warfare in the future as it may lead to more informed decision making, autonomous operations as well as help in increasing the scale and tempo of operations, at the same time, there are serious challenges with respect to the indiscriminate use of such systems in conflict situations. Though robotic systems lessen the probability of military casualties, the moot question is whether machines should be allowed to make life-and-death decisions in battle? Who would be accountable for the actions of completely autonomous systems; the programmer, the machine, or the state that deploys these weapons?[57]

Even though the ability to discriminate would be high, , the ethical issue would be whether we can give AI systems complete freedom to be autonomously employed indiscriminately with the help of pre-programmed algorithms or do we require some form of human intervention to ensure that there is a degree of inbuilt safety for proportionate use? If we employ human intervention, then it would not be truly autonomous. The other key issue is that if AI-based systems due to deep learning take autonomous action, though appropriate in a hostile situation, but due to their precision and speed may attack unintended targets that are also present in that area that may actually escalate the conflict further as the adversary may have no choice but to react accordingly.

The other important issue is that artificially intelligent systems are data dependent and data is mostly man-made or data is collected, identified and coded by humans. This implies that there may be biases; often unconscious in data.[58] This also implies that its employment could lead to seriously embarrassing situations, when the systems go haywire. This also implies that there could develop a link between AI and cyber warfare, wherein if cyber operations are employed, then AI systems could be corrupted and thereafter it could lead to disastrous consequences or create such situations that a large number of neutrals could get affected. It is therefore essential that some form of human intervention is necessary to ensure that large collateral damage is prevented and the cyber warfare and countermeasure techniques that are used do not affect correct decision-making or lead to embarrassing situations including friendly fire.

Doctrinal Principles of AI and Cyber Use

AI application does raise a number of ethical issues. Use of AI and cyber weapons therefore should ideally follow the principles of war and humanitarian laws, perhaps more stringently. Currently, the UN Group of Governmental Experts that included representatives from the USA, Russia and China has been unable to come to a common platform as regards whether international laws on state responsibility and Humanitarian Laws should apply in cyberspace and also for Lethal Autonomous Weapons including killer robots. There is, however, a need to clearly identify application of internationally accepted rules for operating in the cyber domain and for Lethal Autonomous Weapons.

Assessed doctrinal principles for the application of AI-based autonomous systems and exploitation of cyberspace for military use are enumerated below:

(a) ***Principle for Non Offensive Use During Peacetime and Against Systems and Services Used for Humanitarian Purposes***. During peacetime, autonomous systems should not be used for offensive purposes, but only in defensive roles. In addition, cyber hacking should not be carried out to disrupt essential services both during peacetime and during conflict situations, which could lead to a serious humanitarian crisis.

(b) ***Principle of Proportionality***. Disproportionate use of AI-based systems and cyber warfare should be avoided. Only proportionate use commensurate with the emerging situation should be carried out.

(c) ***Principle of Discrimination***. A distinction should be created between using such systems against war-waging capability and assets and indiscriminate use those results in large-scale humanitarian losses. Indiscriminate use of AI-based systems needs to be highly restricted.

(d) ***Principle of Validation Before Use***. AI-based autonomous systems need to be validated and tested before widespread use so that their autonomous use does not lead to friendly losses or large-scale collateral damage.

(e) ***Principle of Human Intervention and Control***. Autonomous weapons must be under human control and judgment to prevent embarrassing situations, friendly fire and large-scale loss of human lives.

(f) ***Principle of Non-Linking With Weapons of Mass Destruction***. The AI based autonomous systems should not be linked with weapons of mass destruction including nuclear, biological and chemical weapons so that even by mistake, a nuclear, biological or chemical war does not get triggered.

(g) ***Principle of Minimum Collateral Damage***. The data fed into autonomous systems must not only include reducing the probability of attack against friendly forces and neutral elements, but also on an adversary's civilian population.

(h) ***Principle of Permanence and Ubiquity***. The quantum of data continues to increase with time and the source of data should always be able to be traced. The storage capacity would need continual enhancement. The value of the datasets also increases with structural complexity and, with time, new datasets would need to be curated.

There are also principles that need to be identified with the integration of AI and Cyber Operations in conflict situations so as to enhance the efficiency and effectiveness of combat operations. These are enumerated as follows:

(a) ***Principle of Multi-Domain Dominance***. The operational concepts will now need to move forward from aerospace superiority to multi-domain dominance that not only includes air, space and sea/ underwater dominance, but also dominance in the AI and Cyber domain. This should be the first priority of any force at the commencement of operations in any future conflict so that the war is won at the lowest threshold while keeping the nuclear factor in mind.

(b) ***Principle of Concentration of Effect***. The effectiveness of a friendly operational action will depend on the ability of a side to mass the appropriate combination of multi-domain forces seamlessly across all the domains so as to create a large effect on the adversary at the commencement itself.

(c) ***Principle of Integration***. Since multiple elements and platforms will be operating in different domains, they would need to be seamlessly integrated with the help of AI-based systems and software for the smooth and efficient conduct of combat operations and to prevent friendly fire or fratricide as well as large collateral damage.

(d) ***Principle of Focus on Attaining Functional Paralysis***. Usually, combat operations focus on attaining physical destruction; the focus in future would be at the hearts and minds of the enemy and the adversary should feel defeated even when he still has large physical forces available with him. His will to fight would need to be targeted. This is where the use of AI to remain within the OODA loop of the adversary becomes extremely important and control of the cyber domain would make a large difference.

(e) ***Principle of Controlling the Cyber Domain***. The controlling of the cyber domain would become extremely important and it is here that it would need to be considered as a separate dimension and not just an enabler. Mission plans to control this domain would also need to be evolved well before the commencement of combat operations. These plans would need to be integrated with operational plans during conflict situations.

(f) ***Principle of Using AI to Control Cyber Domain***. AI technologies help in verifying codes and in spotting bugs and vulnerabilities, thereby making electronic systems robust and less prone to hacking. AI can use machine and deep-learning techniques to detect hacking attempts and identify suspicious behaviour on the network, shut off that part of the system and issue an alert for the same so as to take remedial action, while taking offensive action against the adversary.

Conclusion

There are two key characteristics of AI systems; first the ability to use data to make decisions and second, to be autonomous. Autonomous means the freedom to choose its own course of action or attack target systems freely without human intervention. AI, big data, additive manufacturing, virtual and augmented reality, remote sensing, unmanned systems, hypersonic technologies, electro-magnetic weapons and quantum computing are central to the efforts of most modern militaries to enhance the effectiveness of people, platforms and systems in a technologically advanced battlefield.[59] In future, AI would make a deep impact in Command and Control systems, advanced weapon systems, transportation, logistics and maintenance, unmanned drones and grey zone/hybrid warfare.

While AI would create a significant impact on future warfare, there are also serious challenges with respect to its indiscriminate use in conflict situations. Though robotic systems lessen military casualties, the moot question, however, is whether machines should be allowed to take life-and-death decisions. Furthermore, Artificially Intelligent systems are data dependent and data can easily be corrupted or destroyed. This also implies that there would be a link between AI and cyber warfare, wherein, if cyber operations are employed, then AI-based systems could be corrupted and thereafter it could result in disastrous consequences. Cyber weapons are therefore likely to be used at the beginning of combat operations. It is here that computer systems, communication platforms, campaign planning digital systems and command and control networks would be vulnerable.

This is where a number of protective measures need to be taken and firewalls created along with a battery of cyber warriors prepared for offensive and defensive operations.

Since AI enhances the decision-making process, it ensures that battles fought in integrated battle spaces of multi-domain operations would be fast and deadly to remain well within the OODA loop of the adversary. This would enhance the speed of response and exploit emerging opportunities quickly. Multi-domain operations at the tactical level involve the lowest war fighting echelon to take advantage of the secondary domains, viz., land, sea, air, space, or cyber and to deliver effects more strongly across its primary domain.[60] This would require a significant amount of integration and synchronization. It is here that AI technologies would make a large difference in bringing this synergy, synchronization, integration and speed of response. The only element that can still disrupt combat operations is an adversary's cyber warfare. AI and cyber operations would therefore assist considerably in shaping the integrated battle space and make conventional wars far more ruthless and deadly. This would, over a period of time, bring in a significant change in the fundamental nature of how wars are fought at the tactical level. It is here that the Indian armed forces need to understand this change that is taking place in warfare and quickly adapt to it.

NOTES

1. Jake Frankenfield, Artificial Intelligence, 22 Jan 2020, accessed from https://www.investopedia.com/terms/a/ artificial-intelligence-ai.asp on 05 Mar 2020.
2. R.L. Adams, 10 Powerful Examples of Artificial Intelligence in Use Today, accessed from https://www.forbes.com/ sites/robertadams/2017/01/10/10-powerful-examples-of-artificial-intelligence-in-use-today/#56178415420d on 05 Feb 2020.
3. Lt Col Ashutosh Verma, How China is moving Towards Intelligentized Warfare, accessed from the site https:// www.geospatialworld.net/blogs/how-china-is-moving-towards-intelligized-warfare/ on 06 Apr 2020.
4. Ed Oswald, What is Artificial intelligence, accessed from the site https://www.digitaltrends.com/cool-tech/what-is-artificial-intelligence-ai/ on 05 Mar 2020.
5. Melissa K. Chan, China and the US are Fighting a Major Battle Over Killer Robots and Future of AI, accessed from the site https://time.com/5673240/china-killer-robots-weapons/ on 10 Mar 2020.
6. M.L. Cummings, Research paper, Jan 2017, p. 5, Artificial Intelligence and the future of warfare, accessed from site https://www.chathamhouse.org/sites/files/chathamhouse/publications/research/2017-01-26-artificial-intelligence-future-warfare-cummings-final.pdf on 09 Dec 2017.
7. Kartik Bommakanti, AI in the Chinese Military: Current Initiatives and the Implications

for India, accessed from the site https://www.orfonline.org/research/a-i-in-the-chinese-military-current-initiatives-and-the-implications-for-india-61253/ on 06 Apr 2020.

8. Ibid.
9. Accelerate the Development of Military Intelligentization, accessed from the site https://www.wired.com/ beyond-the-beyond/2020/01/accelerate-development-military-intelligentization- on 06 Apr 2020.
10. Ibid.
11. Kavita Nagpal, Robotics and Artificial Intelligence in Defence Sector, accessed from the site https:// defproac.com/?p=6000 on 06 Apr 2020.
12. Abhishek Bhalla, Indian Army Pushes For Robust AI Mechanism to Minimize Human Error, accessed from the site https://www.indiatoday.in/india/story/indian-army-pushes-for-robust-artificial-intelligence-mechanism-to-minimise-human-error-1601475-2019-09-20 on 06 Apr 2020.
13. Vishal Chawla, AI in Defence: How India Compares to US, China and Russia, accessed from the site https:// analyticsindiamag.com/ai-in-defence-how-india-compares-to-us-china-russia-south-korea/ on 06 Apr 2020.
14. Ambuj Sahu, Artificial Intelligence in Military Operations: Where does India Stand, accessed from the site https://www.orfonline.org/expert-speak/artificial-intelligence-military-operations-where-does-india-stand-54030/ on 06 Apr 2020.
15. Shaurya Karanbir Gurung, Army Pans to Induct AI to bolster Capability, accessed from the site https:// economictimes.indiatimes.com/news/defence/army-plans-to-induct-ai-to-bolster-capability/articleshow/7129887/ on 06 Apr 2020.
16. Maj Gen P.K. Chakravorty, Artificial Intelligence and Its impact on the Indian Armed forces, 05 May 2017, accessed from the site http://www.indiandefencereview.com/news/artificial-intelligence-and-its-impact-on-the-indian-armed-forces/ on 09 Dec 2017.
17. Johan Schubert, Conference Paper at Conference: 23rd International Command and Control Research & Technology Symposium at Pensacola, Fl, USA, in Nov 2018, Artificial Intelligence for Decision Support in Command and Control Systems.
18. GLOBSEC, Future Now, How AI is Already Changing the Global and Military Landscape, accessed from the site https://www.globsec.org/2018/02/06/future-now-ai-already-changing-global-military-landscape/ on 15 Mar 2020.
19. Matthew R. Voke, Major, USAF, Artificial Intelligence for Command and Control of Air Power, accessed from the site https://media.defense.gov/2019/Nov/27/2002218265/-1/-1/0/WF_72_VOKE_%20ARTIFICIAL_INTELLIGENCE_ FOR_ COMMAND_AND_CONTROL_OF_AIR_POWER.PDF on 10 Mar 2020.
20. Dr. Gordon Cooke, Magic Bullets: The future of Artificial in Weapon Systems, accessed from the site https:// www.army.mil/article/223026/magic_bullets_the_future_of_ artificial_intelligence_in_weapons_systems on 10 Mar 2020.
21. Ibid.
22. Wikipedia, Lethal Autonomous Weapon accessed from https://en.wikipedia.org/wiki/Lethal_autonomous weapon on 10 Mar 2020.
23. Michael T. Clare, Autonomous Weapon Systems and Laws of War accessed from the site on 10 Mar 2020 https://www.armscontrol.org/act/2019-03/features/autonomous-weapons-systems-laws-war.
24. Ross Davies, Dumb or Smart: The Future of Military Robots, accessed from the site

https://www.army-technology.com/features/dumb-or-smart-the-future-of-military-robots/ on 03 Apr 2020.

25. Chris Opfer, Are robots replacing human soldiers, accessed from the site https://science.howstuffworks.com/robots-replacing-soldiers1.htm on 03 Apr 2020.
26. Ross Davies, Dumb or Smart: The Future of Military Robots, accessed from the site https://www.army-technology.com/features/dumb-or-smart-the-future-of-military-robots/ on 03 Apr 2020.
27. Anuj Mishra and Simpy Kumari, Military Robots Play a Pivotal Role as Tactical and Operational Tool For Armed Forces, accessed from the site https://blog.marketresearch.com/military-robots-play-a-pivotal-role-as-a-tactical-and-operational-tool-for-armed-forces on 03 Apr 2020.
28. Michael Abrams, Top 5 Aerospace Trends of Now and the Future, accessed from the site http://www.asme.org/ engineering-topics/articles/aerospace-defense/top-5-aerospace-trends-now-future on 24 Feb 2018.
29. Sally Cole, Artificial Intelligence can help warfighters on many fronts accessed from the site http://mil-embedded.com/articles/artificial-intelligence-help-warfighters-many-fronts/ on 15 Mar 2020.
30. Marcus Roth, AI in Military drones and UAVs – Current Applications, accessed from the site https://emerj.com/ ai-sector-overviews/ai-drones-and-uavs-in-the-military-current-applications/ on 10 Mar 2020.
31. J.R. Wilson, AI in Unmanned Vehicles accessed from the site https://www.military aerospace.com/home/article/ 16709577/artificial-intelligence-ai-in-unmanned-vehicles on 10 Mar 2020.
32. Artificial Intelligence for Military Simulation, https://www.nlr.org/flyers/en/f523-artificial-intelligence-for-military-simulation.pdf on 14 Mar 2020.
33. ACM SIGSIM, accessed from the site https://www.acm-sigsim-mskr.org/MSAreas/AIBased/aiBased.htm on 14 Mar 2020.
34. Gavin Wilkinson, Integrating Artificial Intelligence With Simulation Modelling, accessed from the site https:// www.anylogic.com/blog/integrating-artificial-intelligence-with-simulation-modeling/ on 14 Mar 2020.
35. Matt Shipman, How AI Will Help Train Soldiers in Future, accessed from the site https://news.ncsu.edu/2019/ 10/ai-training-future-soldiers/ on 15 Mar 2020.
36. Sally Cole, Artificial Intelligence can help warfighters on many fronts, accessed from the site http://mil-embedded.com/articles/artificial-intelligence-help-warfighters-many-fronts/ on 15 Mar 2020.
37. Millicent Abadicio, Artificial Intelligence for Military Logistics – Current Applications, accessed from the site https://emerj.com/ai-sector-overviews/artificial-intelligence-military-logistics/ on 15 Mar 2020.
38. Tejaswi Singh and Amit Gulhane, 8 Key Military applications for Artificial Intelligence, accessed from the site, https://blog.marketresearch.com/8-key-military-applications-for-artificial-intelligence-in-2018 on 15 Mar 2020.
39. Congressional Research Services, accessed from the site https://fas.org/sgp/crs/natsec/R45178.pdf on 15 Mar 2020.
40. Cyberwarfare, accessed from the site https://searchsecurity.techtarget.com/definition/cyberwarfare on 06 Mar 2020.
41. Ibid.
42. Information accessed from the site https://en.wikipedia.org/wiki/Cyberwarfare on

06 Mar 2020.

43. Caleb Townsend, Cyber warfare: Modern Front-Lines, accessed from the site https://www.uscybersecurity.net/ cyber-warfare/ on 07 Mar 2020.
44. Ibid.
45. IT Pro Team, What is cyber warfare, accessed from the site https://www.itpro.co.uk/security/28170/what-is-cyber-warfare on 07 Mar 2020.
46. Ibid.
47. Sue Halpern, How Cyber Weapons are Changing the Landscape of Modern Warfare, accessed from the site https://www.newyorker.com/tech/annals-of-technology/how-cyber-weapons-are-changing-the-landscape-of-modern-warfare.
48. Ibid.
49. Maxwell Davies, What is the future of Cyber Warfare, accessed from the site https://blog.v-hr.com/blog/what-is-the-future-of-cyber-warfare on 08 Mar 2020.
50. Anna Granova, Marco Slaviero, Cyber Warfare, accessed from https://www.sciencedirect.com/topics/computer-science/cyber-operation on 08 Mar 2020.
51. Ibid.
52. Heba Soffar, Military Artificial Intelligence (Military Robots) Advantages, Disadvantages and Applications accessed from the site https://www.online-sciences.com/robotics/military-artificial-intelligence-military-robots-advantages-disadvantages-applications/ on 03 Apr 2020.
53. GLOBSEC, Future Now, How AI is Already Changing the Global and Military Landscape, accessed from the site https://www.globsec.org/2018/02/06/future-now-ai-already-changing-global-military-landscape/ on 15 Mar 2020.
54. GLOBSEC, Future Now, How AI is Already Changing the Global and Military Landscape, accessed from the site https://www.globsec.org/2018/02/06/future-now-ai-already-changing-global-military-landscape/ on 15 Mar 2020.
55. Todd South, DARPA to use Artificial Intelligence to help Commanders in Gray Zone Conflicts, accessed from https://www.armytimes.com/news/your-army/2018/03/27/darpa-to-use-artificial-intelligence-to-help-commanders-in-gray-zone-conflicts/ on 15 Mar 2020.
56. Outreach at DARPA.MILMaking Gray Zone Activity More Black and White, accessed from the site https:// www.darpa.mil/news-events/2018-03-14 on 15 Mar 2020.
57. Louis A. Delmonte, Genius Weapons: Artificial Intelligence, Autonomous Weaponry and the Future of Warfare, accessed from the site https://rowman.com/ISBN/9781633884526/Genius-Weapons-Artificial-Intelligence-Autonomous-Weaponry-and-the-Future-of-Warfare on 10 Mar 2020.
58. Alexandra Brzozowoski, Autonomous weapons, AI are future of defence but require ethical debate, accessed from the site https://www.euractiv.com/section/defence-and-security/interview/autonomous-weapons-ai-are-future-of-defence-but-require-ethical-debate-says-expert/ on 10 Mar 2020.
59. Aerospace Defence and Security, Defence Technology Innovation and the future of military capabilities, accessed from the site https://ihsmarkit.com/research-analysis/defence-technology-innovation-and-the-future-of-military-capabilities.html on 23 Feb 2018.
60. Maj Albert A.C. Harris III, Preparing for Multi-Domain Warfare, accessed from the site https://www.airuniversity. af.edu/Portals/10/ASPJ/journals/Volume-32_Issue-3/V-Harris.pdf on 01 Apr 2020.

15

Information and Psychological Operations: Emerging Force Multipliers

Lieutenant General PR Kumar

> *"We must recognize the new realities of modern warfare and modern landscape of a battlefield."*
>
> **—Susan Davis**

Preamble

The emerging multi polar world with increasing nationalism, authoritarianism and bilateralism is changing the international security landscape. The established rules based liberal democratic world order is being challenged, ironically by its creators. Emerging and dynamic geo-political and strategic alliances, 24x7 competitive and confrontationist multiple domain activities by nations, niche and COTS (commonly available off the shelf) technologies, potency of both kinetic and non-kinetic/cognitive instruments, has changed the scope of security and enlarged the spectrum of operations in geographical area, space, time, levels of conflict, while creating an ever-growing overlap between the military and civil domains, and most importantly blurring the distinction between peace and war. Creating, retaining and expanding strategic space is an essential pre-requisite for India's status as a regional power and leading balancing power. Confrontation/conflicts have moved from attrition to manoeuvre and now to a combination of the above along with the cognitive domains of Information (Influence) Operations (IIO/IO) and

Psychological Operations (PSYOPS). Nations would always prefer achieving their strategic aims without warfighting in the traditional sense, and impose their will using cognitive/non-kinetic domains. This chapter would focus less on addressing the importance of IO and PSYOPS which is a sine qua non in today's security environment, but on growing scope, potency, application, military structures and functions, and its ubiquitous presence and effects in all domains.

Unique Non-Kinetic Domain. Their uniqueness lies in the fact that questions of sovereignty are ambiguous at best in IO and PSYOPS. The domains cannot be segmented into a military and civilian sphere in ways that we do in traditional areas like land, sea, or air. One cannot declare an 'exclusive information zone' or even a "war zone" in information domain. It's the best space for conducting grey zone operations, as attribution, intentions and even final impact are very difficult to discern. That makes calculating proportional responses problematic. Ubiquitous social media (the elixir of IO), through the internet is changing war and politics, just as war and politics are changing the internet[1]. Terrorists livestream their attacks, "Twitter wars" produce real-world casualties, and viral disinformation alters not just the flow of battles, but the very fate of nations. The result is that war, technology, and politics have blurred into a new kind of battlespace that plays out through our media, smartphones, onto our minds, groups and society[2]. IO can paralyse/degrade Nations (specially its leaders and people) capability and capacity to wage war and more easily stay within the boundaries of adversarial Nations and its allies red lines for military retaliation. Our immediate neighbours specially China and its client Pakistan are prosecuting IO and PSYOPS against India as I write. Countering them as also prosecuting counter IO is a challenge specially against opaque, digitally isolated China. Military capabilities alone may not be an effective tool to deter a particular adversary's action, making other instruments of power the primary deterrent, of which IO and PSYOPS are pivotal and often deciding constituents. Many illiberal/authoritarian nationalistic smaller nations or even groups have created an exponential impact on the world stage mainly by IO and PSYOPS (North Korea, Iran, Pakistan, Al Qaeda, Taliban, IS), staying below the threshold of actual war/conflict. Organisation and structures for IO and PSYOPS at the national and military level needs to reviewed and made responsive to current and future wars, the contours of which is being discussed later.

Overview of Information Operations (IO) and Psychological Operations (PSYOPS)

Information Operations (IO) is the integrated employment (including military), of information-related capabilities in concert with other lines of operation to influence, disrupt, corrupt, or usurp the decision-making of adversaries and potential adversaries while protecting our own[3]. Currently in the Indian Army, IO subsumes electronic warfare (EW), cyber warfare, perception management and psychological warfare. The US military in its Joint Publication 3-13[4], "describes IO as the integrated employment of electronic warfare (EW), computer network operations (CNO), military deception (MILDEC), and operational security (OPSEC). Enlarging the scope, their information-related capabilities include military information support operations (MISO), operations security, public affairs, civil affairs operations (CAO), and cyberspace operations. EW contributes to the success of IO by using offensive and defensive tactics and techniques in a variety of combinations to shape, disrupt, and exploit adversarial use of the electro-magnetic spectrum (EMS) while protecting friendly freedom of action in that spectrum. As the use of EMS has become universal in military operations, so has EW become involved in all aspects of IO. Maximum control of the EMS, including the capability to disrupt all current and future communication systems, sensors, and weapons systems can prove decisive. As the scope and technology expands, some western countries are now using the term Information Environment Operations (IEO)[5]. 24x7 operations (strategic to tactical and multi domain) are on to seize, retain, and exploit the initiative in the information space and consolidate gains, to achieve a decisive information advantage over enemies and adversaries. IO coupled with PSYOPS can provide commanders additional ways and means to influence adversaries command, control and decision making, attenuate threat potency (physical and cognitive), enemy formations and populations and their will to fight; in sum enhance probability of domination/achieving the strategic objective without fighting.

Psychological Operations (PSYOPS) are operations to convey selected information and indicators to individuals/leaders, audiences to influence their emotions, motives, and objective reasoning, and ultimately the behavior of governments, organizations, groups, and individuals[6]. PSYOPS has become dispersed and democratized. And the target audience for psychological warfare has expanded globally. People everywhere might be motivated or affected by what they see, read or hear, to support one side or the other in a given conflict, pressure their government to do so, or even join in directly, as was seen in the flood of foreign fighters into Syria's civil war. In our armed forces, PSYOPS is a part of IO. In the US, psychological operations form part of the Combat Arm Manoeuvre, Fires and Effects Branch (MFE) showcasing its importance. After all human minds (specially leaders and military commanders and local populace) are principal cognitive elements of decision making. IO and PSYOPS are mutually inclusive dealing with information and the mind.

PSYOPS conducted at the tactical level can have strategic effects and must follow a process/protocol that must be understood, and the necessity for timely decisions is fundamental to effective PSYOPS and IO. This is particularly important in the early stages of an operation given the time it takes to develop, design, produce, distribute, disseminate, and evaluate PSYOPS products and actions. All PSYOPS are planned at the strategic or operational level and should generally be executed/conducted under the supervision of sanctioning authority. Each nation has its own traditional and cultural way of conducting PSYOPS. PSYOPS for counter insurgency/ terrorist operations are a vital component and targets the local population, fence sitters, terrorists, their runners and adversarial nations conducting proxy war. The same is being conducted by the adversary nation or terrorist organisations. PSYOPS can be white when it is overtly official or acknowledged as an act of the Government or sources close to it, obviously its effectiveness is based on truth; Grey operations are deliberately ambiguous and true source (Government or military not revealed); Black operations appears as if it emanates from a known adversary and where there is a measure of plausible deniability.

Social Media (SM); Media Weapons [can] actually be more potent than atomic bombs: Propaganda Handbook of the Islamic State

SM has emerged/positioned itself as an inescapable, powerful and ubiquitous tool for IO and PSYOPS. It is the lynchpin of this seismic change in the character of conflict. As journalist David Patrikarakos notes[7], platforms like YouTube, Twitter and Facebook allow individuals to "resonate globally, with a power and reach once reserved for large media institutions or governments." SM, according to security experts PW Singer and Emerson[8], has "become a battlefield where information itself is weaponized." This makes the psychological dimension of conflict exceptionally complex and fast-changing. To remain effective in this new environment, our Government, intelligence agencies and armed forces need narrative shaping capacities and capabilities. To fight and win on the battlefield of SM, the military must have the ability to affect perceptions both in a military area of operations and to a global, domestic, regional and adversarial audience, rapidly shifting themes and messages for maximum effectiveness. Most armed forces around the globe including the US (which was the first of the block) and India are grappling with how to set an aim/end state, plan, coordinate, finetune, prosecute timely, and institutionalise structures, develop and train manpower and use SM to prosecute IO and PSYOPS.

Recent Geo-Political Events where IO and PSYOPS impacted Outcome[9]

USA-Iran Standoff and Role of Russia. Recent events including the US-Iran standoff have highlighted the pivotal role of IIO and PSYOPS. For decades due to reasons of real politik (energy, domination of Middle East and SLOCs et al) USA has used IO and PSYOPS to paint an "outcast/ rogue narrative" about Iran, and recently has upped the ante with the seeming intention of seeking a regime change. Russia under Putin has very ingenuously wedged itself wherever there seems to be a power vacuum/political/diplomatic friction to rise again as a catalyst power. Russia-Iran relations is a paradox, as Russia benefits immensely and strategically from the standoff and Iranian isolation, but would try to support Iran both covertly and overtly to stay firm on its stand-off with USA. With negligible physical intervention but by employing IO and PSYOPS, Russia and China are undermining US credibility and expanding their footprint, with the intention of becoming the most influential players.

Balakot. While kinetic means were used by India to carry out the air strikes into Pakistan, the narrative and optics played out by both India and Pakistan were done using the domain of IO and PSYOPS. There are two opposing views by security strategists regarding optics of Balakot air strike inside Pakistan. Pakistan's pro-active and timely responses in terms of media coverage, submission of proof, producing witnesses, internalising, centralising and coordinating a plausible narrative of deniability of shooting down of F 16, capture of IAF pilot, quick release of Wg Cdr

Abhinandan, a pragmatic retaliatory air strike showcasing restraint did provide necessary optics of a reasonable, mature Nation acting against a desperate India led by a warmongering political party. On the other hand, India for political reasons and expediency made an operational blunder which soon took strategic dimensions. India after the attack, laid emphasis on the effect of the raid in terms of infrastructural and terrorist casualties, whereas the act of conveying to its own public, international community and most importantly Pakistan (both Army and public) that 'enough is enough' of the proxy war took a backseat. By the time India realized it, Pakistan had seized the opportunity and took the initiative in denying, obfuscating and casting doubts on the very 'surgical air strike deep into Pakistan air space' which was the 'cause celebre and raison de' etre', and a brilliantly thought out and executed geo-politiacal and strategic manoeuvre. This was naturally made worse by a questioning and skeptical intelligencia and opposition. In the end, India's standing as a mature, democratic, rising, responsible nuclear weapon state following a liberal world order helped her, while it also took some sheen of its image.

Wuhan and After: A classic case of IO and PSYOPS. Doklam (2017) incident was qualitatively different (involving a third country, Bhutan) and proved a testing ground for China's and India's IIO and PSYOPS capabilities. Beijing was uncharacteristically vocal with an unprecedented propaganda push often involving ultimatums, and the use of slogans such as "border line is the bottom line." Chinese military officers spoke of this as a "no smoke battlefield" and China used a number of outlets; Xinhua, People's Daily, the PLA Daily, foreign and defence ministries, and Embassy in New Delhi to issue coordinated messages. This was followed by a sudden lowering of temperatures after the standoff was resolved and in the run-up to the Wuhan Summit in 2018. Wuhan is a classic case of Chinese mastery and penchant for IO and PSYOPS (3 Warfare strategy) to achieve strategic goals. The high profile visit and meeting between President Xi Jinping and PM Modi at Wuhan, followed by Mamallapuram, while not producing any substantial outcome/assurances/benefits for India, did lull us into a state of complacency. The political hierarchy, MEA, China experts and watchers (even international) and our defence forces believed what was essentially a smokescreen, to be a major milestone in India-China border rapprochement. It led to the current standoff along the LAC in East Ladakh which is by far the most challenging and serious security lapse since the 1962 debacle. The government (CCS), intelligence agencies, NSA and the armed forces could not gather the intent of the massed Chinese troops close to the LAC ostensibly conducting routine training. It goes to the credit of the PM and the Army that with bold and resolute operational pro-active actions, the scales are about even, or else the strategic ramifications could have been tragic and irretrievable for India. The Chinese almost pulled off a copybook manoeuvre, employing IO and PSYOPS for achieving strategic victory without fighting. The jury is still out, on how the impasse will end. India always believed in strategic restraint and strategic autonomy which it has reviewed based on Chinese escalation. India is actively and successfully conducting its own counter IIO and PSYOPS both internally and internationally, and it would be fair to state that it is currently winning the battle.

Another extremely vivid and game changing event in history where IO and PSYOPS played the pivotal part is the Capture of Northern Iraq by ISIS[10] (terrorism/ fundamentalism played out with a twist, which included occupation of real estate). In the summer of 2014 the IS (ISIL/ISIS or Daesh in Arabic) roared into Northern Iraq in pick-ups and fully armed (even swords), and blew away four fully trained and equipped Iraqi divisions which vanished overnight into thin air. But, contrary to tradition, they did not keep their operations a secret but wanted the world to know everything about it. The IS succeeded in subverting the minds of all commanders and the local population psychologically, and used the internet as a weapon to carry out a blitzkrieg. There is a lot of talk of 'cyber security and cyberwar', but the IS had no real cyber capabilities but won a victory which was not possible, it hadn't hacked the network but hacked the information on it.

Ubiquitous SM (integral component of IO and PSYOPS) is affecting the interplay of Nations, and by extension the entire global system. Along with diplomats and heads of state an increasing number of military leaders from the strategic to even tactical levels (in fact it now forms part of military operations with requisite structures, staff and equipment), have embraced the social media revolution. They have left behind the slow moving, ritualistic system that governed international relations for centuries. A multi-layered-ethnic-lingual-religious-diverse India with its geographical span can very easily spin into instability with adversaries' IO and PSYOPS, concurrently threat to sovereignty and integrity would coalesce/ strengthen unifying bonds (like in Pakistan against India).

IIO, IW and PSYOPS Concepts and Organisations of Major Powers and Pakistan

China. PLA approach to modern warfare to include training, organisation and equipping for over the past two decades has been thoroughly influenced by systems thinking. For them 'War has changed drastically from the traditional wars to a contest among numerous adversarial operating systems and referred to as systems confrontation'. Chinese most recent White Paper states that the PLA'S "integrated combat forces .... [are to be] employed to prevail in sys-vs-sys operations featuring dominance, precision strikes, and joint operations."[11] PLA is also preparing to conduct "political warfare," including what is termed the "three warfares": public opinion warfare, legal warfare, and psychological warfare. Psychological warfare is in some ways the most far-reaching of the "three warfares[12]." The primary objective of the Chinese to paralyse enemy's operating systems is to degrade or disrupt the flow of information within the adversary's operating systems. The book *'Unrestricted Warfare'*[13] (published 1999! cyber and information space has revolutionized warfare and security concepts since then) illustrates their adoption of multi-domain warfare/ operations (MDW/O) with special emphasis on IIO, PSYOPS and cyber operations decades ago. However, this very closed information environment if penetrated can reap mega dividends, and we must do so at the strategic level concurrently conducting counter IO.

Russia. They have always been masters of the art of disinformation, deception, information influence operations and perception management. They use the concepts enunciated in their 'Reflexive Control Theory'[14] having both military and civil uses, which makes it more apt for MDW which in itself is a concept to control the political and military will of a Nation. They have been studying it for decades and used it for interference with the decision-making capability of a political or military leader, and can be employed on the human-mental and computer-based decision-making processes. Russia has managed to synchronise both the strategic to tactical security actions, as also multi domain synergy when it comes to national interests, and is undergoing rapid structural and organization changes. Undeniably, grey zone operations and IO has allowed Russia to punch much above its current weight and be a big player in Middle East, Africa and other parts of the world.

USA. The US Army is preparing to carry out major, organizational changes to its force structure within the next five years, according to the Futures and Concepts Centre Director. "There is going to be a fundamental change in the organizational structure to conduct multi domain operations, the new concept of warfighting," Lt. Gen. Eric Wesley told an audience at the Centre for a New American Security in Washington on 04 March 19[15]. Open sources state that they are focusing on non-kinetic forces like cyber, information, computer, big data, PSYOPS, deception, and operational security, and are currenly examining how to create functional structures by clubbing and combining into basic Corps. In terms of organization and structures the US Army has both integral information operational staff above Division and also has the following:

- **1st IO Command (Land).** Provides distinctly tailored IO and cyberspace operations planning, synchronization, assessment, and feedback support to the Army.
- **56th, 71st and 151st Theater IO Gp (TIOG).** TIOGs maintains regional focus but can deploy elsewhere too. It has same composition as the 1st Bn, and deploys purpose-built IO field support teams designed to provide the necessary IO support required by the requesting comd. You can call it a theatre resource.

In 2017, the Chief of Staff of the Army directed the design and testing of Multi-Domain Task Forces (MDTFs)[16] as forward- stationed formations able to execute aspects of MDO. Designed to deliver long-range precision joint strike as well as integrate air and missile defense, electronic warfare, space, cyber, and information operations, the MDTF operates across all domains, the EMS, and the information environment in both competition and conflict to provide the Joint Force and coalition with new capabilities to enable the defeat the Chinese anti-access and area denial strategies. Most significantly, the MDTF demonstrated methods of employing layered non-kinetic effects (EW, space, cyberspace, and information and psychological) operations.

Pakistan. ISI, Pakistan according to many experts, think tanks, articles is rated as one of the best, most dangerous and powerful intelligence agencies (its staffing is disproportionately large given its size and strategic requirements) in the World with very vast and sweeping powers answerable only to the COAS Pakistan Army[17]. Historical and geo-strategic compulsions and existential reasons (both externally and internally) in

Pakistani perception dictate a larger than life role to IO and PSYOPS to achieve its strategic objectives without crossing the red line/threshold of conflict. Pakistan mainly through ISI has been waging relentless proxy war against India. It has carried out terrorist and IO globally (US, UK, France, Afghanistan, Iran, Iraq, Bosnia, Nepal to name some) and supports multitude of terrorist organisations (HM, LeT, Al-Badr, HuM, Haqqani Network). The organisational structures and departments can be found online. Apart from its three wings (internal, external and foreign relations !) it has many departments viz covert action, joint intelligence (int), joint int bureau, joint counterint bureau (for India), sigint, techint, SS Directorate (using SSG for terrorist activities) and Political Internal Division. Pakistan (ISI) uses psychological and unconventional/hybrid operations in a synergistic role. Surprise, deception and IO have always formed an integral part of their military operational plans.

IO and PSYOPS in the Indian Context

Where are we & what needs to be done to meet future Challenges. Organizational structures and reforms for IO and PSYOPS both at the strategic realm and military are a work in progress even amongst the pioneer powers, and so it is with India. IO and PSYOPS during peace, competition and confrontation stage is planned and tasked at the national and strategic level. The Armed Forces continue to mainly focus on war fighting (including the present extra focus on grey zone/hybrid/counter terrorism operations) and attrition activities, with increasing capability and capacity to prosecute offensive and defensive non-kinetic MDO at all levels down to tactical. Therefore, the organisational and structural reforms envisaged, need to be rooted in the current structures, cause least turbulence, and be phased depending entirely on our increasing synergy, jointness, capabilities and capacities. Change for the sake of change and peer pressure needs to be avoided as our threat scenario, technological threshold, HR management, economics, geo-political landscape and geography are unique. This methodology hopefully will be adopted in India due to strategic and operational compulsions, due to our rather dynamic regional security environment. Each system and interlink should be unique and mission specific; and only some or all the systems may be created depending on the adversary and mission. Naturally the systems need to be 'seamlessly linked'. The systems and organisations of great powers specially China need to be analysed in detail. India must carry out a pragmatic holistic assessment of allies and foes alike (*real politik* - numerous plausible threat contingencies from peace to war and MD) to proactively shape conditions in our favour, building from its strengths, and respond effectively when vulnerabilities are exploited. This naturally requires improvements in our government policies, authorities, and capabilities, and structures and organisations at the National level. They exist but need a road map, focus and synergy.

Information, Media, Cyber Policies and Regulations[18]. Decision-making power in the Indian media regulation is fairly centralized, with the central Government and ministries making the final call when it comes to new policies and appointments. Politicians have a keen interest in news media regulation owing to the high degree of political ownership in the sector. Thus, political and electoral logic shapes media regulation. The New Media Wing (NMW) and the Electronic Media Monitoring Centre (EMMC) come under the Ministry of Information and Broadcasting (MIB) and are involved in media surveillance along with the Ministry of Home Affairs (MHA). The National Intelligence Grid (NATGRID) which keeps all sorts of citizen data in a single database that can be accessed by officers from RAW, CBI, IB and comes under the MHA. The National Cyber Coordination Center (NCCC) and the National Crime Records Bureau (NCRB) also come under this ministry. The Ministry of Communication and Information Technology controls CERT-In, the Indian Computer Emergency Response Team that performs emergency cybersecurity functions and releases annual reports of security incidents. The proposed National Media Analytics Centre (NMAC) and Digital Swachhata Kendra (DSK) will also come under the MCIT. NMAC will monitor and analyse content on the internet and counter negative content, while DSK will look to deal with malware and botnets. The Department of Electronics and Information Technology (DEITY) operating under the MCIT is responsible for ensuring cyberspace security, other than delivering government services online and promoting the IT sector. Given its strategic importance the Govt has ordered establishment of the 'Defence Cyber Agency'[19].

Operational Philosophy for IO. Our operational philosophy should be; "the application of specific and special information and media, in consonance with physical action, to realise a strategic goal and in support of political and military objectives". Such efforts are aimed at a variety of potential audiences and usually involve operational missions against an opponent's psychological and cognitive capacities (Note: There are myriad targets and objects; it is applied against the enemy, but also against friends; it targets externally, but also internally). Strategic IO and PSYOPS for security and military purposes will mainly be dealt at the PMO, NSA, CDS and service HQs level with valuable inputs from all concerned Ministries (mainly MEA, MHA, MoD, I&B, Science and Tech, Aviation etc) and Intelligence Agencies. Execution will be left to field formations/ units (in all domains, not just armed forces) overseen centrally or by Mission Control based on task.

Our Government and Armed Forces have already begun the process of reforms by way of creation of DPC and CDS who has a three-dimensional charter, giving him a pivotal task of implementation of the process. The charter of CDS is not being elaborated upon which in itself if allowed to be actioned is a major reform and concrete step towards civil-military integration, military structural and organizational reforms, push towards indigenization and pragmatic PPP, economic powers and reforms, and impetus and prioritization to modernization. There is an absolute necessity of clearly established chain of command, control and communications and necessary authorities and permissions to operate in competition and rapid transition to conflict effectively. Based on the National Security Strategy (NSS) and National Military Strategy (NMS) promulgated by CCS and NSA/CDS, the CDS and PCCOCS (Permanent Chairman, Chiefs of Staff Committee) should prepare Conflict Prevention including Deterrence, Conflict Management and Conflict Termination Strategies of which IO and PSYOPS against specific threats is an essential ingredient.

Develop Multi-domain Rapid Response Mechanism[20]. There is a requirement of a central cognitive/non-kinetic operations centre (NKOC) where all information is collected, collated, planning and decision making is taken and loop is completed where 'after action effect' is analysed and the circle continues. Staff for the NKOC starting from NSCS (will provide inputs to the CCS and DPC) and PCCOSC will be a mix of military, bureaucracy and core domain experts. At the Services, MO and Theatre level it can be tri-services manned. At Army Corps and Divisional level, we can have Col GS (NK) and/or GSO 1 (NK) who will be in charge of non-kinetic domains. Advisors from other Arms and Services like engineers, signals, EW, PI will get linked from within the HQs. The important aspect is to institutionalise the process so it becomes an integral part of operational planning, which will happen due to the changing dynamics of security and conflict. PSYOPS will be directly under the Commander and his chosen staff while execution is left to specifically tasked formations/units/sub-units (including cyber and IO units). The setting up of a tri-services 'Cyber Defence Agency', and DGIW under a freshly structured DCOAS (Strategy) in Army HQ who will also oversee functioning of DGMO, DGMI and DGPP underscores the growing awareness of the vital role of IO and PSYOPS within the Govt and Armed Forces both in peacetime and conflict[21]. Accordingly, HQ IDS and each service HQs are reviewing IW and IO functional organisations and structures[22].

Electronic Warfare (EW)[23]. Strategic and tri-services tasks are executed by ADG SI (along with services assets) with independent SIGINT/EW resources tasked by DG DIA/NSA/CCOSC. For perception management/ PI we have the NIB (National Information Bureau) reporting to the NSA. This is supplemented by inputs from NTRO, R&AW, IB and NIA (National Intelligence Agency). For EW, the Army has EW Groups and Sub Groups under the Theatre Commander and one to two Sub Groups with active Corps (along LAC, LC and IB) which carry out EW tasks envisaged by the theatre and corps commanders. Keeping the EW groups modernized so they function and fulfill their mandated tasks is a challenge in this fast-paced technological field. A review of its affiliation (should it become a part of DGIW?), organization, number of units to meet strategic and operational tasks, modern technological equipment and manning/career growth needs to be carried out expeditiously. For IO presently in the Army, we have the ADG PI operating under the DGMI and the ADG IW under the DGMO. IW branch has a section looking after communications including strategic and an IW section, along with an autonomous unit operating under the DGMO looking after cyber defence and whenever mandated limited cyber offence. The DGMI too has cyber warfare capabilities. The IAF similarly has the ACS E&IW (Electronic and Information Warfare) at Air HQ and the IN has ACNS (Ops and IW) who apart from coordination operations operates an IW Cell comprising of a dozen officers and 20 odd seamen, and an independent SIGINT unit. However, in active HQs Northern and Eastern Command and their affiliated Corps, IW sub-branches headed by a Brig/Col are actively engaged in IO operations with special focus on SM. There are no formal or institutionalized units below that in all three Services. There is a certain amount of ambiguity existing in specific nuances of terminology and tasking, which naturally leads to some diffusion in operations. With the advent of MDO, we will need to bring more clarity in the organisation and structures as also operational employment.

Raising of Information and Cyber Operational Units/Sub Units. Similar to EW units and sub units at Service HQs, and integral to Theatre and Operational (pivot and strike corps) formations, we need to raise IO and Cyber units to carry out planning, tasking and execution of offensive and defensive operations. Pro-active actions in both domains will provide exponential gains at the national to tactical levels, and defensive operations can protect us from highly destructive/damaging adversarial operations. US, Russia, China and many modern armed forces have these units in their orbat for decades. A battalion at the Army HQ level with a coy at theatre and corps level ab initio with expansion based on experience and operational necessity. Operational discussions on whether structures and organisations for IO should be tri-services ab initio should be held, though at this stage service specific would prove more effective, but costly financially and in HR. While writing out the pioneering paper and charter of Cyber Defence Agency and DGIW, due thought must be given to ab initio tri-services structures for SF Division, strategic forces, long range missile/rocket formations with bricks for lower formations and contingencies. We also need Information Warfare/ Operations Officers, JCOs and NCOS deployed at all levels of seniority and formations up to brigade level in a phased manner.

Case for a Specific Corps. Till such time a Corps of Information Operations is established, officers and OR from all arms and services with adequate aptitude and training can man these appointments. Due thought on training, creation of tri-services and individual services training nodes for conduct of basic and advanced courses for Officers and all ranks be given and put down to make it a comprehensive time bound phased organization and structure for IO, IW and PSYOPS. Serious consideration needs to be given to creating basic corps for IO, IW (including EW), Cyber, PSYOPS, Space and Strategic Forces by grouping of similar fields (need not have basic corps individually but similar functional and interrelated fields can be grouped)[24]. This will ensure clear career growth prospects, meet HR aspirations and optimize officer and soldier HR mgt. Here, we have the option of creating a tri-services IO Corps ab initio which will be a very complex process given the lack of jointness as also diverse IO requirements, but enjoys great advantages as intrinsically IO are essentially tri-services specially at the strategic and operational level, and in future too, MDO will be joint operations. Second option which is more pragmatic and implementable is to create individual Service oriented IO Corps.

Military Operations Other Than War (MOOTW). IO and PSYOPS are essential operations for Military Operations Other Than War (MOOTW) to include Aid to Civil Authorities, HADR, IS duties, UNPKO, Out of Area Contingency (OOAC) tasks including assistance to Friendly Foreign Countries (FFCs), assistance in 'Non Combatant Evacuation Procedures, Force Projection Capability (India's role as a regional security provider); and Grey Zone Operations in Dense Urban Environment[25].

Training and Courses. Great thought needs to be given, as this will actually create the desired effect at the ends. Both service specific and tri-services level modules need to be created from the basic to advanced to include field training under battle conditions. At the national level, all players need to be provided with a road map by NSA/NSCS.

Conclusion

History and wars have taught us that Nations and groups will respect India based on their perception of India's strength and vitality of our alliances and our will and intent to protect our national interests (ergo the need for IO and PSYOPS!). The world has entered a multi polar era, where nations are carrying out MDO 24x7 against friends and foes alike to create and maintain their strategic space in order to achieve their national aspirations and some just to survive. Non-kinetic/cognitive domains coupled with technology are emerging as perennial players of which IO and PSYOPS are the pivots, which form the grid/base on which other domains operate to achieve strategic to tactical objectives (including military), during cooperation, competition, confrontation and conflict. No doubt, when and if required kinetic/physical domains would be the final arbiter. IO and PSYOPS which target the mind of leaders and people are ubiquitous today. Our Nation and military have to analyse, plan, train and execute 24x7 IO and PSYOPS tailored for specific targets, missions and time, as it's not a one size fits all exercise. For this we need well thought out structures from the strategic to tactical level for optimum and effective operations. It would not be incorrect or dramatic to state that 'prosecution of and protection against IO and PSYOPS has become existential for the Nation and our Armed Forces'. This requires adoption of a shared war fighting philosophy across the Services (and the Government). Changing a Service's war fighting philosophy requires time and a shared vision across layers of successive leadership across all Services[26]. Initiation of the whole process will need approval and cooperation of multitude of agencies to include armed forces, the establishment and other security and domain actors. Leaders at each level must embrace the concept to provide the organizational, intellectual, and cultural space to establish and evolve the new tenets of competition and confrontation. A foundational joint education rather than a service-flavoured learning experience may be a more professional approach. While IO and PSYOPS have been prosecuted for centuries, even the global powers are finding their feet in creating formalised organisations and structures and current talk/writings on the subject are mainly aspirations. There is no doubt that transformation of our polity, bureaucracy, and people, and the Armed Forces is a must for fighting future wars, as Nations fight wars and not the military. We in India are just sinking our teeth into the capabilities of both mediums, and are already working on putting systems in place. History, geography and our security environment are the main drivers which are automatically prodding India to prepare for future wars, of which IO and PSYOPS will play game changing roles.

NOTES

1. 'The Operational Environment and the Changing Character of Future Warfare'; TRADOC paper, 2017.
2. 'Like War: The weaponization of Social Media' by PW Singer and Emerson T.Brooking, An Eamon Dolan Book, Houghton Mifflin Harcout, 2018.
3. Derived from Wikipedia; US-Information Operations in Doctrine-jstor; www.jstor.org> stable; Field Manual 100-6, Information Operations, www.hsdl.org>abrstract; The Conduct of Information Operation, www.fas.org.irp.doddir.atp3-13-1.
4. 'The US Army in Multi Domain Operations 2028', 06 Dec 2018, TRADOC Pamphlet 525-3-1.
5. IEO is the integrated employment, during military operations, of information related capabilities (IRC) in concert with other lines of operations to influence, deceive, disrupt, corrupt, or usurp the decision making of enemies and adversaries while protecting our own; to influence enemy formations and populations to reduce their will to fight; and influence friendly and neutral populations to enable friendly operations.
6. Wikipedia, RAND Corporation, US Field Manuals specially FM 3-05.301 (FM 33-1-1) MCRP 3-40.6A; Psychological Operations Tactics, Techniques, and Procedures (www.fas.org.com).
7. 'Social Media Has Democratized Psychological Warfare. Can the US Military Adapt?'

Steven Metz, Friday, Nov. 16, 2018; https://www.worldpoliticsreview.com/insights/26772/social-media-has-democratized-psychological-warfare-can-the-u-s-military-adapt

8. 'Like War: The weaponization of Social Media' by PW Singer and Emerson T.Brooking, An Eamon Dolan Book, Houghton Mifflin Harcout, 2018.
9. All events being covered are major international issues covered widely in both print, TV and social media and by Think Tanks and security analysts and writers.
10. The event is widely covered and also paraphrased from 'Like War: The weaponization of Social Media' by PW Singer and Emerson T.Brooking, An Eamon Dolan Book, Houghton Mifflin Harcout, 2018.
11. 'China's Military Strategy', Beijing: The State Council Information Office of the People's Republic of China, 2015.
12. 'Winning Without Fighting: The Chinese Psychological Warfare Challenge' by Dean Cheng, 12 Jul 13, The Heritage Foundation, accessed on 01 Feb 20 on www.heritage.org.
13. 'Unrestricted Warfare' by Qiao Liang and Wang Xiangsui (Beijing: PLA Literature and Arts Publishing House, February 1999). English translation, 18 Jan 2000 – CIA FBIS (www.cryptome.org/cum.html).
14. 'Russia's Reflexive Theory and the Military' by Timothy L Thomas; Journal of Slavic Military Studies; 17-237-256-2004 published by Taylor and Francis Group.
15. 'The US Army is preparing for major changes to force structure' by Jen Judson on 06 Mar 19; https://www.defensenews.com/land/2019/03/06/major-army-force-structure-changes-afoot/
16. Accessed numerous TRADOC documents and articles (Think Tanks, Magazines and even articles on mainstream print and online media) on Multi-Domain Warfare/Environment/Operations to include 'The US Army in Multi-Domain Operations 2028'; Tradoc Pamphlet 525-3-1; www.tradoc.army.mil; Multi-Domain Battle: Evolution of Combined Arms for the 21st Century 2025-2040, Version 1.0 December 2017; Modern War Institute at West Point; www.mwi.usma.edu; Putting the Enemy between A Rock And A Hard Place: Multi-Domain Operations In Practice by Curt Taylor and Larry Kay; 27 Aug 19. Also finds ref from own article on 'Organisational Reforms for the Grey Zone Concept In the Indian Context' for CENJOWS.
17. Wikipedia on ISI; top 10 intelligence agencies in the world forbes rates Pakistan No 1 and numerous reports online. No shortage of credible sites citing terrorist and IO and PSYOPS activities by Pakistan.
18. Notes from numerous papers and publications to include 'Policy Making in India: Who's behind it?' By Archit Puri dated 26 Aug 2017 in Indian National Interest; www.nationalinterest.in accessed on 17 Jan 20; RSIS Monograph No. 27, 'National Security Decision-Making In India' by Bibhu Prasad Routray; S. Rajaratnam School of International Studies, https://www.files.ethz.ch/isn/163172/monograph27.pdf accessed on 10 Jan 20. 'National Security Decision Making: Overhaul Needed' by Gurmeet Kanwal, 26 Aug 14 and 'Organisational Reforms for the Grey Zone Concept in the Indian Context' by Lt Gen PR Kumar (Retd) for CENJOWS.
19. India to have Defence Cyber Agency in May; Rear Admiral Mohit to be its first chief; Asian News International dated 30 Apr 19 and numerous national mainstream media.
20. Paraphrased from 'Organisational Reforms for the Grey Zone Concept In the Indian Context' by Lt Gen PR Kumar (Retd) for CENJOWS.
21. India to have Defence Cyber Agency in May; Rear Admiral Mohit to be its first chief;

Asian News International dated 30 Apr 19 and numerous national mainstream media
22. Also peruse 'Organisation And Structures For IW and Influence Operations In Indian Context' by Lt Gen PR Kumar in CENJOWS Synergy Magazine of August 2019.
23. Paraphrased from 'Organisation and Structures For IW and Influence Operations In Indian Context' by Lt Gen PR Kumar (Retd) for CENJOWS magazine SYNERGY.
24. Ideas have been taken from 'Land Warfare Doctrine-Indian Army 2018' accessed in the net on 08 Jan 20, and from the Dissertation 'Org the Army for IW' by Col Maxell S Thibodeaus, US Army, USAWC Class of 2013 Dissertation.
25. 'Land Warfare Doctrine-Indian Army 2018'.
26. 'Multi Domain Warfare in Indian Context', USI National Security Paper 2018, by Lt Gen PR Kumar (Retd).

16

Disruptive Strategies: A Key Ingredient for Success in Future Conflicts

Lieutenant General (Dr.) JS Bajwa

Strategy is ultimately about exercising power.

—Gregory D. Foster

ABSTRACT

In the face of globalisation, the 'modern state' is shedding many of its responsibilities to non-state actors and even private actors. Postmodern wars are fought by a disparate array of fighting forces, many with no territory. While the nature of war (violent, interactive, and fundamentally political) remains constant, its character (technology, law, ethics, culture, methods of social, political, and military organization) is ever changing.

Though not a panacea, technology will remain an essential element of gaining advantage and an important driver of military change. Technological developments will be the most important factor to enable formulating disruptive strategies. Strategy is oriented towards the future by declaring intent and an indication of possible means to fulfil that intent related to securing 'national interests'. Political institutions declare war but military institutions fight them. Therefore, strategy must be made on political considerations.

The mind-set of not "losing an inch of territory" ties down forces. In the future technological-laden battlefield "boots on ground" will not mean as much less. The ground forces will need to be more distributed, more flexible and responsive in a larger battlefield geographic space. In future, the doctrines and capabilities of the adversaries will be less predictable and more ambiguous. To outmatch the adversary, adopting a pre-emptory offensive defence posture will disrupt the adversaries' plans. Take the battle into the enemy's territory.

Preamble

War has been a perennial feature of human history. It is condemned as an evil activity in which human beings show the darker side of their nature by using violence and killing to achieve their ends. Modern wars reflect a symbiotic relationship between a well-organised structure of governance and industrialisation. It developed along with what became the character of modern societies along with the power of the state through processes of centralisation, bureaucratisation and, to some extent, democratisation. It was influenced by the rise of powerful ideologies such as nationalism (Baylis, 2013: 33). Modern wars were state controlled, but in the post-Cold War era of the post-modern world, the era of industrialised great power war has passed and with it there has been an end of the last bastion—nuclear deterrence.

In the face of globalisation, the 'modern state' is shedding many of its responsibilities, including military responsibilities, to non-state actors and even private actors. Modern wars were fought by formally organised hierarchically structured armed forces of the state (Baylis, 2013: 48). Post-modern wars are fought by a disparate array of fighting forces which include guerrilla forces, foreign mercenaries, kin/clan-based irregular forces, terrorist networks with no territory. Recognising the blur of state and non-state actors and the fusion of interstate and intrastate conflicts, Frank Hoffman portrays modern wars as "hybrid wars" while Martin Shaw chose the term "degenerate warfare". A host of euphemisms for these 'new age' wars have emerged—Nuclear Biological Chemical War, $4^{th}/5^{th}$ Generation War, Asymmetric War, Hybrid War, Space War, Cyber War, Effect Based Operations, Low Intensity War, Special Forces Operations, Limited War, Non-Contact War, Guerrilla War, Sub-Conventional War, Counter Insurgency and Non-Traditional War, to name a few. Which war or combination of wars does a state prepare for will pose a strategic dilemma. There is a school of thought that while modern wars originated in the pursuit of perceived national interests and driven by geopolitical assumptions, post-modern wars are now focussing on 'identity politics'—religiously inspired or civilisational wars. These are generally more violent and do not have a defined beginning or end but are, nonetheless, political. The emergence of nuclear weapons had initiated a process of neutralising the most powerful weapons possessed by the leading powers and encouraged a security policy of restraint. So while the *nature of war* remains constant, its *character* is ever changing.

Technology

Though not a panacea, technology will remain an essential element of gaining advantage in the future operating environment and an important driver of military change over the next 20 years. The tempo of technological change will accelerate and human interaction with technology will increase significantly. (Joint Concept Note 1/17, *Future Force Concept: 1*). New military technologies have a destabilizing effect particularly on those who do not have a robust defence R&D and military industrial complex. When one party introduces a new technology, potential adversaries believe they are at risk until they can match or counter the innovation. Here again, weapon-importing nations are at a disadvantage. Military innovation can create a new dynamic for calculating risk among potential adversaries, leading them to reassess their views on deterrence and the role of nuclear weapons. Forces and understandings that once seemed adequate to produce stability are called into question. Since the middle of the nineteenth century, change in military technology has become a constant, through what Martin van Creveld has called 'invention of invention' (Baylis, 2013: 125). Undoubtedly, technological changes are bringing about a change from *quantity* to *quality* across the board. However, for institutional reasons, military organisations tend to fit new technologies into old doctrinal and operational frameworks. Quality of equipment is fully exploited by an apt combination of manpower and technology. Old systems of estimating military power by simplistic means of bean count or scientific calculations of attrition-driven models may no longer apply.

Technology is the key driver of change. Computerisation, by its awesome power of computing, has accelerated the rate of change in technological developments with widespread impacts on both individuals and societies. It will be the single most important factor that will affect any formulation of disruptive strategies. The nature of our workforce, how we fight wars, the risks posed by disease, and even our bodies and brains are all being transformed by new technology, and we can expect the future to bring even more dramatic changes. It is vital to understand the nature of technological change, its directions and possible impacts for humanity. It is necessary to be able to usefully predict and analyse the long-range trajectories and limitations of transformative technologies and establish how best to prepare for the societal influences, both positive and negative, that these will bring. Future technologies, such as machine learning or machine super-intelligence, human enhancement, synthetic biology and biosecurity, surveillance technology, quantum technologies, nanotechnology, Big Data analytics and computational neuroscience will begin to affect the world in less than a decade. Technology developments will offer the Armed Forces opportunities as well as pose challenges. Pressure on defence budgets, weapon proliferation and adversaries who choose to focus their capabilities in specific environments will all be contributing factors to technological challenges.

Human Factor

Human behaviour, undeniably, has a pivotal role to in the planning, preparation, declaration and execution of wars. There is an ongoing debate about the relative importance of *'nature'* versus *'nurture'* (heredity versus environment) as a determinant of human behaviour (Baylis, 2013: 72). Liberal thinkers prefer to emphasise the importance of *'nurture'* and are naturally attracted to the idea that aggression and war can be tamed. Conservative thinkers tend to believe that aggression is basic human *'nature'* and are therefore sceptical about possibilities of ridding the world of war. Even Albert Einstein and Sigmund Freud agreed that the roots of war were to be found in an elemental human instinct for aggression and destruction.

Basics of Strategy

It is evident from the discourse in the preceding paragraphs that it is the political institutions that will continue to take recourse to use of military force for securing their national interests. And then, human proclivity will dictate the prosecution of war. While the nature of war will remain unaltered, its character will continue to change. Technology will influence the outcome of battles. With a combination of skilled and well-trained manpower ably led by competent leaders who have been educated in the complexities of warfare and not merely trained at the tactical level, the outcome will be military success. With this as the highly complex dynamic environment, strategy for future conflicts will need to be formulated with circumspection.

Strategy is oriented towards the future. It is a declaration of intent and an indication of possible means to fulfil that intent. The intent relates to securing 'national interests'. Strategies function with political consequences. Political institutions declare war but military institutions fight them. Therefore, strategy must be made on political considerations.

The immediate purpose of strategy is to constrict adversaries' choices and exploit them for political purposes. An adversary is not a static entity. He too has a dynamic ongoing process formulating his strategy in relation to his adversaries and so may not always respond along rational and expected pathways. A nimble cunning adversary will make sure of this. Ipso facto, the strategic culture of a nation plays a role too.

World leaders have often, independently, stated that the present global security situation is 'complex'. It is just in the beginning of the twenty-first century that there has been mention of new forms of war—fifth generation war, hybrid war, transnational terrorism or cyber war—and competition that spans the entire spectrum of conflict require a suitably structured force to match this reality. Therefore, any strategy to deal with future wars will need frequent revisions. Thus, formalising a security strategy is feasible for just the near-term time span.

The Challenge

In a technologically charged environment, assessing the global and regional strategic environment in a time frame of 20 years presents a significant challenge. Trend analysis indicates an increase in globalisation, inter-connectivity and urbanisation. A wide range of potential threats appears that are complex and ambiguous. Lack of dynamism at any level can result in a 'strategic shock' by an unforeseen disruptive event. There are likely to be significant challenges resulting from population growth, demand for food, migration, greater demand for energy, climate change, shortage of water, continuing globalisation, rapid urbanisation, an unprecedented global pandemic and the exponential rate of change in some readily-available technologies. In the Indian context, internal stability is driven by political compulsions. A divisive society is more fragile and prone to external interference. These broad trends are pointers where the government will use its military force.

The global balance of power is shifting from America and Europe to Asia. Global institutions created by the victorious powers at the end of the Second World War had their interests in mind. The West is reluctant to make them more inclusive in sync with the reality of ongoing geopolitical changes. While the USA is likely to remain the world's leading military power for the foreseeable future, its military advantage is likely to be reduced and challenged increasingly by China. Any new World Order should protect the global commons and ensure it is available for all. As is being now visualised, "other rising powers, such as Brazil and India, will take a strategic interest beyond their own regions in pursuit of resources" (Development, Concepts and Doctrine Centre's Strategic Trends Programme—Ministry of Defence, UK: Future Operating Environment 2035. 2).

Smart Power

China is a strategic competitor using predatory economics to intimidate its neighbours. To be of relevance, India has to decide as to what extent it is willing to exercise its hard and soft power in the global arena. Its influence will be bolstered by the system of government and its diplomatic, cultural and commercial weight, as well as the professional reputation of its Armed Forces. Through its Diasporas, India has strong cultural, social and ethnic links across the globe—such connections will be invaluable to continue to use 'soft-power' as a tool for influence worldwide. Soft power seems more and more important in a more connected world (Treverton, 2005: 9). Economic power is more a facilitator of another power, especially military, than usable power in its own right. (Treverton). This is manifest in the active role that India plays within international institutions such as the United Nations (UN), the Commonwealth and the regional forums in Asia. India's Armed Forces should expect to continue to contribute to its soft power in numerous ways as part of Government strategy, including defence engagement with countries in the Asian region as well with the USA, UK, France Japan and Australia. Military soft power will have greater credibility if underpinned by hardpower. Combat-credible military forces are needed to deter war and protect the security of the nation. Should deterrence fail, the Armed Forces need to be prepared to wrest the initiative. Reinforcing the nation's traditional tools of diplomacy, the Armed Forces provide military options to ensure that the Government and the country's diplomats negotiate from a position of strength.

External Threats

Post the Cold War, the developed countries of the West now neither have disputed boundaries nor hostile neighbours. Consequently, they are looking to deterring threats from unconventional forces which are often ambiguous and illusive. Formulating a strategy and structuring their forces for such threat contingencies require agile and flexible responses. On the contrary, India has disputes regarding the alignment of the boundary with

China as also its illegal occupation of Aksai Chin in Ladakh. On the other hand, Pakistan had surreptitiously occupied Indian territory in the Indian state of Jammu and Kashmir way back in 1947 and continues to do so. The borders are active and India will, in some time the in future, need to get its lost territories back. For this, India has to formulate its strategies and structure its forces suiting the requirement at hand.

The Chinese armies marched into Tibet in 1950, fragmenting historical geographies, and fracturing people-to-people contact in the India-China borderlands. By China's brazen annexation of Tibet it, willynilly, became India's largest neighbour along an International Boundary/Line of Actual Control running nearly 4,056 km in the high Himalayas. The boundary dispute remains unresolved since the first meeting of officials in 1960 which was duly recorded as the India-China Officials Talks 1960. The document summarises India's case and is worth repeating: '*The facts therefore demand respect for this boundary, defined by nature, confirmed by history and sanctified by "the laws of nations"*' (Rao, 2014: 4). The Chinese had raised no claim in regard to the Indian depictions of the boundary, and "far from doing so", as Dr. S. Gopal (the Head of the Historical Division of the Ministry of External Affairs of India, which did the research for the Officials Talks of 1960 with China) observed, "had affirmed their respect for the territorial integrity of India" (Rao, 2014: 6). Dr. S. Gopal's view was that at the heart of the failure to disclose Chinese claims on Indian-claimed territory during Mr. Nehru's visit to China in 1954 was evidence of China having "no desire for long-term friendship" (Rao, 2014: 7) with India. The boundary remained disputed and not much later, led to a war between India and China in 1962. India's relations with China in the future will remain fluctuating between 'cold' and 'luke warm'. Militarily, China will remain a threat and diplomatically a formidable challenge.

India's neighbours have, over the last decade or so, drifted away from their erstwhile close bilateral relations, which, in a way was largely one-sided. In the process, some of these countries have reached out to China to hedge against India's so-called hegemony in the region. Besides having occupied Indian territory [Pakistan Occupied Kashmir (POK)], Pakistan has been abetting, supporting and orchestrating a proxy war in Jammu and Kashmir (J&K). With the advent of the China-Pakistan Economic Corridor (CPEC) under the ambit of China's Belt and Road Initiative (BRI), Pakistan has virtually become a 'protectorate' of China. Consequently, there is a perceptible bias in its relations with Pakistan vis-a-vis India which has emboldened Pakistan in its activities in J&K. This poses a significant diplomatic challenge for India and a major military threat too. Collusive action by China to bail out Pakistan is not an unlikely possibility.

Nepal has, of late, tilted towards China which has made deep inroads into Nepal in various fields under the guise of infrastructure development. The Chinese presence may not construe a military threat per se; but it allows China to carry out close electronic and digital surveillance of India, round the clock, which it can easily switch into active offensive cyber operations. Nepal has also become a safe and secure staging area for Pakistani Inter Services Intelligence (ISI) backed terrorists to enter and exit Indian territory.

As regards Sri Lanka, it was compelled to turn to whoever could help it in its last stages of its fight to destroy the LTTE Tamil militants. Due to internal political compulsions, India did not come to Sri Lanka's assistance by way of supplying it with military hardware to combat the Tamil insurgents. Sri Lanka got that assistance from Pakistan and China. Consequently, Sri Lanka tilted towards China. In fact, Bangladesh too, sources its military hardware requirements from China. That notwithstanding, there is no real military threat from these countries. However, non-traditional threats remain a possibility, particularly through Nepal.

Internal Threats

Internal security entails keeping peace within the borders of a nation by maintaining law and order and defending its people from internal security threats. The responsibility to maintain it lies with the State Government through the Civil Administration which is assisted by the local Police, State Armed Police, Central Police Forces, paramilitary forces (Assam Rifles and Coast Guard), and in demanding circumstances, the military itself. The State and Central Intelligence Bureau along with the National Investigative Agency (NIA) augment the effort. A majority of India's internal security challenges are state-centric. A poor criminal justice system and large-scale corruption leads to a nexus between criminals, police and politicians with the result that organised crime goes on unabated. In the Northeast States of India, a demographic inversion was politically orchestrated by way of large scale migration from Bangladesh that has resulted in a serious security threat. Illegal movement in many of the bordering districts has brought about a total demographic transformation as the original inhabitants are being forced to sell their lands and flee to safer places. Coastal security is poor and lacks coordination making the long coastline and EEZ (Exclusive Economic Zone) vulnerable. Left Wing Extremism has emerged as the country's most serious internal security challenge. It assumed serious proportions after 2004 when the PWG (People's War Group), MCC (Maoist Communist Centre) and Party Unity, along with other splinter groups, merged together to form the Communist Party of India (Maoist). While some of these are externally sponsored and supported, others are by-products of political mismanagement, lack of governance and corruption. Vote bank politics has fractured the fabric of society into aggressive groups based on caste, clan, cult, religion, language, region and political leanings. Religious fundamentalism is on the rise due to a sense of insecurity among individuals, thus, making society vulnerable to subversion by inimical anti-national elements.

Future Weapon Technologies

Future weapon technological developments will, undoubtedly, dictate the course of the conflict. A robust military R&D complemented by an equally advanced civil industry R&D is the sin qua non for maintaining an edge over any adversary. The rate of technological change will adversely affect a procurement system that is not adaptable. The obsolescence of legacy systems in service will increase; therefore, superior technologies will need to be quickly and affordably integrated to retain capabilities. Defence budgets, already tight, will need judicious optimising. Alongside developing new weapon systems, counters to render enemy weapons ineffective will also have to be developed. By that logic, own weapon systems can also be rendered ineffective with counters by the enemy. Secrecy of development projects both in the public and in private sector defence industries will therefore be an important criterion.

A 2018 US Defence Intelligence Agency report stated that China "leads the world" in some weapons systems. Under the process of Chinese People's Liberation Army (PLA) transformation, the erstwhile Second Artillery was changed to Rocket Force for strategic and conventional deterrence and precision strike missions. The PLA Rocket Force has also developed an imposing conventional ballistic and Cruise missile force and elaborated concepts for its employment to conduct precision strikes and for deterrence and coercive diplomacy. Some of the weapon systems being developed by China include MOAB (Massive Ordinance Air Blast) bomb (claimed to be an improvement to the US "Daisy cutter" bomb used in Afghanistan); anti-ship ballistic missiles, supersonic Cruise missiles, hypersonic glide vehicles carrying missiles; medium and long range stealth bombers; massive Wireless Electromagnetic Method (WEM) radio antenna for sending out extremely low frequency (ELF) radio signals for communications with submarines without having to surface; ship-borne rail-gun firing a projectile upto 100 km at nine times the speed of sound; super-cavitating torpedoes; stealth drones and mini and micro autonomous drones; advanced unmanned surface vessels and submarines. China's Anti Access Area Denial (A2AD) will dwell on the reliance of long-range conventional missiles and precision guided munitions in a non-contact duel. It will deploy weapons to deny access to, and freedom of movement within operational areas. The aim of the adversaries is likely to be to be a deterrent by raising the potential cost of action. China is likely to employ offensive space or ground-based anti-satellite systems that will be able to disrupt India's own space assets and rupture the satellite-based navigation systems. Offensive and defensive cyber capability will offer specific advantages—disrupting networks and systems, while countering offensive cyber operations. Less technical methods will include conventionally-armed terrorist attacks and proxy warfare methods that open alternative fronts.

Disrupting the Adversaries Strategies

These multitudinous factors are in a complex way linked to affect formulation of a national security strategy. Military power is the ultimate yardstick of national power. Military capabilities allow the governments of countries to protect their territorial sovereignty and their people against external and internal threats. It simultaneously enables governments to pursue whatever interests they wish, if necessary, over and against the preferences of other competing entities. Peter Paret summarized it thus, "military power expresses and implements the power of the state in a variety of ways within and beyond the state borders, and is also one of the instruments with which political power is originally created and made permanent." (Paret, 1989: 240).

The ultimate "output" of national power should be, ideally, the ability of a military force to successfully prosecute a variety of operations against a country's adversaries. Whether a force is in fact capable of overwhelming these adversaries would be the result of an analysis of the balance of power, the circumstances under which the engagement occurs, and the relevant constraints and objectives that condition the overall interaction between the two sides. However, in the overall context, if state power ranges from coercion to coaxing to cajoling, then the last is the most cost effective; it means convincing others that your aim is also theirs.

Defending every inch of territory is a term of reference which compels the ground forces to deploy excessive resources to hold their ground. The IB/LAC and the LC runs along the rugged high mountain ranges of the Himalayas, and it is an accepted military dictum that mountains 'eat up troops'. In defending in those areas, there is a need for a large deployment of forces in the 'show window'. China's military presence in Tibet is more limited. In accordance with its doctrine on frontier defence, China stations most of its conventional forces in its interior, to be surged in times of crisis. (Rehman, 2017: 108). With modern technology, these locations are easily identified and acquired as targets for destruction by indirect fire. Deception by the attacker is easier and it allows the other ground forces of the enemy to bypass the forward tiers of defences. Also, the indirect supporting fire resources of the defender are thinly distributed all along the front. The terrain does not permit rapid redeployment. Reserves too are, perforce, held forward due to which their employment is restricted.

To outmatch the adversary, adopting a pre-emptory offensive defence posture will be a major factor in disrupting the adversaries' plans. Take the battle into the enemy's territory. During the Kargil war, the political restriction to not cross the Line of Control resulted in fierce attrition battles which could have been avoided. Wars are as much about defeating the enemy's mind and inflicting casualties.

In event of a war with China, Tibet Autonomous Region (TAR) will be the battle area that will need to be isolated. China has the advantage of strategic interior lines in Tibet against India's exterior lines if the entire LAC is activated. Isolating TAR will force China to operate on exterior lines with inherent strategic disadvantage. The three main highways (Eastern, Central and Western), Gormo-Lhasa railway line and the six airfields should be the strategic assets targeted in the first phase. At the operational level, to exercise viable military options, there will be a need to have uncommitted forces held well forward, the constraints of the lay of terrain and altitude (where troops will be required to be acclimatised) necessitate this. Integrated Battle Groups located well forward within the theatre of operations will enable an effective riposte. The Mountain Strike

Corps will need to be reconstituted to make available these resources abinitio, while retaining the capability for a quid pro quo in a suitable sector. Employment of Scouts battalions to conduct guerrilla operations behind enemy forward line must be built into the operational plans. Special Forces augmented by Tibetan volunteers should be inducted deep into Tibet from the word 'go' to disrupt the long vulnerable logistic chain. Long range conventional vectors should target the vital choke points on the Tsang Po which flows more or less parallel to the LAC in Sikkim and Arunachal Pradesh and the railway line from the north to Lhasa. Pakistan is equally vulnerable in POK.

Disrupting communications and seeking to target the adversaries' satellite communications network will cripple the forces dependent on these links. At the tactical level, the PLA is more accustomed to a detailed command system. Operating under a directive style of command is likely to be its vulnerability. On the other hand, Pakistan is adept at employing irregular forces operating more or less independently but effectively. The 'Maginot Line' syndrome is deeply embedded in the Indian military psyche which is attributed to the political 'No Loss of Territory' term of reference.

Militaries that do not have access to the political leadership tend to be more attrition minded and rigidly hierarchical. The Indian military has this weakness. The 'Make in India' initiative has not taken root as expected. Depending on imported weapon systems and defence technology seriously constrains India against China.

Military training is not the same as education in war. Presently, the junior leaders at section and platoon level are not capable of leading small teams in a future offensive in a directive command style battle environment. A large majority of the Non Commissioned Officers of the Infantry (who will be required to fight the battle) have not attended any professional training course during their service! Marching down Rajpath on the occasion of every Republic Day in flashy 'plumage' with arms swinging forty-five degrees into the sky does not necessarily make good fighting soldiers in a future hybrid war.

Conclusion

It would be evident from the arguments put forth that formulating a disruptive strategy for a future conflict is not an exercise on paper but requires serious holistic consideration and remodelling of minds, procedures and organisations. It requires revamping the existing set-up of higher direction for war, political mindsets, civil-military relations, national economy, defence industrial infrastructure, harmonising all elements of national power and military studies as against military training and a quick thinking unencumbered military leadership.

NOTES

1. John Baylis, James. J. Wirtz & Colin S. Gray, *Strategy in the Contemporary World* (Fifth Edition), Oxford University Press, UK, 2016.
2. Future Operating Environment 2035 (First Edition), Development, Concepts and Doctrine Centre's Strategic Trends Programme – Ministry of Defence UK, 2017.
3. Joint Concept Note 1/17, *Future Force Concept*, Development, Concepts and Doctrine Centre's Strategic Trends Programme – Ministry of Defence UK. 2017.
4. Peter Paret, "Military Power," *The Journal of Military History*, Vol. 53, No. 3 (July 1989).
5. Nirupama Menon Rao, Third Dr. S. Gopal Memorial Lecture, Kings College, London, Kings India Institute, 13 May 2014. https://www.nirupamamenonrao.net/uploads/4/2/6/7/42673355/s_gopal_lecture_final.pdf
6. Gregory F. Treverton & Seth G. Jones, "Measuring National Power", RAND, National Security Research Division, 2005.
7. Iskander Rehman (2017), "A Himalayan Challenge," *Naval War College Review*, Vol. 70, No. 1, Article 6. https://digital-commons.usnwc.edu/nwc-review/vol70/iss1/6

Notes on Editors and Contributors

EDITORS

Lieutenant General A K Singh, PVSM, AVSM, SM, VSM (Retd), is a Distinguished Fellow with Centre for Land Warfare Studies (CLAWS) and an Advisor with OP Jindal Global University. The General is the erstwhile Lt Governor of the Andaman & Nicobar Islands and Puducherry, Ex GOC-in-C Southern Command and has been an alumni of Staff College Camberley, UK, Malinovsky Tank Academy, Moscow & the Higher Command & National Defence College courses in India. He is one of the few officers to have trained with both the NATO & Warsaw Pact at the height of the Cold War. Known for his high integrity and professionalism, the General is looked upon as a role model by large numbers in the Armed Forces. The General has commanded the 7th Cavalry, a T-90 Tank Brigade, an Armoured Division and the most powerful Strike 1 (Corps), and has the distinction of conceiving and executing some of the largest ever manoeuvres in recent times. After a distinguished service in the Armed Forces, the General was entrusted with the responsibility of Lt Governor of A&N Islands in Jul 2013 and later concurrently assumed the charge of Lt Governor of Puducherry in Jul 2014, where he made a great difference with his unique qualities of head & heart. He has been a member of Prime Minister's Team India, as also a member of the National Development Council and Inter-State Council. The General is a frequent speaker at defence and civil forums and also contributes to the print media. His first book as editor, *'Military Strategy for India in the 21st Century'* was published in 2019. His blog may be accessed at: http//ak7cav.in

Brigadier Narender Kumar, SM, VSM (Retd), is a Visiting Fellow at CLAWS. The Brigadier served in counter insurgency and counter-terrorism operation area in J&K and Northeast. He has authored two books- "Challenges in the Indian Ocean Region and Response Options." and "Rise of China: A Military Challenge to India." He has authored more than 200 research papers/ Chapter's for various books/ articles journals and web portals. He has edited a book "India-Nigeria Experience in Combating Terrorism". He is the Founder Editor of *Sammaan Journal*. He was a former Distinguished Fellow at USI of India.

CONTRIBUTORS

Lieutenant General Ashok Bhim Shivane, PVSM, AVSM, VSM (Retd), is an alumnus of National Defence Academy, Pune and joined the Indian Armoured Corps in Dec 1978. A scholar warrior with over 39 years of outstanding career in the Indian Army, he has represented India at the United Nations Peace Keeping Force in Guatemala, handled anti-terrorist desk in J&K, held the appointment of ADG PP and finally superannuated as the Director General Mechanised Forces. An alumnus of National Defence College, he is an acclaimed expert on manoeuvre warfare and operational art. He commanded 50 Armd Regt, an Indep Armd Bde, Armd Div and the elite Strike Corps at Mathura. The General post retirement was Consultant with the Ministry of Defence (Ordnance Factory Board). He is an acclaimed motivational cum leadership speaker, defence analyst and prolific writer on matters national security, and has over eighty publications to his credit. The Officer is a Senior Advisor and Board Member to several institutions.

Lieutenant General Anil Chait, PVSM, AVSM, VSM (Retd), has forty-one years of service with the military. He has been the Commander-in-Chief of a Field Army and also the Chief of Integrated Defence Staff. Practicing art and science of warfare, he has been a conceptualiser, creator, and implementer of military strategy at the Apex level. Post retirement, he has been actively engaged with many major defence manufacturing companies as an advisor and a consultant.

Brigadier Arvind Thakur (Retd), is a cavalry officer, and a regular contributor to the defence and strategic journals. He is also an alumni of the US Army War College.

Colonel (Dr.) Michael Padgett (US Army) (Retd), is North Carolina based and is President of Bilbee Consulting Enterprise, which focuses on teaching the US Government employees on government contracting. He is also a Professor Contracts, Defence Acquisition University, Fort Belvoir, Virginia, USA.

Lieutenant General (Dr.) Rakesh Sharma, PVSM, UYSM, AVSM, VSM (Retd), is currently a Distinguished Fellow with CLAWS. The General has forty years of service in the Indian Army and commanded the 'Fire and Fury Corps' in Ladakh. He superannuated as the Adjutant General of the Indian Army. He is a prolific writer and regularly gives lectures on geo-strategic and military matters.

Lieutenant General (Dr.) VK Ahluwalia, PVSM, AVSM, YSM, VSM (Retd)**, is presently the Director, CLAWS. The General superannuated as the Army Commander, Central Command in March 2012. Thereafter, he served as a Member, Armed Forces Tribunal (AFT). He commanded an infantry brigade, mountain division and corps in Uri- Baramulla, Kargil and Leh-Ladakh sectors respectively. He has authored a book titled *Red Revolution 2020 and Beyond* and co-edited a book on Kargil titled *'Surprise, Strategy and Vijay; 20 years of Kargil and beyond'*. His latest co-edited book is titled *'COVID-19 and Its Challenges: Is India Future Ready?*

Vice Admiral Satish Soni, PVSM, AVSM, NM (Retd), is a distinguished fellow at the United Service Institution of India and a member of the USI Governing council. The Vice Admiral superannuated from the Indian Navy on 29 Feb 2016 after 40 years of service. He has held the appointments of Flag Officer Commanding in Chief- Eastern Naval Command, Flag Officer Commanding in Chief- Southern Naval Command, Deputy Chief of Naval Staff, Commandant National Defence Academy and Chief of Staff Eastern Naval Command in the rank of Vice Admiral. Post retirement he has been writing, travelling, participating in Seminars/ discussions and is mentoring students of schools/ college run by the Dyal Singh Trust.

Air Commodore (Dr.) Ashminder Singh Bahal, VM, (Retd), is Consultant Dean, ICAI. He has worked as Deputy Commandant, College of Air Warfare, DS at Army War College, Executive Director at Doon Business School, Dean School of Business Studies, Sharda University and Director at Amity University. The Air Commodore was also former Distinguished Fellow at USI of India. The officer was awarded Vayu Sena Medal (Gallantry).

Lieutenant General DS Hooda, PVSM, UYSM, AVSM, VSM (Retd),** is an infantry officer with an Army career spanning forty years. During his service, the General acquired vast experience of serving in active counterinsurgency areas of both Jammu & Kashmir and the North East Region. He was the Northern Army Commander from June 2014 to December 2016. During this period, he was responsible for handling the disputed and troubled borders with Pakistan and China as well as the counterterrorist operations in J&K. The surgical strikes of September 2016 were launched under his leadership.

Lieutenant General Dushyant Singh Chauhan, PVSM, AVSM (Retd), is a former Director General of the Defence Intelligence Agency. He worked closely with the premium intelligence organisations in India and numerous friendly foreign countries. He commanded an independent Armoured Brigade, a RAPID Division, Uttar Bharat Area and a Corps in the Western theatre.

Lieutenant General PR Kumar, PVSM, AVSM, VSM (Retd), superannuated as the Director General of Military Operations (DGMO). The General keeps himself updated on international and national strategic security issues. He writes for numerous Think Tanks and delivers talks in educational institutions.

Lieutenant General (Dr.) JS Bajwa, PVSM, UYSM, SM (Retd), is the editor of the Indian Defence Review. The General has held various appointments in the Military Operations and Perspective Planning Directorates of the Army Headquarters. He is a Doctorate from Madras University. He has Authored three books (two on the Chinese PLA) and edited one on China.

Index

*